Father Leopoldo
of Castelnovo

The Servant of God
Father Leopoldo
of Castelnovo
Capuchin

FATHER PIETRO DA VALDIPORRO, O.F.M. CAP.

TRANSLATED FROM ITALIAN
BY STEPHEN DEACON

WITH A FOREWORD BY THE LATE
CARDINAL WILLIAM GODFREY
ARCHBISHOP OF WESTMINSTER

Roman Catholic Books
Post Office Box 2286, Fort Collins, CO 80522

Original title:

Il Servo di Dio P. Leopoldo da Castelnovo, cappuccino
(5th edition, Padua, 1960)

S. RITUUM CONGR.
CAUS. SERVORUM DEI

(Tab. n. 510-46), - Romae, 3 Iunii 1963

Nihil obstat

[L. S.]

NICOLAUS FERRARO, S. R. C. Adsessor
Fidei Sub-Promotor Generalis

ISBN 1-929291-11-6

CONTENTS

FOREWORD

In recent years, the story of the life of Padre Leopoldo da Castelnovo has become more widely known, not only in Italy but also behind the Iron Curtain.

His great desire had been to work for the reunification of the Orthodox Churches with Rome; his wish was never granted and, instead, he had to offer his priestly life, spent almost entirely in Padua, for those outside the true Church.

Padre Leopoldo was one of those priests whose mission in life, it seems, is to be an apostle of the confessional. People came to Padua from all over Italy and from every class of society in order to go to confession to him. Many striking stories are told of his seemingly miraculous gifts in the confessional, but much more striking was his ability to inspire true contrition and his own fervent love of God and His Mother in his penitents.

Padre Leopoldo is little known in England and I am pleased, therefore, to commend this translation of his life, in the hope that it will inspire in those who read it some of the charity and humility of Padre Leopoldo.

[Rome,] October, 1962

† WILLIAM Cardinal GODFREY
Archbishop of Westminster

AUTHOR'S NOTE

For nearly fifteen years I lived with Fr. Leopoldo.

He was really a chosen person, full of God's gifts and so overflowing with grace that he communicated to all who knelt before him his own awareness of the Resurrection and the Life. Hidden away in his tiny confessional cell, he became a centre of attraction for millions who sought him out there and who came away transformed.

In these days of self-glorification when the simplest decent gesture is transformed by propaganda into headline news, there is scarcely praise enough left for one who sacrificed himself for his neighbours as few others have done and who did it in the greatest secrecy, hidden from all eyes save God's.

The first version of the Life ran quickly through four large printings in Italian and was translated into the principal languages of the world, the German version running into six printings. God wished to glorify his servant to the extent that there is now no corner of the globe where he is not known.

The present work is not so much a new edition as a completely new study, made possible by a new collation of documents and a reorganization of the archives. In it I have tried to bring out Fr. Leopoldo's spirituality by making use of his own writings and the reminiscences of those who knew him. In this way I have been able to confirm certain aspects of his spiritual life jealously concealed by himself.

I do not wish to make of him either a hero, a martyr, or a saint; these terms are too frequently applied to worthless subjects and have thereby lost their meaning. I leave the reader to decide if they can be applied in their true meaning to Fr. Leopoldo.

My work in this matter is of no great significance, but at least it is an expression of the love I always bore Fr. Leopoldo.

P. Pietro da Valdiporro

Padua, 1st June, 1960

TRANSLATOR'S NOTE

This is the first edition of the full-length Life *to appear in English. A translation of the 4th (Italian) Edition was made, but it was finished such a short time before the completion of the radically new 5th Edition that it was thought better to scrap it and pass directly to the latter.*

In the Italian Edition every quotation is supported by reference to the relative item in the Archives. These footnotes have been omitted from the English version on the assumption that anyone wishing to consult the sources, which are in Italian, will be able to and prefer to study the Italian text.

In the preparation of this translation I have been assisted by the helpfulness and unfailing patience of Fr. Umile of Valstagna, of the Capuchin friary in Padua, and by the suggestions and corrections of Fr. Bernardine, of the friary at Crawley, Sussex.

The work, imperfect despite their assistance, expresses my gratitude to Fr. Leopoldo for enduring comfort and many favours.

STEPHEN DEACON.

Maundy Thursday, 1962.

Chapter I.

TOWARDS THE GOAL

By our faith in Christ we pay homage to God, and this act of submission to the God Who has spoken to us is a blow against the pride of Satan, whose sin was pride. But above all else Satan fears our charity, our love: it is the love of a friendship in which two hearts love each other, each becoming the sole object of the other till both are fused into one heart. Such a love puts to flight Satan, our bitterest foe.

Fr. Leopoldo.

On the Northern shore of the entrance to the Gulf of Cattaro, like a jewel in an enchanted setting, rises the picturesque township of Castelnovo. Before it lies the Adriatic, sometimes ruffled by squalls but more often gleaming calmly in the sun; to the east, the Gulf continues to lose itself in the delightful fjord; to the north, rise the rough peaks that guard the town closely from the bitter winds of the uneasy Balkans.

The climate is exceptionally mild and the town is almost submerged in the lush green of Mediterranean vegetation. An ideal place for a peaceful holiday, and much patronized by those who wish for nothing better than to spend their time between the calm of the town and the radiant beauty of the beaches.

Castelnovo was founded in 1382 by Tvrtko, King of Bosnia, who wanted to be independent of the great trading centres of Ragusa and Cattaro. Castelnovo was to be his access to the sea, a staging point for caravans, a centre for manufacture and a salt depot. A few years later Castelnovo passed under control of the noble Bosnian family of Kosacia, who, becoming Dukes of Herzegovina in the 15th century, made it one of the most beautiful and best found centres in their country.

When Herzogovina came under Turkish domination in 1482, Castelnovo was the last stronghold to fall. Under Turkish rule its character changed somewhat and it became more of a military base than a centre of commerce. In 1538 the Christian allies decided to attack it, and it was taken by the Venetians, but they were in turn driven out when the Turks retook the town the following year. From then until 1587, when the Venetians again managed to add it to their Dalmatian dominions, it was a nest of Turkish Corsairs.

When Venice fell, the town suffered a variety of unpleasantnesses, being often the scene of fierce fighting. In 1814 it was occupied by Austria, but in 1918 was assigned to Jugoslavia.

As a harbour of some consequence, Castelnovo housed within its walls at various times people of all countries and all religions, and suffered frequent and prolonged Turkish occupation. As a natural result of all this, the people are of a complex character, combining the strength and weaknesses of the East with some more native characteristics. It is a turbulent people, always ready for vendetta.

The Catholic Church is represented in Castelnovo by numerous churches, monasteries and friaries. For more than two hundred years it was the Capuchins of the Province of Venice who kept alive Catholicism and the Franciscan ideal. They had come first in 1688 as chaplains on the ships of the Venetian Republic, which built them a hospice there.

They were responsible for the spiritual welfare of the Venetian troops stationed at Castelnovo and along the Gulf and of those passing through on their way to the East. By definition apostolic and missionary, the Capuchins also went all out for the conversion of Turks and schismatics, both resident and passing through, but alas! without notable success. Their real work, however, was the maintenance of Christianity among the inhabitants of the City and among those from the hinterland who flocked to the port and attended the Capuchin church. Their voice was heard raised in all the churches scattered along both shores of the Gulf. At the fall of the Venetian Republic, they remained at Castelnovo to ensure the spiritual welfare of the Italian Community. The Hospice was finally abandoned in 1903.

Such was the birthplace of Fr. Leopoldo.

* * *

He was born on 28th May, 1866, such a thin and delicate child that it was a month before he could be taken to the church of Saint James to be baptized. He was christened Bogdan, which means gift from God, God's gift to the world for the salvation of innumerable souls, though his parents cannot have foreseen that.

The Mandić family was a very old Bosnian noble family and it was Bogdan's great-grandfather who settled in Castelnovo early in the 18th century, coming probably from Almissa originally though he seems to have spent some time at Poglizza before settling down to maritime commerce in Castelnovo. He seems to have done fairly well, for his son John, Bogdan's grandfather, was the owner of a fleet of deep-sea fishing-boats and coastwise traders.

Another Catholic family in Castelnovo was Zarević, also nobly connected and well-off. They traded throughout the Adriatic and possessed a very flourishing dye-works in the region of Lazzaretti Vecchi, in an area which is still called *Tinturium.* In 1845 Mandić's son Peter married Caroline Zarević.

They had twelve children of whom Bogdan was the last. The Peter Mandić family was not rich. For all that his father had been a ship-owner and his wife's family no less well placed, political unrest was bad for trade, and in time, from being less rich, they faced real poverty.

We have confirmation of this from Fr. Leopoldo himself: consoling some unfortunate man who was financially ruined, he said: "I understand your feelings because, you see, my own family was rich and then lost everything and was reduced to poverty. So I know what it's like."

Riches and influence disappeared but two things remained, their natural nobility of spirit and their religion, two very positive things which Bogdan inherited in full measure. Well aware of their responsibility in this matter, his parents gave their children a sound Christian education.

For some reason Bogdan was their favourite and he seems also to have been under the special protection of Providence, for his sister relates how when he was two years old his mother fell headlong down a flight of stairs with him in her arms. She received various injuries, but the child remained completely unhurt.

It was early apparent that Bogdan had a very strong character, but also an even stronger will to keep it under control. He had a great love of his parents and obeyed them promptly in all things. Very early, too, his piety and love of prayer manifested themselves. Any time he was not in evidence, his mother knew she would find him on his knees in his room.

His parents, themselves very good people, encouraged his piety, fostering particularly devotion to Our Lady and to the Blessed Sacrament. Many, many years later Fr. Leopoldo said, "My mother was a woman of outstanding piety. To her especially I owe what I am today."

SAINT PHILOMENA,
Powerful with God,
Pray for us!

The Story of St. Philomena

On May 25, 1802, excavators in the ancient Catacomb of St. Priscilla in Rome came upon a well-preserved shelf tomb sealed with terra-cotta slabs in the manner usually reserved for nobility or great martyrs. The tomb was marked with three tiles, inscribed with the following confusing words: LUMENA / PAXTE / CUMFI. However, if one places the first tile last and separates the words properly, the very intelligible sentence emerges: *Pax tecum, Filumena*, which is "Peace be with you, Philomena." Also inscribed on the tiles were symbols: a lily, arrows, an anchor and a lance, which would appear to indicate virginity and martyrdom. Inside the coffin there were discovered the remains of a girl of about twelve or thirteen years of age, along with a vial or ampulla of her dried blood.

Transferred to the Treasury of the Rare Collection of Christian Antiquity in the Vatican, the remains were soon forgotten by the public, especially since no record existed of a virgin martyr named Philomena. But in 1805, a Neapolitan priest, Don Francesco di Lucia, traveling to Rome with his newly appointed bishop, requested and, after a brief delay, received the relics of this martyr "Philomena" to enshrine in his village church at Mugnano, near Naples.

Immediately upon the official donation of St. Philomena's sacred remains, signal favors began to be granted through her intercession and unusual events to occur. The favors, graces and even miracles started to increase, even before her enshrinement at Mugnano, and they steadily grew in number thereafter—such that this virgin martyr soon earned the title, "Philomena, Powerful with God." In 1837, only 35 years after her exhumation, Pope Gregory XVI elevated this "Wonder-Worker of the Nineteenth Century" to sainthood. In an act unprecedented in the history of Catholicism, she became the *only* person recognized by the Church as a Saint solely on the basis of her powerful intercession, since nothing historical was known of her except her name and the evidence of her martyrdom.

St. Philomena has been successfully invoked by her supplicants in every sort of need, such that she has become another patron of "hopeless" and "impossible" cases, like St. Jude or St. Rita, but she is known to be especially powerful in cases involving conversion of sinners, return to the Sacraments, expectant mothers, destitute mothers, problems with children, unhappiness in the home sterility, priests and their work, help for the sick, the missions, real estate, money problems, food for the poor and mental illness. But truly, as her devotees have discovered, no case, of whatever matter, is too trivial or too unimportant to concern her.

Among her most devoted clients was St. John Vianney (the Curé of Ars), whose childlike devotion to this virgin Saint played an intimate part in his daily life. Other Saints who were always devoted to her, prayed to her and sang her praises were St. Peter Julian Eymard, St. Peter Chanel, St. Anthony Mary Claret, St. Madeleine Sophie Barat, St. Euphrasia Pelletier, St. Frances Xavier Cabrini, St. John Nepomucene Neumann, Blessed Anna Maria Taigi and Ven. Pauline Jaricot.

A number of Popes have also shown remarkable devotion to St. Philomena as well: **Pope Leo XII** (1823-1829) expressed the greatest admiration for this unknown child-saint and gladly gave his permission for the erection of altars and churches in her honor. **Pope Gregory XVI** (1831-1846), who authorized her public veneration, showed his esteem and devotion to the Saint by giving her the title of "Patroness of the Living Rosary." A Mass and proper Office in her honor were approved by him in 1834 or 1835. This is an extraordinary privilege granted to comparatively few Saints. **Pope Pius IX** (1846-1878) proclaimed her "Patroness of the Children of Mary." **Pope Leo XIII** (1878-1903) made two pilgrimages to her shrine before his election to the papacy. After he had become the Vicar of Christ, he gave a valuable cross to the sanctuary. He approved the Confraternity of St. Philomena and later raised it to an Archconfraternity (which is still headquartered at her shrine at Mugnano, Italy). **Pope St. Pius X** (1903-1914) spoke warmly of her and manifested his devotion to her in various ways. Costly gifts were given by him to her shrine.

Truly, St. Philomena is a powerful intercessor—seemingly held quietly in reserve by Our Divine Lord during these many centuries—for especially strong help in our times, when so much confusion and absence of faith are manifest. Her principal feast day is August 11. *St. Philomena, powerful with God, pray for us!*

NOVENA PRAYER TO ST. PHILOMENA

O FAITHFUL VIRGIN and glorious martyr, St. Philomena, who works so many miracles on behalf of the poor and sorrowing, have pity on me. Thou knowest the multitude and diversity of my needs. Behold me at thy feet, full of misery, but full of hope. I entreat thy charity, O great Saint! Graciously hear me and obtain from God a favorable answer to the request which I now humbly lay before thee . . . (*Here specify your petition.*) I am firmly convinced that through thy merits, through the scorn, the sufferings and the death thou didst endure, united to the merits of the Passion and death of Jesus, thy Spouse, I shall obtain what I ask of thee, and in the joy of my heart I will bless God, who is admirable in His Saints. Amen.

✠ Carolus Hubertus Le Blond
Episcopus Sancti Josephi
January, 1952

It is easy to read into the accounts and reminiscences of his relations and contemporaries the description of a pietistic prig. One can well imagine that they, searching back in their hearts for memories of the child who has now become a candidate for the Altars, tend to dredge up the extraordinary and to forget the ordinary. We thus get a picture of a precocious young boy, not joining in the games of his fellows but preferring to walk apart in prayer and contemplation, a model pupil at school, a joy to the Franciscans who gave him religious instruction, a delight to his parents who set him up as an example to his eleven older brothers and sisters—in fact a thoroughly unnatural little prig whose contemporaries must have wanted to throw him in the horse-pond. But the fact is that they did not want to throw him into the horse-pond. They loved him. Of course he was different, though he did sometimes join in their games to please them, but he was not self-righteous and they accepted his difference, accepted him even as an arbiter of their childish quarrels and differences.

Children are the quickest to see through hypocrisy of false attitudes, but with young Bogdan there was nothing to see through. He was genuine.

It would be nice to be able to back this statement by recounting incidents from this period rather than just enthusiastic remarks such as "Every one said he was a Saint and I thought so too." Two things are perhaps significant: after he had made his first Holy Communion, he went every day to Mass and Holy Communion, not something one does to bolster a pose; in 1947 Joseph Bogdanović, who emigrated to America in 1902, came across a Life of Fr. Leopoldo and wrote at once to recount how when they were at school together he had been very poor and Bodgan, his senior by a year, had shared his food with him.

When he entered the Seminary, his Parish Priest wrote: *Young Bogdan is of excellent character and exemplary behaviour and could well be a model for his contemporaries.*

And the Bishop of Cattaro, Mgr. Casimiro Forlani: *Young Bogdan applied his whole soul from his tenderest years to the attainment of Christian perfection; he was an example of every virtue.*

But for me the best evidence of his genuineness, of the fact that his piety was not pietism and his recollectedness not an attitude, remains that his contemporaries accepted him as he was and showed no tendency to 'debunk' him.

* * *

The boy was growing up. While still a mere lad he was aware of the sorry state of religion in his native town, among the whole of his people, the whole of Eastern Europe. Devoted to the Catholic Church, he saw the misery of schism and felt very strongly that it was the lack of the true Faith that made his compatriots so violent. He had personal experience of fratricidal battles and vendettas of such bloodiness that their memory remained with him all his life.

Compassion for this state of affairs gradually crystallized into one shining idea: why should he not try to lead these poor errant people back to the one true fold and provide them with the consolation of the one true Faith? He thought long about it, and prayed, and came to a decision.

"Very well," he said, "I shall dedicate myself to the salvation of all these unhappy people. I shall be their missionary."

One of the things that may have influenced this decision was perhaps the centuries-old family custom of celebrating on the Feast of Saint Nicholas of Bari their introduction to Christianity. This is the Saint who, outside the Church, survives in the Anglo-Saxon culture as Santa Claus, but for Fr. Leopoldo his feast day had much greater significance. In 1906 he wrote on a picture of Saint Nicholas: *On this day, on which my family celebrates according to ancestral custom our introduction to the Faith, I Leopoldo Maria, formerly Bogdan John Mandić, renew my vows in perpetual memory of the event.* (1)

---

(1) The origin of this custom goes back a very long way. In pagan times the people of the region devoted a whole week to feasts in honour of their *Lares* and *Penates.* When they were converted to Christianity, the festival was transferred to the name-day of the head of the family. The head of the Mandić family at that time was called Nicola, so the feast of St. Nicholas became the family patronal feast. Doubtless there was much talk of the grace of belonging to the Catholic Church in contrast to the Orthodox all round them. In any case the celebrations must have made a great impression on the young Bogdan for him to recall it after so many years away from his family and to make it the occasion for a renewal of his vows for the redemption of the Eastern peoples.

Archives of the Vice-Postulation at the Capuchin Friary in Padua. Documents concerning Fr. Leopoldo are classified by subject and numbered in alphabetical order in plastic folders kept in twelve wooden boxes.

Before this great plan could be realized, however, everything else had to be abandoned—brothers, sisters, and his beloved parents. This must have been a great wrench, but sustained by grace, he was able to say, "Here I am, Lord! Send me where Thou willst."

Once the idea was clear in his mind, decision followed quickly. He decided to become a Capuchin which would give him, he thought, the best chance of realizing is ideal. His parents were delighted. Naturally, they too felt the break of losing him from their midst, but the thought that their favourite child had been chosen by God and would one day serve at His Altars, more than offset their human sorrow.

Application was made to the Father Provincial at Venice, who accepted Bogdan. 16th November, 1882, was fixed for his entry into the Seminary at Udine. He was sixteen years old (2).

Delighted at the news of his acceptance, Bogdan rushed off to Church to give thanks.

When the time came for him to leave, his parents half reproached him.

"You're leaving us without a tear, Bogdan?" "Tears?" he replied. "I'm going to my Father's house and you expect me to weep!"

---

(2) Towards the end of the 19th Century the Capuchins of the Province of Venice were in difficulties due to the fewness of vocations. Until the suppression of 1866, vocations had been numerous and always among grown men, most of whom had already completed their studies at diocesan seminaries. After the suppression, however, there was an abrupt change and entries into the Order by those who had completed their studies dwindled almost to vanishing point. In order to survive, the obvious course was to establish their own seminary where youngsters who showed a vocation for the religious life could be educated. It was not all that easy, however, for it was feared that, should they prove unable to bear the rigours of the Capuchin life as led by grown men, the final result might be irreparably worse. Unwilling to take such a weighty decision on their own, the Superiors caused special prayers to be said in all the friaries, and canvassed the opinion of all their members. The majority, trusting in God, were in favour, so in 1878 a small seminary was started at the friary in Udine.

To start with, results were not very encouraging, for most of the boys, for health or other reasons, had to be sent back to their families. But the Capuchins just prayed the harder and God finally rewarded their efforts. In a short time the seminary, later transferred to Rovigo, was turning out a line of good and holy religious, who later became distinguished in many fields.

Undersized, frail, and awkward in his gait, Bogdan immediately aroused pity on his arrival at the seminary. How could he stand up to the long hours of study and the strict discipline? Soon, however, pity was forgotten in the admiration and respect of his fellows and his Superiors. He knew where he was going and, now that his feet were on the path, he pursued it with single-minded devotion.

Of him at this time, Archbishop Cuccarollo writes: *I met Bogdan first when I joined the seminary at Udine in 1883. Fr. Guglielmo of Mandrisio, our Master, and even more Fr. Cesario of Villafranca, the Director of the seminary and a man with an enlightened knowledge of souls, held him in boundless esteem. We seminarians were well aware of this but we did not mind a bit, for he really was a model of discipline, application and composure at work and recreation, but most of all in his recollection in chapel where he prayed like a saint, seeming at times to be transfigured.*

In the discipline of the tongue he was particularly strict with himself until it became an absolute habit. He never uttered a word outside the proper times, but this did not prevent his sharing our fun or occasionally joining in our games to please us.

Even in those days he suffered from physical defects, but they were compensated for by his perfect courtesy of manner and by an interior beauty which, unknown to him, shone through to win the affection and even veneration of everyone.

Of the same period, Fr. Odorico of Pordenone, one time Provincial of the Venetian Province, writes: *I was with Bogdan at the seminary and even in those days he was already a saint. I can assure you that right from those earliest days he was most careful not to commit the slightest deliberate fault. Anything which he knew to be less than good was impossible for him. He was always recollected, as if wrapped up in God.*

After two years at the seminary, Bogdan's studies were so advanced and his conduct so exemplary that his Superiors found him fit to enter the novitiate proper and take the habit of Saint Francis. The Director wrote at that time: *From his entry the seminary Bogdan Mandić has behaved in the most praiseworthy manner, his conduct has been uni-*

formly edifying and he shows clear signs of a true vocation to join our Order.

Although he was only two years at the seminary, his virtues were long remembered. Another Capuchin wrote: *When I joined the seminary in 1888, Bogdan Mandić had already been gone two years, but the memory of his exceptional goodness was still very much alive. The two venerable old Lay Brothers who served the seminary were always saying, "Ah, that young Mandić! He was a real saint!"*

* * *

It may be of some interest to the reader to insert here a brief note on the severity of the Capuchin rule in the Province of Venice in those days. This will help to give a better appreciation of the heroic courage required by Fr. Leopoldo to face the life with his frail constitution.

As soon as they began to recover from the suppression of 1866 the Venetian Capuchins thought that the best thing to do in order to deserve God's blessing and that of Saint Francis and to repopulate their half-empty friaries and rekindle the ancient fervour, was to go back to the original strictness of the Capuchin Rule. And this they did with all their heart.

The habit was that permitted by Saint Francis' rule. A gown of coarse stuff, coarse indeed for it was woven in the friaries, so coarse that the habit stood up on its own with nobody inside it. Under this was another sort of tunic coming to the knees, or a bit lower in winter, but so badly made that all the winds of heaven had free play, and so coarse that it was in effect a hair shirt. Shirts or underwear were absolutely forbidden. No socks. In the depths of winter the sick were allowed to cover their feet, but with old rags not socks.

There was no heating in the friaries and the small windows had oiled paper instead of glass. Only on the coldest winter nights were they allowed to gather round a fire to thaw out their frozen extremities after the two hours of nocturnal prayer.

For mattress they had a simple straw-filled sack. One blanket, but no linen. No question of not conforming to the rule of sleeping in their habits summer and winter alike. At midnight they were awakened for a good two hours of prayers in choir. In winter this was sheer martyrdom.

Fasting was also hard. Absolutely nothing was taken before midday. The midday meal was adequate, but supper was no more than a piece of bread and a glass of wine. The principal fasts were also completely meatless. After nearly six months of such a regime, when it came to Easter the friars were in no very good heart for singing!

This was only a part of the austerity. In addition there was absolute silence, the discipline, and a hundred other things that made the life a real crucifixion. No one dreamed of holidays, or jaunts, or rest cures in the mountains or at the sea. The life was the same for all, older Frati and young students alike (3).

* * *

Such was the life which Bogdan was entering on when he reported to the Capuchin Friary at Bassano del Grappa on 20th April, 1884.

After a 10-day retreat, he took the habit on 2nd May, assumed the name of Fra Leopoldo, and began the year of the novitiate.

The novitiate, common to all religious orders, is a time of testing. The novice experiences every aspect of the life of his Order and at the same time is subjected to a special discipline so that he may be fully cognizant of the life he is embracing and he and his Superiors convinced of the genuineness of his vocation.

We have seen what the life was like, and we can imagine Fra Leopoldo, his thin and delicate frame bundled up in the coarse habit, his misshapen feet shuffling awkwardly in the rough sandals, frozen stiff in winter by the bitter blasts sweeping down the Valsugana from the Brenta.

People were sorry for him, but he had a strengh of mind that more than compensated for the deficiencies of his body and could face any-

---

(3) Adapted from the reminiscences of Fr. Gerardo of Villafranca.

thing. No question of dispensations for him: on the contrary he obeyed every last rule down to the minutest detail.

However, what mattered in this year was not Fra Leopoldo's external faithfulness to the Rule but his interior spiritual development. We cannot, of course, know much about this except from certain external manifestations, but we do know that he was already accustomed to the interior life and that in this year must have been laid the foundations of his holiness.

In his long hours of prayer he realized that the mission to which he felt called could be accomplished only by a soul steeped in God. He therefore strove towards holiness with all his might, basing his efforts on humility, faith, charity to all, devotion to the Blessed Sacrament and a filial love of Our Lady.

He was fortunate in having an exceptionally gifted Master, Fr. Pietro of Avesa, a man of oustanding virtue and a great knowledge of souls. He recognized at once that Fra Leopoldo was destined by God for great things, and with fatherly solicitude set his feet in the path of perfection. In his turn, Fra Leopoldo saw the angel of the Lord in the person of his instructor and faithfully followed his advice, holding him in reverence and affection till the end of his days.

We know how decisive the influence of this year of the novitiate was in Fr. Leopoldo's life because he made resolutions then which he kept till his death and which were to lead him to great heights of virtue and enable him to do untold good.

At the end of the canonical year of novitiate, the Chapter considered Fr. Leopoldo and found him worthy. On 4th May, 1885, he took the first real step towards his goal when he made his Simple Profession.

No one seeing this insignificant little Frate that day could have imagined that before long thousands of people, men and women of every class and profession, would be flocking to him for comfort and inspiration.

The next day Fra Leopoldo received his Letter of Obedience from the Father Provincial. Among other things it ordered his immediate transfer to Padua.

In Padua, Fra Leopoldo began to study philosophy (4). For an entire year his whole thought had been for his soul: now he had to enrich his mind as well with that knowledge needed by a priest and indispensable to his cherished mission.

Let us again hear from Mgr. Cuccarollo, who studied with him:

As I had found Fra Leopoldo at the seminary, so I found him during our studies in Padua and Venice, except for an increase in sanctity and religious intensity.

He was the type of perfect scholar learning from book as well as from our instructors, and meditating on what he learned. During recreations he liked to talk 'shop', asking for clarification of a point or with the greatest humility putting forward some thought of his own. In the inevitable discussions that followed, he was never ruffled nor did he in any way give the impression of trying to override the opinions of others. He was in complete control of himself and his passionate temperament, almost as though he had no temperament, whereas in fact the turbid Dalmatian blood still coursed in his veins.

---

(4) As has already been noted (Footnote 2) the Capuchins were at this time facing the problem of educating their own ordinands instead of accepting fully-fledged priests into their houses. The seminary at Udine solved only a part of the problem: it did not deal with that of higher education, let alone theology. Their efforts to solve this problem were not immediately crowned with success. There was a dearth of instructors among their own number and they were loth to have lay teachers in the Friaries even for secular subjects. So it was that the education of their students in the humanities suffered somewhat, often being largely dependent on the enthusiasm and self-discipline of the individual, though even these might often prove inadequate without proper guidance.

As soon as it became possible, the more promising young men were sent to the International College in Rome and, gradually, a competent teaching faculty was built up.

Such was the climate in which Fra Leopoldo completed his training.

His own literary education was by force of circumstances somewhat limited, but he did learn Latin, which he used for his personal writings, and Italian, which he wrote correctly. On his own account he also learned some East European languages such as Croat, Slovene, Serbian and a smattering of modern Greek. All these languages he could also speak. As far as philosophy and moral and dogmatic theology were concerned, he was in better case, for there were suitable instructors aided by his own intelligence and enthusiasm. In fact, as we shall see, he continued to study the Fathers and Doctors of the Church throughout his life.

He had no use for books that had no intrinsic doctrinal value, preferring above all the great writers and thinkers, of whom he often spoke, though his defective pronunciation made it difficult for him to express his thoughts very clearly.

Here then is a picture of his mentality, contemplative, analytical, rational, discarding external forms and embellishments for the core of truth. Yet we must not think that concentration on his work was to the exclusion of his soul; on the contrary.

On 20th October, 1888, he made his Solemn Profession at Padua and was then transferred to Venice to study theology and prepare himself for the priesthood.

From his parents Fra Leopoldo had learned at an early age to hold the office of priesthood in veneration. His studies and his own spiritual development had by now revealed to him the true sublimity of the office and one can well imagine that, feeling himself called by Almighty God to enter the ranks of the ministry, his preparation for it both in study and in prayer was exceptional. His humility made him tremble at the very idea of himself in such a situation, yet the call was clear and he set himself to obey it as worthily as possible.

As the time approached for his ordination, his parents wanted to participate as far as possible in his intense joy. On 5th July, 1890 his mother wrote: *I cannot tell you, dearest son, how much joy and consolation your letter gave me, nor how great a consolation it is to a mother's heart to know that her son is about to reach the happiest day of her life when he first celebrates Holy Mass.*

It will be a day of a great happiness for the entire family.

Pray to Our Lady for your loving mother who sends you a thousand kisses and cannot wait for the day when she will once more hold you in her arms.

On 14th September, mother and father wrote a joint letter: *You can imagine, dearest son, what consolation, joy and happiness it has brought us to hear that you are to be ordained on the 20th.*

Praise and thanks be to the Giver of all gifts that your desires will be fulfilled and that a son of ours will be mediator between Heaven and Earth. When you are at the Altar, dearest son, and hold the

Inmaculate Lamb of God in your hands, remember your parents, your brothers and sisters, and all your relations. We in our turn shall unite our feeble prayers to yours that God may bless you and us abundantly.

We send you our paternal blessing and, once you are a priest, we kiss your anointed hands and beg a blessing of you.

On 20th September, 1890 at S. Maria della Salute in Venice, Fra Leopoldo was ordained priest by Cardinal Agostini.

The new priest was moved to tears. Wonder that the insignificant little Frate was now a priest of God? Or just tears of gratitude for the grace accorded him?

Once he had completed his theological studies and received faculties for preaching and hearing confessions, Fr. Leopoldo was ready to start his life's work. He lost no time in making known to his Superiors his ardent desire to work in the East European mission field, but in view of his frail constitution they would not for the moment consider it. Not for the last time he accepted in obedience and humility until it should please God to clear the way for him.

Since his speech made it impossible for him to be a preacher, he preferred to make himself useful in the confessional. Thus it was that, almost to fill in time as it were, he was led to start what was to be his life's work, his apostolate.

He was in various friaries at this time, but in each he went quietly about his work in the confessional and about the task of his own spiritual improvement. In his great humility he used also to help the lay-brothers with their work about the house kitchen and also went out collecting alms for the friary.

In September, 1897 he was appointed head of the Capuchin Hospice at Zara. He went off at once, overflowing with joy, for this was one step nearer his still-cherished goal. He felt the day not far off when he would be able to start his mission of reclaiming the schismatic Easterners and bringing them back to the one true fold. He started work at once, making contact with the Orthodox people in order to enlighten them and attract them to the Church. Often when a ship came into port, he would go down to the harbour and talk to the Orthodox in transit, sowing the seed of truth in their hearts. His work began to be known and even people from the interior came to talk to him. The rosiest hopes began to blossom in his heart, but in October, 1899, obedience called him back to Veneto and posted him to the friary in Thiene.

This friary, reopened after 40 years of suppression, had since the 17th century had charge of the adjacent shrine of Our Lady of the Elm. For Fr. Leopoldo the possibility of serving a shrine once blessed by the presence of Our Lady was consolation enough for leaving his beloved East.

At Thiene he spent every spare moment at Our Lady's feet. When the others went off to siesta, he was to be found on his knees at the Lady Altar.

At that time the shrine was open even during the siesta period and working women returning to their tasks after the midday meal made a habit of looking in to say a prayer. Finding Fr. Leopold always there at prayer they began to conceive a certain respect and veneration for him and to ask him to hear their confessions.

He was always ready to excercise his ministry at whatever sacrifice and at whatever time, but unfortunately his conduct caused unfavourable comparisons with his fellows priests and the Father Guardian felt obliged to order him to retire to his cell as the others did at this time of day.

Fr. Leopoldo bowed to authority and prayed in his cell instead. And from then on never prayed before the Lady Altar but went instead to a side aisle where he would not be seen by the public.

In 1903 he was transferred to Bassano del Grappa where he continued to hear confessions and to pray. Fr. Ruffino of Cadore who was Father Guardian at the time, says that Fr. Leopoldo was an example to all and spent his whole time in prayer. When the others went to their cells for the siesta, he slipped into the choir and remained there in prayer until Vespers. Study was not neglected either, for he considered it a way of raising one's mind to God. Fr. Ruffino says he often came upon him in his cell studying Saint Augustine on his knees on the bare floor.

He offered for as long as he was at Bassano to say the last Mass on Sundays.

His love and devotion in the confessional at this time can best be attested by the fact that forty years later many of his then penitents made the 25 mile journey to Padua to go to confession to him.

In 1905 the Provincial Chapter nominated him Vicar of the friary at Capodistria where, too, he left an ineffaceable memory. Giuseppe Norbedo, a servant at the friary, writes. *Fr. Leopoldo was in great demand as a confessor. Everybody knew him and considered him a delightful person and a holy one as well. When he was not in the confessional, he was in the choir praying. His was a jovial temperament and he got on well with everyone. He was really a good man among good men.*

Often he would seek me out when I was working in the garden in order to cheer me up with his conversation or to thank me profusely for some small service I had been able to render him. Another thing, he would never hear a word said against anybody: he was much too good.

In 1906 he was transferred to Padua where he remained, apart from enforced absence during the war, till his death.

* * *

In October, 1910 he was nominated Director of Students at Padua and held the post for four years. At the same time he gave instruction on the Fathers of the Church.

In the control of the young men in his charge, Fr. Leopoldo's standards were generous but precise; his aim, to give them a sound basis of firm conviction and to inspire them to the apostolate. He was so fatherly in his treatment of them that some people saw in his rule a falling away from the Order's traditional austerity, but if he relaxed certain material rigours it was with the twofold object of producing men healthy and strong enough for the work they were to undertake and to be able to demand of them even greater interior mortification.

Fr. Ilarione of Melilli recounts that Fr. Leopoldo did his best to protect his students from the worst rigours of the winter and, for example, sent them off to bed after the evening recreation, dispensing them from the customary visit to the Chapel. "I'll do penance for you," he said, "I'll pray for you."

He loved his students like a mother, foreseeing their needs and providing generously for them. Often he used to go into the kitchens when the meals were being prepared and urged the cooks to be a bit extra generous with the portions for the students, giving himself less.

Fr. Gregorio of Villa writes: *As Director he was most diligent in his spiritual assistance to us students. He wanted us to carry out our tasks from love and not from fear. It was impossible not to fall under his charm, not to follow wherever he led. His piety and mortification were always in evidence. His care for us was almost motherly and his love for us as a body and for each of us as an individual knew no bounds. Among those who were his students his memory never fades, as the odour of sanctity never fades.*

He sought God's blessing on his beloved students by prayer and sacrifice, offering himself to God as a victim for their good.

When the four years were completed in October 1914, he devoted himself solely to the confessional.

* * *

The first world war was a time of great trial for Fr. Leopoldo. Padua was a target for the Austrian air force and air raids were frequent. The danger was great, but Fr. Leopoldo would hear nothing of moving to another friary: he wanted to stay near his penitents and help comfort them in a time of so many sorrows. In 1917, however, he had to move. The Italian Government ordered that all persons of Istrian or Dalmatian origin resident near the Austrian frontier must either take Italian nationality or be confined to an area south of Florence. They would not be prosecuted, nor interned, only as a security measure sent away from the vicinity of the front.

Fr. Leopoldo, being very attached to his native country, refused to take Italian nationality and was therefore ordered by the police to leave Padua. Various influential persons intervened, pointing out to the authorities that he was not interested in politics and confined himself to purely spiritual works; moreover, he would be of great value in sustaining the morale of the sorely tried city.

But the authorities were adamant, and towards the end of July, 1917, Fr. Leopoldo set off for Rome accompanied by one lay-brother, Fra Simone of Sebenico.

A slight digression is in order here to explain Fr. Leopoldo's attitude on his point of nationality, a point that has aroused considerable discussion and misunderstanding.

In 1866, when he was born, Castelnovo was under Austro-Hungarian rule. He was born, therefore, an Austrian, but this Austrian nationality was a purely formal, political thing unconnected with his lineage, automatically imposed, not chosen. Had Fr. Leopoldo agreed to become an Italian citizen, he would have been changing from the nationality of one country to which he did not really belong to that of another country to which he did not belong either—but with this all-important difference: Austrian nationality was imposed upon him, whereas Italian would have been a matter of his own free choice. Now, he was neither Austrian nor Italian, but Croatian.

This may seem a niggling point since Croatia was in those days a geographical rather than a political concept, but the Croats firmly believed that with the defeat of Austria they would regain their independence or at least become part to a Balkan Slav hegemony. In that case Fr. Leopoldo would automatically have been granted the nationality of his own native land, Croatia.

Politics as such had no interest for him, but he loved his country and would not have renounced it for anything, all the more since he knew that once the special circumstances of the war were over, the Italian authorities would make no difficulties about his remaining as a foreigner in Padua.

Not everybody understood this and some remonstrated with him for not accepting the situation and with it the mere formality of taking Italian nationality. He contented himself with saying that blood was thicker than water, that one did not betray one's blood. Whereupon he got the reputation of being pigheaded enough to accept all the bother entailed for a matter of supreme unimportance.

But there was another, nobler motive which he disclosed to nobody, knowing that it would not be understood. He had never forgotten the goal he had set himself, the reconversion of Eastern Europe. He wrote of "the reconversion of my people" and among his people he included all who had become detached from Rome. He daily awaited the summons to the eastern mission field: how could he go among his fiercely proud people and earn their trust and lead them back to unity with Rome if he had forsworn his nationality, their nationality, to join himself to a strange people?

Nothing in all this diminished his love for his second country which had made him so generously welcome and which was to surround him with affection and devotion for more than sixty-six years, treating him as a favourite son. He had a particular love of Italy as the seat of the Papacy and the heart of the Church. He was overjoyed when the Lateran Treaty of 1929 reconciled the Vatican and the Quirinal and, quite exceptionally for him, studied the newspapers in order to read everything that was written about the event.

* * *

But it was still a great wrench for him to leave Padua where so many penitents, to whom he felt bound by ties of a great affection, wanted him in the confessional. In addition, the long journey and his always precarious health were the source of physical suffering, but he bore it all heroically without a murmur.

The Father General of the Order was not there when he arrived in Rome, so while awaiting his return, Fr. Leopoldo visited the Roman basilicas and the catacombs, celebrated Mass on the tomb of Saint Pius X and had the great joy of being received in private audience by Benedict XV.

When the time came, he was ordered to Tora Presenzano, near Foggia. Here he remained until after the disastrous defeat at Caporetto. The local masons made this the occasion to accuse him of having publicly rejoiced in Italy's discomfiture. Fr. Leopoldo was most indignant at this suggestion and immediately sent his companion, Fra Simone, to the local authorities to indicate his intention of changing his residence by way of protest. The reply came that although all

Capuchins without exception were held in the greatest esteem, given the considerable masonic influence in the neighbourhood, it might be a good thing if he were to move. They suggested Nola.

In due course, with the authority of the Father General, Fr. Leopoldo transferred himself to the friary at Nola where he remained until German aircraft bombed S. Brigida in Naples and all foreigners had to leave. He took refuge then in the friary at Arienza al Cancello, near Naples, and remained there until the end of the war.

Fra Simone tells us that during all this time he was suffering considerable abdominal pain but bore it with exemplary and edifying fortitude.

Fr. Odorico, Guardian of the friary, wrote to him: *You feel the gap in your life, but I assure you we feel it in ours too, I myself especially. How true it is that one only really appreciates one's blessings when they are taken away.*

Mgr. Perin, Professor at the Seminary, for his part wrote: *You are badly wanted here in Padua. The day before yesterday the good Parish Priest of S. Croce asked me, "What about Fr. Leopoldo? They really seem to have stolen him from us." Which will give you some idea of the affection and esteem in which we all hold you.*

Towards the day of his return Fr. Leopoldo contributed his own earnest prayer which was rewarded by the intervention of the Hon. Boselli, who had the greatest regard and affection for him and managed it so that he was one of the first to be released from the residence restrictions at the end of the war.

So it was that after a devout pilgrimage to Monte Vergine, Pompeii, S. Filomena at Mugnano del Cardinale, Camaldoli, Assisi, S. Rose at Viterbo and S. Catherine at Bologna, Fr. Leopoldo came back with tears of joy to his beloved Padua.

Here he returned with more enthusiasm than ever to his ministry of the Sacrament of Penance, though his heart was still set on his East European peoples and he never ceased to pray that his dream might be realized.

In 1923 it seemed as if his prayers had been answered. With Italy's annexation of Fiume, the friary there passed from the jurisdiction of the

Slav Capuchins to that of the Venetian Province. The friary had assumed responsibility for a large parish and Fr. Leopoldo with his knowledge of various Balkan languages was sent there to help with confessions.

The *Annals of the Capuchin Province of Venice* contain the following passage: *Among those transferred by the Provincial Chapter held on 16th October, 1923, was Fr. Leopoldo who was sent to Fiume to act as a confessor of the Slavs. For nearly twenty years he had been in Padua where, as everywhere he had been before, he did enormous good by his holy administration of the Sacrament of Penance.*

This is in fact his mission in life, for his frail constitution is not adapted to other forms of ministry. In the confessional he exercises what one might almost call a fascination, so great is his culture, so fine his intuition and so manifestly holy is his life. Everybody flocks to him, not just simple people but particularly intellectuals and aristocrats, university students and professors and the clergy both secular and regular.

Small wonder that the city greeted his departure with dismay. He on the other hand, was delighted, and hurried off to S. Croce to say a *Te Deum* before the Lady Altar.

One can imagine Fr. Leopoldo's joy, but the consternation of the City at what amounted to a civic calamity was not left to the imagination. So many representations were made to Mgr. Dalla Costa, the recently appointed Bishop, that he felt constrained to write to the Father Provincial on 23rd October in the following terms:

I feel obliged to ask you a great favour. The posting of the excellent Fr. Leopoldo to Fiume has let loose in the city a flood of bitterness and unease. Many very distinguished persons, both clerical and lay, beg of you, Most Reverend Father, to allow him to remain here. I know the exigencies of your Holy Rule, but it seems to me that for the good of this great city an exception might be made, an exception that everyone would greet with the greatest enthusiasm.

The Father Provincial, Fr. Odorico of Pordenone, considered the matter and consulted his advisers, and decided to recall Fr. Leopoldo. He knew, it is true, what a blow it would be for him to leave his new apostolate, begun at last after so many years of longing, but equally he had no doubts about his immediate obedience.

On 11th November he wrote from Villafranca:

This letter, or at any rate its contents, will come as a surprise to you. God is asking another sacrifice of you, but I am sure you will meet the demand with the words of our Divine Master, Ecce, adsum *and* Fiat voluntas tua.

Due to pressure from the clergy and the Catholic laity of Padua, and in response to a direct request from His Lordship the Bishop, I have had to go back on my decision about you and recall you to Padua. You are greatly needed there by many prominent people, religious and pious people: in others words you were, to quote the Bishop, doing "a heap of good" here and your task is not yet finished.

History repeats itself: even Saint Anthony wanted to go and preach to the heathen and find a martyr's death, but the Lord's winds drove him to our shores when he was on his way to Africa.

Obviously he wants your company! So accept the will of God and come home.

What must Fr. Leopoldo have felt! Here he was on the point, it seemed, of realizing his ambition when once more it proved no more than a dream. But the decisions of his Superiors were the will of God and there was no question but of immediate return. Padua was delighted. Their holy and beloved Fr. Leopoldo was back; but they did not know what a sacrifice the return had cost him, for outwardly he was content and as happy as if his dearest wish had been granted.

CHAPTER II.

THE MEANING OF THE RELIGIOUS LIFE

Anyone who will not obey can give up hope. Every superior is such by authority of his superior who in turn has the approval of the Pope: the Pope is the Vicar of Christ. Superiors therefore are the representatives of God: in obeying them we are certain of not being in error; in honouring them we honour God through Christ His Son.

FR. LEOPOLDO

To someone who said he would go to Holy Communion every day but that he was afraid it would become mere habit, Fr. Leopoldo replied, "I say Mass every day, and every day it is a new experience."

The greatest grace that God can give a human being is a vocation to the religious life. Although the good one can do in other states of life is certainly something, the immolation of embracing the religious life has much greater value and merit before God.

These words, written by Fr. Leopoldo to a penitent, give a clear idea of his conception of the religious life. First it is a *grace,* a free gift from God, about which there is no call to boast. He often said, glancing at the Crucifix, "We didn't choose Him; He chose us." It was this idea that impelled him to a continous striving to be worthy of the gift, to correspond to the grace.

But it is also a grace which demands complete *immolation* by the recipient. "The religous life is a martyrdom," he once said, "and we must be dead while still living." He realized fully the weight of this charge, but also that the victim must remain on the altar of sacrifice till the very end. "It was God who called me, and I, by His grace, was able to obey. Now I must die, but still be here."

When all temporal satisfactions have been set aside, it is only the thought of eternal reward that keeps the religious on the hard road of perfection. A Franciscan who by following Fr. Leopoldo's advice had got over a crisis that threatened his vocation, wrote to him: *You told me several times, and later wrote to me, that even while retaining my full freedom of choice I would do better to choose sacrifice, even to the extent of accepting death to be faithful to the ideal. I chose sacrifice and now I am happy.*

With such an heroic concept of the religious life, he exercised the greatest prudence in judging whether someone had a real vocation or not, for, as he often said, the religious life is a very serious matter and without a true vocation one can destroy oneself and bring others down with one.

The story of a man from a village near Padua is significant.

"I was rising twenty and uncertain what to do with my life. Quite often one of the questing Brothers used to come to the house and always suggested very strongly that I should follow in his footsteps and join the Order. I was in doubt and went to Fr. Leopoldo. I made my confession and before I could begin to explain my problem, he asked me my profession.

"I have none," I said. "I was thinking of joining the Order."

"When becoming a Brother becomes merely a sort of trade or profession like any other", he said suddenly very serious, "you also will become a Brother. Pay no attention to the words of that Brother; he is himself not suited to this life."

I followed his advice and remained in the world. I married and now have a family and I am happy. Two years after this incident the Brother who had urged me to join the Order put aside his habit and returned to the world.

His esteem for the religious life and his love of his own Order did not blind Fr. Leopoldo to the value and necessity of other ways of life and other Orders of regular clergy.

The *immolation* of the religious life, upon which Fr. Leopoldo insisted, is essentially a function of the three vows of poverty, chastity and obedience, each of which demands the sacrifice of something, the loss of a part of one's personal liberty. Fr. Leopoldo loved his vows, renewing them verbally every day and often in writing as well. He studied their practical application according to the strict Capuchin rule. Before all else he wished to be a good, perfect religious.

* * *

His observance of the vow of *Poverty* was scrupulous. By the Capuchin Rule, the religious owns nothing. He has the use only of such things as are necessary to life and his ministry. What is considered necessary by the Capuchin constitution is really only the barest essentials, and Fr. Leopoldo obeyed to the point of scrupulousness. His cell was bare, though he could have filled it with gifts from his penitents who begged for the honour of being allowed to help him, but he would accept none of them, not even the small things that even his most conscientious fellows allowed themselves.

A lady from Padua recounts that after she had insisted and insisted that there must be something he needed, he finally gave way and admitted that an umbrella would be useful when he had to go out in the rain. But he in his turn insisted that it should be the simplest, cheapest sort of umbrella, befitting his humble state of poverty.

When he had to have glasses, it was a great business to find frames suitably modest for him.

Finally when he was very ill, she managed to persuade him to accept a pair of woollen socks.

But these things he did not possess for himself. He accepted them for the friary and used only with permission of his superiors.

Poverty was particularly evident in his dress. It was usual in the Venetian Province to apply for a new habit every three years, but Fr. Leopoldo made his last much longer, while his undergarments were so patched that the tailor hardly knew where to attach the next patch. When his arthritis made it necessary for him to keep his feet covered, he would not wear socks but used old rags roughly cobbled together. Threadbare and patched his clothes certainly were, but also scrupulously clean, for, as he said, they were frequently touched by other people.

In all his sickness and right up to nearly the end of his life he insisted on using the straw mattress prescribed for the healthy brethren.

In money matters, of course, he was also scrupulous. "Money," he used to say, "is the passport that will get you anywhere—except into Heaven. It is the source and origin of many things—but not of happiness." All offerings that came into his hands went straight to the Fr. Guardian and even if he received money to pass on to some needy third party, he only undertook the commission with the Fr. Guardian's approval.

Towards the end of his life, showing a friend an offering of money given him by a penitent, he said, "I have had so many of these offerings in the course of my life and mostly they want me to use them for my own benefit, but by the grace of God I have never spent a farthing on myself."

In the confessional he was constantly recommending to his clerical penitents, secular as well as regular, complete detachment from earthly goods.

St. Francis had a worthy follower for his own love of poverty.

* * *

Chastity, the second vow, was one that he cherished as the apple of his eye. The vow of chastity does not remove natural concupiscence. As Fr. Leopoldo once said to a penitent, despairing in his struggle for purity, "My son, temptation doesn't respect even my gray beard nor my habit." So it was his constant endeavour to keep temptation at arm's length or further. Constant prayer and constant vigilance, the avoidance of anything remotely suggestive, discipline of the eyes, and above all charity, love of God and one's neighbour.

So firmly did he keep his glance downwards that practically no one could have told you what colour his eyes were.

His attitude to women was one of respect. Was not the Mother of God also our Mother and a woman? When a woman entered his confessional-cell for advice, he immediately desired her to be seated, while himself remained standing, and usually he left the door ajar.

But he could also be very severe with anyone who dared come to him not dressed according to his standards of modesty.

One summer's day when there was quite a queue of men waiting for confession, a young woman arrived, made up to a ridiculous degree, with no stockings, a skirt above her knees and a generous décolleté.

Curious to see how Fr. Leopoldo would deal with this apparition, the men made way for her.

She entered the confessional but had no time to open her mouth before Fr. Leopoldo ran to the door and showed her out crying, "*Carne da mercato!*" Unfortunately the English niceness in having different words for flesh and meat make an intelligible translation impossible, but no doubt the meaning is clear.

Blushing furiously, the girl tried to make her excuses, but he would not hear a word. "Go home and dress yourself," he said. "Then you can come back."

In the same way he would not allow boys or youths with too brief shorts to enter the confessional thus attired, and if he saw them in church he sent them out.

For himself, he kept his body scrupulously clean and respected it as something offered to God. He kept strictly to the rule of no personal contacts and was very insistent on its being observed by young religious. In his infirmities and old age it was a source of great distress and humiliation to him that he had to be helped by, and receive treatment at the hands of others.

His natural reserve, sustained by constant prayer and mortification, enabled him to withstand the more than fifty years of hearing other people's impurities poured into his ears in the confessional without himself ever being contaminated. Just before his death he was able to say, "By the grace of God and his blessed Mother, I cannot remember ever having sinned against chastity. My soul feels like a child's."

* * *

The third vow, that of *Obedience,* was also one of Fr. Leopoldo's great virtues. In any moment of doubt or difficulty he reminded himself, "I have vowed obedience." At the basis of his obedience was the firm belief that his superiors' words were for him the words of God.

He had the greatest respect for his superiors and never questioned or criticized their decisions. It was a source of hurt to him when the exigencies of the daily time-table cut down the time available for confessions, but he did not query the wisdom of the arrangements. On many occasions he had to refuse or break off interviews, even on the point of entering the confessional. He would excuse himself, apologize for the inconvenience, explain about holy obedience and depart whither the time-table decreed. Such are the workings of Providence that the 'victims' of these incidents were edified rather than suffering the more normal reaction of annoyed frustration.

Not only was he instant in obedience in doing what his superiors ordered, he also wished to have their authority and approval for everything he did, including activities that his confrères would normally do without a second thought.

When the Fr. Provincial visited the friary he would ask his approval for everything, and then perhaps he would ask for some extra favours. These favours were not relaxations or dispensations, but permission to hear confessions an hour longer, to undertake more mortifications, to attend the sick at any hour or any distance, to get up earlier and retire later in order to devote more time to his penitents.

Nor would he ever assume a permission that had not actually been granted. In December 1905, he was going to visit his relations near Trieste. It was raining hard and the icy *Bora* was blowing. It was evening when he arrived in the village and stopped to pay his respects to the Parish Priest of the place. The latter begged him to spend the night and not to go out again in that weather, but Fr. Leopoldo would not hear of it. He had not had permission to sleep outside a friary. So he walked another hour or more in the icy rain and wind until he arrived stiff with cold at the friary in Trieste.

Himself obedient, particularly to his own confessor and spiritual director, he insisted on obedience in his penitents, not only stressing it as a virtue but allowing no argument about a departure from his instructions.

CHAPTER III.

FAITH IS THE BASIS OF SANCTITY

Fr. Leopoldo used to call Our Lord Padrone (*Master*) *and Our Lady* Padrona *(Mistress). It has been commented that these titles do not accord very well with the traditional Augustinian-Bonaventuran theological concept traditionally followed by the Franciscans, but one must realize that, when he used these terms, Fr. Leopoldo had no intention of using technical theological language, but was writing or speaking for ordinary people. He used the terms because he himself was steeped in the spirit of "paternity" with which the* Padroni *of the old Venetian Republic treated their dependents. In the majority of cases they behaved as fathers* (padri) *rather than as masters* (padroni): *their dependents were considered as family and the word* Padrone *signified 'Father' with all the benevolence, providence and tenderness associated with fatherhood. This was the sense in which Fr. Leopoldo used the words.*

Belief in God is the one road to salvation. God himself at baptism sows the seed of Faith in us and then leaves to us the task of fostering it and giving it meaning.

For Fr. Leopoldo, Faith was his daily bread and his reason for living. In 1908 he expressed his thought as follows: *Sanctity, or justice, comes to life only with faith.*

He was determined that his faith should be the expression of his unwavering subscription to revealed truth, based solely on the authority of God who revealed it; but he desired with St. Paul that this supreme homage of the intellect should also be rational. For this reason he did not limit his study of revealed truth to the period when he was learning theology, but made it a subject of research and meditation throughout his life. The Scriptures, particularly the New Testament, were the sources, but to these must be added the clarifications and commentaries of the Fathers and Doctors of the Church. St. Augustine and St. Thomas were his favourites.

For four years, as we have already noted, he taught patrology (study of the Fathers) and the history of dogma at Padua, and this was a further occasion for him to increase his own knowledge. Anything in the nature of a theological discussion interested him vastly and he often sought the opinion of some competent authority. He bent his own acute intelligence to many long-standing difficulties, trying to find new solutions by following the Franciscan School of thought, and would put his findings up for discussion by students in the matter.

His greatest awareness came, however, from his continual meditation on the truths of the Faith. In the long hours of prayer before the Blessed Sacrament, his mind was enlightened by that intuitive knowledge that God accords to the simple and the humble. But this was something that he kept to himself.

For all these reasons, faith was such an integral part of Fr. Leopoldo's soul that when he spoke about belief he gave the impression of not just believing it but of seeing it. Faith informed his whole life and was the source of all his virtues, particularly of his humility; it united him to God and allowed him to share in His life and thought; it was the light of his intellect and the consolation of his will; and it shone out of him whenever he spoke of the things of God.

Such faith could not remain a secret of his own but had to be passed on to others. He wanted everyone to have faith and exhorted everyone, particularly his penitents, to study the Gospels as the prime source of faith. Commenting on the distress felt by Fr. Leopoldo because the Gospels were read so little among the people, and especially among the educated classes, and on his enthusiasm for the efforts made to popularize them by the Association of St. Jerome in the early part of the century, Archbishop Cuccarollo adds that he himself was much moved and as a result developed a greater love of the study of the Gospels and studied the vast commentaries of Cornelius a Lapide which he found a veritable mine of truth.

Fr. Leopoldo wanted to make the Gospels known and to defend them against their numerous and fierce enemies. Word of mouth was not enough, so he took up his pen and wrote a series of eleven articles in the *Bollettino Francescano* between 1907 and 1910. He urged upon the Tertiaries, with apostolic fervour backed by close reasoning, the necessity of living the Faith and defending it courageously.

Then (he wrote) *Faith must be a shield for us. As the soldier of old manipulated his shield to cover and protect every part of his body from attack, so must the Tertiary be able, in the more or less difficult circumstances of everyday life, to shield himself by remembering the teachings of his holy Faith.*

St. Paul said, "I believed, for which cause I have spoken." So *must Tertiaries, and all Christians, behave. We believe in God, so we are ready to do all He asks of us in our daily lives, whether within the privacy of the four walls of our houses or in the glaring light of public life; we are fearless in professing our Faith, in making it known and defending it. If we live our Faith, zeal for the cause of Christ will be born spontaneously in our hearts.*

Aware of the need to accept all methods of apostolate for the defence of the Faith, he understood the need for the help of the laity in carrying the truth to the masses. A layman can penetrate where no priest can in the religio-political and sociological fields. In 1909 he wrote: *What is called Catholic Action is necessary for two reasons. First of all, present day civil society tends to a parliamentary form of government in which, more or less, every group of citizens, whatever the ideas they support, wants to have its representatives among those in power. In the second place, modern society has largely abandoned God and needs to be led back to truth and justice, so that that part of the people that has remained faithful has the duty to take an active part in civil affairs and also to be represented among those in power. Such Catholics are fighting in God's cause for the defence of the Faith, and they need two things: they must be well grounded in the Gospel and they must be in very close touch with the Church whose ambassadors and representatives they are.*

Wise words, and not vainly idealistic, for he realized all the difficulties of putting them into practice and, as a man of faith, could point to the real causes of the first unhappy failures. In fact, not long afterwards, he wrote: *Those who came forward as champions of God's cause would certainly not have come less up to expectations and aspirations had they had a firmer grounding to support their material actions.*

Those of his penitents who seemed fitted for this struggle were encouraged by him to take part. He wrote, for instance, to the Servant of God Guido Negri: *Your soul is full of apostolic ideas... Christ Our Lord chooses certain persons and inspires them, He gives them a generous heart, wide views, and makes them men of action. This special apostolate is particularly found among men called to the priesthood, but also when the times require it, among the simple faithful. You, now, are among those faithful who have been specially chosen.*

And to another penitent: *You know how much I value your work for the Faith and how important before God I consider it. I consider it my duty before God to try to obtain more and more grace for those who are called upon to do great things for His glory.*

'Great things', witness to the truth, and defence of the Faith did not mean for him the noisy emptiness of propaganda, but before everything the example of a holy life. In 1909 he expressed his opinion as follows:

The first way of proclaiming the truth of the Faith is that of the Apostles and their successors the priests: the second way is by holiness of life, by the practice of evangelical perfection, and this is the way par excellence *of the militant Christian. When holiness of life shines through the apostle or the militant Christian, his internal conviction of the truths which he witnesses is manifest. Now the human mind is logical and seeks a cause for this effect, and will give glory to God, the giver of all gifts.*

To know of the joy it gave him to see the lay apostolate in action, we may read what he wrote to his brother Andrea. *It is the greatest consolation to me to see how in the midst of the boundless evil and corruption of the world there are still some chosen souls who bear witness to the Faith, and not just among the old and dying but also among the flower of youth, in the midst of plenty and luxury.*

The propagation of the Faith through the missions was his dream. He longed to go himself and bring back the dissident Eastern Churches, but since this was impossible, he offered his whole life in the confessional to this end. (This in fact is such an important aspect of his life that it is treated at length elsewhere in this book.) He followed the progress of the missions, rejoicing in their successes and sympathizing with all their manifold difficulties. Naturally he was particularly interested in the Capuchin Missions and knew every last detail about them. When the ceremony of consigning the Cross to departing missionaries was held, he always took an active part and one could read in his face a sort of holy envy for the lucky ones who were going.

He supported the missions with prayer and sacrifice and on one occasion, in this connexion, foretold something in a way that has all the characteristics of pure prophecy.

In 1938 Fr. Gaetano of Thiene came back seriously ill from the Ethiopian mission field. As his work had been daily among the members of a leper colony at Harar, the gloomiest fears were entertained for his health. Not unnaturally he himself was in a rather depressed state of mind. Fr. Leopoldo comforted him and assured him he would get better, and added: "My son, when all these political disorders are over, in the name of God ask to go back to the missions. To *our* mission, however, for if you ask to go to any other it will be refused. Your place is with our mission."

Many years passed and the Venetian Capuchins were all removed from Abyssinia and not allowed to return. They opened another mission in Angola, but Fr. Gaetano remained in Italy and it looked as if the mission field had become no more than a dream for him. In 1950, wishing still to go back to his lepers at Harar, on the advice of the Father Provincial he made his request to the Father General. The Emperor seemed ready to allow him to join the French Capuchins who had replaced the Italians and all seemed to be going well when suddenly the Father General opposed a flat refusal. Half of Father Leopoldo's prophecy at least had come true!

In 1954 the other half came true when a further request to be sent to the missions was granted and he was sent to Angola, to their own mission.

Chapter IV.

DEVOTION TO THE PRIESTHOOD AND THE MASS

As Christ our Redeemer redeemed mankind through His sufferings and cross and death, so He wishes his followers to apply His merits to redeemed mankind by use of the same means of suffering, sorrow and sacrifice, united with and sanctified by His sufferings as priest and eternal victim. Every member of the faithful is called upon to cooperate with the divine plan in this manner for the benefit of mankind, for to all of them was given the command to pray one for another and to be a cause of salvation one to another.

Fr. Leopoldo

One thing in particular was the object of a great devotion for Fr. Leopoldo, the Catholic priesthood, that sublime institution founded by Christ for the salvation of the world. For him wisdom, wealth, beauty, everything was but a shadow compared with the one really great thing, the priesthood. His conviction in this matter was profound and he acted accordingly. When he was hearing confessions, advising, consoling people he *knew* that it was not just the insignificant little friar who spoke, but the priest, the minister of Christ, in fact Christ Himself acting through His priest.

This absolute certainty sometimes made his attitude or expressions profoundly disconcerting for people who did not understand them. In difficult circumstances he would sometimes say, "Who has spoken? I, perhaps, a poor friar? No! The priest has spoken, in other words Christ. That's enough!" So great was his own conviction that he never failed to convince his interlocutor and remove all doubts, even in the solution of the most trying cases.

This extremely high regard of his for the priest arose principally from the fact that the priest celebrates Mass and offers the Divine Victim in sacrifice. To Andrea Corner, a childhood friend, he wrote on one occasion:

The glad day is approaching when your son Don Girolamo will be ordained priest. This will be a great joy for you as a father and a Christian. May I be allowed to anticipate the happy event by sending my best wishes and congratulations now? I have not the pleasure of knowing your son, but I know you and I beg you to tell him what friends you and the humble writer of this letter have been from the time we were boys together till our now somewhat advanced years. Give him my best wishes then and say that this old priest, who hopes under Providence to celebrate his Golden Jubilee in two years' time, greets him already as a colleague in the apostolic ministry.

You know well enough how the priest in celebrating the Sacred

Mysteries offers to God His own Son and bloodlessly renews the sacrifice of the Cross, in other words we offer an Infinite Good, the very Son of God, to God the Father. In doing this, the priest is fulfilling the highest office possible on earth. This office your son will shortly be fulfilling. I have every reason therefore to hail with joy now the day when your son will for the first time celebrate the sacred Mysteries.

One more thing I must ask you: when your son has been ordained, please kiss his hands for me.

A little later he wrote again, almost a postscript to the above. *You have long had a priest for an intimate friend in my humble person, Our Lord has now given you a son who is a priest. With your fervent faith you cannot fail to realize what an ineffable favour God has granted you.*

* * *

Fr. Leopoldo's respect for the priesthood was also manifested externally.

In the Venetian Province it was the custom that brothers on meeting a priest would out of respect for his office, make way for him, uncovering if covered, and bowing the head, as an act of faith in the priesthood. Fr. Leopoldo observed this custom scrupulously, not only before ordination but throughout his life, and not only to what might be termed his seniors but also to the newest ordained.

A lady told Fr. Leopoldo once that she was going to Verona to see Don Giovanni Calabria so he charged her to kiss this priest's hand for him.

"That's all wrong!" said Don Giovanni when he heard. "It is I who should kiss his hand, and you will please do so for me as soon as you get back. Fr. Leopoldo is a saint! Do what he tells you, and don't miss a syllable, because Our Lord speaks through him. It is God who guides him. And ask him to pray for this poor priest."

For priests Fr. Leopoldo would do anything. He joyfully answered the demands from various houses to help in the confessional during retreats and he greeted his clerical penitents with the greatest deference and was never tired of comforting them and sustaining them in their difficulties.

On the occasion of his sacerdotal Golden Jubilee, a large number of priests gathered to express their gratitude. Mgr. Schievano, Archpriest of Padua Cathedral, spoke for them all when he said, "Venerable Father, you see gathered around you a large part of your spiritual family. The ties which bind us to you are strong and holy and felt by us all. Only on the last day will it be known how much you have sacrificed for us, how much good you have done, how many worries banished and sorrows consoled and softened."

During his last illness, it was principally priests whom he received into his cell for confession. "There's not much I can do now," he said to one of them, "but at least I have still the souls most dear to God, those of His priests."

He reacted strongly to any denigration of priests and even when it was a matter of notoriety he always said, "Let God judge."

Once his reaction to disrespect for the priesthood took a more practical form. In 1935 he was on his way home from the Basilica of St. Anthony via the Botanical Gardens and was on a small bridge over the *canaletta* when he was met by some young toughs who jeered and said, "Let's take the old boy and chuck him in the canal."

"Try!" said Fr. Leopoldo, going on his way.

In due course, walking slowly, he arrived at the Prato della Valle and then retraced his steps.

The youths were still there, like so many statues, unable to move.

As he approached they threw themselves on their knees, begging his forgiveness.

"Don't ask my forgiveness," he said kindly. "It's God's forgiveness you should ask. I am only a poor friar, but you must learn to respect people, particularly God's ministers."

Then he gave them a friendly clap on the shoulder and let them go

* * *

It has already been said that Fr. Leopoldo's respect for the priesthood was based principally upon the fact that priests could celebrate

Mass. And the Mass for him could never become a daily routine. He *lived* the mystery of the sacrificing priesthood. "If only we could see", he exclaimed in several occasions, "if only we could see what happens on the altar! Our eyes could never master such splendour."

This living faith was the result of a long and intense preparation. Archbishop Cuccarollo, who studied with him, recalls the importance that he gave to the treatise *De Eucharistiae Sacramento* by Billuart, to Cardinal Bona's treatise *De Sacrificio Missæ* and to Fr. Chaignon's book *The Holy Mass,* and that he had learned by heart Book IV of the *Imitation* which deals with the Eucharist.

"One must so prepare oneself for ordination," he used to say, "that the life of the priest becomes the life of Christ who offers Himself on the altar, so that he becomes the mouthpiece of Christ when he pronounces the words of consecration. His hands will touch Jesus and will give Him to the faithful, as the hands of Our Lady, of St. Joseph, of old Simeon touched Him; in the Holy Mass the priest performs the most important action of his day.

"For the ordinary Christian sanctifying himself is reduced to two things, dying and coming to life, casting off the old man and putting on the new. For us priests however there is the additional duty of passing on to the faithful the supernatural, divine life derived from Jesus Christ. Sanctifying ourselves therefore means dying, coming to life and giving life, three phases of priestly perfection of which Christ offers Himself as a perfect example every day on the altar in our hands. Thus He teaches us to die to ourselves and to the world, to come to life to a holier existence, and to revivify our neighbour by our zeal."

But, as always with Fr. Leopoldo, it was more than words. Let us see what Mgr. Cuccarollo had to say.

When still a young student he had always before his mind, and often on his lips, the words of Holy Writ: Purify yourselves, who bear the vessels of the Lord. *For this reason his remote preparation consisted of daylong effort to be always in the presence of God and to avoid even the slightest deliberate fault. As a student he repeated fervently the words with which it was customary to preface any important action:* Let us remember that we are in the presence of God, that we received

Holy Communion this morning, and that we shall communicate again tomorrow. *Once he became priest he retained the habit, modifying the words to:* Remember that you have today celebrated Mass and that you will celebrate again tomorrow.

In order really to "purify himself", he went to confession every evening. Supper was always a very light meal for him in order that he should sleep lightly and be clear-headed in the morning for the great office he had to perform. He rose, always with the permission of his superiors, long before the others and spent a whole hour in prayer as his immediate preparation. In that hour of meditation all he did was to intensify the preparation that had being going on all the previous day and a good part of the night as well.

In view of all this it is scarcely to be wondered at that for him the celebration of Mass was really a "feast of soul" and for the congregation a source of the greatest edification. Particularly after the Consecration, when his face was transfigured and his eyes often filled with tears, one could sense that he often had direct contact with the Victim he held in his hands. He would have liked to remain long at the altar, but did not out of consideration for others and so as to not to keep the crowds of penitents waiting.

His idea of participation by the congregation was not they should indulge in vocal prayer but that they should concentrate on the sacrifice being performed, for this was everything. When he himself touched the Sacred Host, he felt an increase of grace in his soul and of sanctity in his body.

A lay-brother who often served his Mass, on returning to the sacristy, wanted to kiss his hand, but Fr. Leopoldo always withdrew it and hid it in his sleeve, although the custom is common enough in Europe.

"Father, mayn't I kiss the hand that has so recently touched Our Lord's Body?" asked the Brother one day.

At this Fr. Leopoldo gave way at once, and thereafter always offered his hand to be kissed.

Exery day it was with the same enthusiasm, the same fervour that Fr. Leopoldo celebrated Mass. He often repeated the words of the

Imitation: The good priest who wishes to honour God, rejoice the angels, edify the Church, help the living, obtain rest for the departed and himself share in all good, never allows the celebration of Mass to become a habit.

He himself celebrated his last Mass with the same fervour as he gave to his first Mass.

His thanksgiving after Mass was commensurate with the fervour of his preparation and celebration. He wrote: *There is no more precious moment than that of thanksgiving after Mass. Jesus, infinitely rich though He be, cannot give more than He gives each day to the priest celebrating Mass. It is only just to make adequate return. Some through lack of love or of faith have lost the habit of thanksgiving. Jesus when He was in the world healed the sick who merely touched His garments; what good will He not do to us, if we have faith, who hold Him under the Sacramental species, in our hearts? We are the official distributors of His divine largesse: let us therefore use His power on behalf of sinners, on behalf of our neighbour and for the faithful departed. So long as the Sacramental Species remains in being, He is within us. What a feast for our Faith!*

In fact Fr. Leopoldo did not spend a long time over his thanksgiving, but went almost immediately to the confessional. "After Mass," he explained once, "I start hearing confessions almost immediately because there are so many people waiting, but I also hear the Masses of my fellow-priests." In fact if some other priest was celebrating while he was in the confessional, he stopped hearing confessions from the *Sanctus* to the Consecration, rising to his feet and withdrawing into himself in such a manner that his internal devotion was manifest. This without regard to who might be in the confessional at the time, so that there are plenty to witness his habit and their own resulting edification.

In fact it is true to say that Fr. Leopoldo *lived* his Mass in an unending thanksgiving for the last and preparation for the next, his belief being so vivid that he could not keep his mind from it.

Our Lord had his own way of rewarding such faithful devotion to the Sacrament of His love. In his last illness constriction of the oesophagus made it impossible for him to take any solid food, and even liquids had to be introduced by tube; nevertheless in his Mass he was always able to consume without difficulty the Sacred Species and the purification. Not even the specialists could offer any natural explanation of this.

* * *

Strong in his faith, Fr. Leopoldo knew that he had in the Mass a weapon which even God Almighty could not resist. He knew that when he asked a favour, however great, while offering up the Divine Victim, refusal was impossible.

"*Since the Divine Victim Who offers Himself in the Sacred Mysteries is infinite,*" he wrote to a friend, "*what is asked for will never be as great as the Victim Who offers Himself.*"

And to another, "*When I say Mass, my thoughts are for all who have consulted me. At the culmination of the Sacred Mysteries I fold them all in my heart and I know that my prayers will be answered because what I ask for is nothing compared with what I offer.*"

There are plenty of incidents to confirm this statement.

On 7th March, 1925, Signorina Evelina Berto from near Padua caught influenza which rapidly developed complications in the form of arthritis, nephritis and endocarditis. High fever and excruciating pains caused the unfortunate woman to scream in agony. The local doctor called in a second opinion, a Professor from the Padua Clinic; the prognosis was far from reassuring. Danger of death at any moment, and in the unlikely event of a cure it would never be complete. For eleven days the agony continued for the helpless patient and her distracted family.

On 18th March the girl's father had to go to Padua and decided to go to the Basilica of Saint Anthony, go to confession and place his daughter under the protection of the Saint. He got as far as the Prato della Valle and got out of the tram to go to the Basilica when some mysterious force made him board the tram again and go on to the Capuchin friary and see his confessor Fr. Leopoldo.

He made his confession as usual, but said nothing about his daughter. Fr. Leopoldo, however, asked him why he was not his usual cheerful self, and Signor Berto told him.

Fr. Leopoldo, usually so apt to join himself to the sorrows of others, remained smiling in the face of Berto's distress, and said:

"Signor Berto, don't be afraid. Have faith, as you always have had. Tomorrow is the feast of St. Joseph. I shall remember your daughter in my Mass and she will be cured. And you will bring an *ex voto* to St. Joseph. Do you believe me?"

"Yes, Father. I believe you."

He went home happy, secure in the belief that his daughter would be cured next day.

During the night the girl grew worse, with higher fever, increased pain and muscular spasms. But at six in the morning, just when Father Leopoldo would have been saying Mass, the patient's mother watching at her bedside observed an improvement. Fr. Leopoldo was right, she thought, she is cured.

And she was. The doctor was sent for at once and could not believe his senses. He took her temperature three times before being convinced that the fever had really subsided. However, he examined her thoroughly and, still astounded, pronounced her cured. In a few days she had regained her strength and sat down with her family to Easter Sunday dinner completely herself.

In the meantime the girl's father had rushed off to Padua to tell Fr. Leopoldo the good news. The latter was all smiles.

"I told you St. Joseph was good at that sort of thing, didn't I?"

The incident had wide repercussions. A well-known industrialist from Conegliano who was far from practising his religion, hearing Berto's account of his daughter's cure, was so moved that not long afterwards he was reconciled to the Church and later left the world and entered religion.

Another case concerns a Signora Anselmi, of Padua, who after the birth of a son in 1934 had been constantly ill for a number of years.

She had twice been in hospital and all known treatments had been tried, but without success. She ended up bed-ridden and subject to high fevers and acute pain. Two specialists now examined her and recommended surgical intervention though, they said, they could not guarantee the outcome. Faced with the possibility at only 26 years of age of having to leave her husband and small son for ever, the poor woman could do nothing but weep, till a good friend of hers brought Fr. Leopoldo to her bedside. He heard her confession and then, as if inspired, said, "Madam, don't cry any more. Go to hospital and have the operation. I shall remember you every day in my Mass and I assure you you will be completely cured."

From that moment everything changed. The patient cheered up, went to hospital and insisted on having the operation. The two professors told the husband they could accept no responsibility and only performed the operation at the insistence of his wife. However, perform it they did, and it was a long and tricky business—but completely successful.

On the day of the operation Fr. Leopoldo had said Mass for the patient and it was to him that, as soon as possible, she came with her husband and son. He was, of course, delighted to see them, blessed them all and urged them to hear Mass frequently.

In 1940 Giacomo Lampronti, from Udine, a man of Jewish origin, found himself in a hopeless situation on account of the social laws. He had been dismissed from his employment and found it impossible to get another job. Having heard of Fr. Leopoldo, he came to Padua and, full of despair, put his case to him.

"Have faith," said he. "Providence will not abandon you. And since you have no job for the moment, go to Mass every morning and Providence will not be wanting. It is not I who tell you this, but God Who speaks through me. Only don't forget to hear Mass every morning."

Lampronti believed Fr. Leopoldo and heard Mass every day, and the whole time he remained unemployed he never lacked necessities for himself and his family, help often arriving in an apparently miraculous manner.

First light on 6th April, 1935. Signor Amerigo Alibardi, living in a suburb of Padua, came into the city in search of a doctor for his wife. She should have given birth two days before, but now a natural birth seemed impossible. The wife's agony was terrible and it seemed she must die. Her husband rushed off to find help, but at that unearthly hour he didn't know where to apply.

Finding himself outside the Capuchin church, he remembered Fr. Leopoldo and went in to find him. Fr. Leopoldo was already in the confessional and when he had heard the story, remained a moment in thought and then said:

"Have you faith?"

"Yes, Father."

"Good! Then go at once to the Basilica of St. Anthony and hear Mass at the Tomb. Then, go home and see how things are. And then come back and tell me."

"Father, I'll gladly go and hear Mass later, but right now I must go and find a doctor for my wife. She's dying."

"I told you to go and hear Mass at once."

Moved by some unknown force, he obeyed. Then he rushed back home, to find that his wife had given birth to a beautiful child without the slightest difficulty. The birth took place, they reckoned, just as he was leaving the Basilica after hearing Mass.

When the delighted father duly reported to Fr. Leopoldo, the latter smiled. "Didn't I tell you to have faith in the Holy Mass?"

* * *

Fr. Leopoldo *lived* the Mass and always tried to instill into others the same vivid faith in what he rightly considered to be the source of all grace and blessings. Probably every priest who came to him to confession was frequently exhorted to celebrate Mass well and to make it the central point of his spiritual life.

Mgr. Giuseppe Manzini of Verona wrote: *I was a young priest when I first went to Fr. Leopoldo. He spoke to me with great wisdom about the Mass, recommending me to celebrate with great devotion and to make it the centre of my spiritual life. "If you do this," he ended, "the fruitfulness of your priestly office is assured and you will work endless good for your own soul."*

To another priest Fr. Leopoldo wrote: *See that you celebrate Mass with ever more and more fervour so that it will be more and more fruitful. Live always in terms of the Mass you have celebrated or the one you are going to celebrate, almost a continuous Mass, since we priests are carrying on the eternal priesthood of Christ.*

To lay persons he recommended frequent, even daily, attendance at Mass, following it by meditating on its great mysteries. *We should,* he wrote to a penitent, *keep our whole mind and our whole heart in the presence of the Divine Victim Who offers Himself every hour of every day and night. He is the Lamb of God Who takes away the sins of the world. If for one moment this sacrifice were withdrawn, the world would tumble in the ruins of its own wickedness. We must cling ever closer to the divine Victim-Priest and I, as I celebrate, and you, as you attend, must be generous-hearted and embrace all mankind. The divine charity of Our Lord Jesus Christ in the Holy Sacrifice of the Mass overcomes, in infinite measure, our human delinquencies and satisfies the Divine Majesty for our so numerous sins. Keep these thoughts always in mind.*

He wrote to Luigi Maggia of Padua: *At every moment of time, somewhere in the world, Christ is offering Himself up in the Holy Mass. You have only to unite yourself in spirit with the celebrant to partake of the special graces accorded to this Sacrifice.*

To Signora Anna Bertoliero of Padua he sent the following, recommending her to read it often: *Always think of the Divine Love with which Our Lord Jesus Christ gave His life for us, and of how He perpetuates this Sacrifice by continually renewing it in the Mass. Then consider this point: the first sacrifice He made alone; the rest He makes through the ministry of His priests celebrating the Divine Mysteries, and He makes them in conjunction with the faithful present at Mass.*

CHAPTER V.

DEVOTION TO THE BLESSED SACRAMENT

Jesus told the Jews that if they kept His commandments they would know the truth, and the truth would set them free. This truth is none other than the grace of the Holy Ghost, the grace promised by Christ to the Samaritan woman under the simile of the living water. Let us therefore approach God, Who is Truth and Light, and we shall be illuminated. Before the splendour of this Light, Satan, who is darkness, will be put to flight, and the kingdom of God and the Gospel of Christ will be safe within us.

FR. LEOPOLDO

Great was the mystic joy with which Fr. Leopoldo held the Sacred Host in his hands and consumed It. But this did not last long. After Mass he folded his arms across his breast as though trying to retain the treasure of which he had partaken, but before long the Sacramental Species lost their identity and the Real Presence dissolved with them. Jesus, truly present in Body and Blood was, however, not far off: He was always still there in the tabernacle, and it was to the tabernacle that Fr. Leopoldo now turned his attention, never turning it away. Whatever he did during the day, wherever he might go, his heart remained in adoration before God. He was constantly aware of the call of the tabernacle and the necessity of it for the spiritual life. (1)

At any time when he was free of other duties, he went immediately to the Blessed Sacrament Altar and plunged into adoration. In spite of acute arthritic pains in his legs, he always knelt upright without the support of the bench, and very often on the bare floor. He remained completely immobile, like a statue, and his face, turned to the tabernacle was ecstatic; often tears poured down his cheeks.

The archives are full of written descriptions; all agreed on his devotion to the Blessed Sacrament and the ecstatic nature of his adoration.

Even in his genuflexions when passing before the altar, one could see that here was no routine gesture, no everyday acknowledgement of a belief however firmly held, but a genuine, almost spontaneous act of adoration.

From his great devotion to the Blessed Sacrament stemmed a desire to ensure that, as far as he was concerned, everything to do with

---

(1) Fr. Leopoldo had a saying, "Senza il fuoco del tabernacolo non può durare la fiamma nel cuore del sacerdote" which cannot properly be translated since 'fuoco' has in the context the double meaning of 'fire' and 'focal point' or centre of interest, 'without which the fire/ardour in the priest's heart must die'.

tabernacle should be perfect. He laid great stress on the proper carrying out of ceremonial rites and gently pointed out any lapses. He always tried to see that the church was kept in good order and scrupulously clean, himself giving a hand with scrubbing and sweeping the floor, when he was still young and able to do so. For a long time he kept in his own hands the task of washing corporals and purificators.

For organists he always had a good word, since they added to the splendours of the sacred ritual.

He suffered visibly if anyone's behaviour before the tabernacle was not all that it should be; one day, coming upon a priest leaning in a slovenly manner on a bench in the choir, he said, "My son, that's not the way to kneel before God."

On another occasion when he was praying in choir, a young Brother in a hurry passed in front of the altar with a rather token genuflexion. He called him back. "My son, doesn't it occur to you that Our Lord is there?"

In 1931 when the friary was being rebuilt, the old infirmary was being demolished and with it the infirmary chapel where Fr. Leopoldo had so often celebrated Mass. He was terribly upset and told Father Venceslao of San Martino that walls which had housed Christ in the Blessed Sacrament should never be demolished. What pained him particularly was that on the site of the chapel a scullery was to be built.

Aware that in the Holy Eucharist was the inexhaustible source of all good, Fr. Leopoldo, moved by his ardent charity, did everything in his power to persuade others to approach the Blessed Sacrament. He often included a visit to the Blessed Sacrament in the penances he gave, and was always recommending frequent Communion as a sovereign aid to perfection.

A priest, member of a religious house, asked him once whether in case of illness he should have Holy Communion brought to him every day as it might make work for others. "What!" said Fr. Leopoldo, astonished. "When so many lay-people are at such pains not to miss daily Communion, can we, for whom it is so easy, do without?"

I recommend daily Communion, he wrote to a penitent. *You'll see what a marvellous effect it has.*

And to Guido Negri: *Our Divine Redeemer asks one thing in particular of you: that every day, when it is possible, you should receive Him in the Most Holy Eucharist.*

To Gino Maggia: *Now that you have recovered from your serious illness, resume your old habit of receiving Holy Communion if possible every day. You know the importance of going to Holy Communion. We only have to think of Our Lord's words when he foretold this ineffable Sacrament, "For my flesh is meat indeed and my blood is drink indeed. He that eateth my flesh and drinketh my blood abideth in me and I in him." When we receive Holy Communion, therefore, we unite ourselves to Our Lord. More than this one cannot say. Keep this thought before you when you go to Holy Communion.*

He recommended frequent Communion as a sure defence against the spiritual dangers among which most of us live. To Armando Bredolo he wrote as follows:

The things around us are not the causes of our desires but only occasions of them, therefore it is possible in any surroundings to be, in one's thoughts, independent of those material surroundings. You must therefore keep your independence of thought and will in whatever company you may find yourself. Since you have faith, pray as hard as you can and above all go frequently to Holy Communion.

Your good intentions are an important gift of God. God, Who has started the good work by giving you these good intentions, will not fail to complete what He has begun. However we must always do our part and cooperate with the grace of God working in us. I repeat, therefore: go frequently to Holy Communion.

CHAPTER VI.

DEVOTION TO THE WORD OF GOD

The Son of God became man to destroy the kingdom of Satan. This kingdom, which began with Adam's sin and will end with that of the last sinner, is nothing tangible, but exists within man so long as he has a mortal sin on his soul. The whole world of irreligious people gives allegiance to Satan and in this sense he is said to be the prince of this world. It is against this supreme enemy of the Gospel of Christ that we are called upon to fight.

FR. LEOPOLDO

In 1908 Fr. Leopoldo wrote: *St. Paul says, "For the Word of God is living... and more piercing than any two-edged sword... and is a discerner of the thoughts and intents of the heart. Nothing is hidden from it."*

This powerful Word of God is effectual, omniscient and omnipotent, for the Word of the Mind of God the Father could not be other, made tangible by the mystery of the Incarnation whereby the Word became flesh and dwelt amongst us and still is with us in the Eucharist.

St. Paul also says, in his own name and in that of all Catholic priests, "We are the ambassadors of Christ, Who by our ministry exhorts and warns you." Quite rightly and properly, therefore, priests make these words of the Apostle their own, being those to whom the apostolic authority has been passed on. For this reason when properly ordained priests carry out their office and preach the Gospel to the people, it is in reality Christ Who speaks and preaches through them. And His Word is living and efficacious, as He Himself is living and of infinite worth. This then is the most effective weapon that we priests, following St. Paul's precept, can employ in the defence of the Gospel.

The regular clergy are in his view particularly called upon for this work of spreading the Gospel. *Those who are called to embrace the religious life,* he wrote in the *Bollettino Francescano* of December, 1907, *are for that very reason called to the apostolic ministry since the religious life is of its nature more adapted to the apostolate. Since, in fact, they are called to a life closer to Gospel sanctity, they are better able to preach it.*

Since defective speech made it impossible to preach the word of God himself, he did his best to arouse enthusiasm and love for this work among others.

Fr. Leopoldo, writes Archbishop Cuccarollo, *although richly endowed with the gifts of God, did not have the gift of speech, but he could arouse in others the taste for preaching based on the Gospel. He admired eloquence and enjoyed the best speakers. He knew well, and often spoke enthusiastically of Bossuet's works, especially his sermons for the feasts of Our Lord and His Blessed Mother. Every year on the feast of St. John Chrysostom, and for days after, our conversation centred on his* Homilies, *and he gave thanks to St. Pius X who had nominated him patron of preachers. Alas, in the last decades of the 19th Century and the first of the 20th, the pulpit had become a sounding board for theatrical oratory. This "synthesis of all heresies" as Pius X called it was introduced into the pulpit by priests who preached not Christ but themselves, being ashamed of the Gospels and the Fathers of the Church.*

Fr. Leopoldo was fired to indignation to think that there were priests who instead of nourishing their flocks with the word of God used the pulpit to show off their worldly knowledge. He spoke of the despair that would come to such priests in their last hour when they knew how they had betrayed the word of God.

He gave thanks to God for having preserved the Capuchins from falling into like error, and he had an especially good word for the Venetian Province which, under the guidance of Fr. Roberto of Nove (1), preached Jesus Christ and not a lot of vain worldly wisdom.

With a love and an enthusiasm that was almost startling in his normally serious and austere manner, Fr. Leopoldo advised and guided young preachers. Fr. Raimondo of Herne wrote: *In 1938 when I was a very young priest, I lived next to Fr. Leopoldo whom I found very generous with advice and encouragement. He was wonderful to listen to on the subjects of study and preaching. And how he pounced on certain traditional faults! He might have been a young priest of my own age, so full was he of ideas and enthusiasm in the search for new ways to success. Astonished, I said to him one day:*

"But, Father, you think like a young man! You have the best and most up-to-date ideas about preaching!"

---

(1) Born 1869. In 1898, already ordained and with honours in philosophy and canon law, entered the Order. A man of vast culture and great gifts, he began his career as a preacher at once, becoming the most famous preacher and most in demand of this time. Died 1939 leaving important writings.

"Well, you know", he said, smiling, "Truth doesn't get old. It's always up-to-date."

Every time I went to see him, he urged me to study, and often he would get up and take some work of St. Augustine which he kept in the confessional, and opening the book which was nearly as big as himself, would point out with his twisted arthritic forefinger some passage of profound truth which would serve as text for a sermon.

When I came back from preaching somewhere, he always wanted to know how it had gone. When things had gone well he rejoiced with me, but when, as sometimes happened, I was depressed by difficulties or criticism, he always managed to cheer me up and sustain me. I felt that he was watching me and that I was the object of his paternal interest, so I could never do less than my best. (2)

As soon as Fr. Leopoldo heard that the son of his childhood friend Andrea Corner was destined for the priesthood, he wrote:

Congratulations that one of your sons has been called to the priesthood and the apostolate. Encourage him in this course. It is certainly a course of sorrows and sacrifice, but He Who calls one to the service of the Holy Gospel takes the greater part on Himself.

---

(2) A brief note on the writer of the above may add value to his testimony. Born in Germany of Italian parents, he came to Italy as a young man and became a Capuchin. His career as a preacher began as soon as he was ordained and his gifts soon made him much in demand. Fr. Leopoldo took a great paternal interest in him and gave him much valuable help and advice. One lesson in particular Fr. Raimondo learned from him: that a priest ought to devote his whole life to the salvation of souls, even if it meant dying of exhaustion in harness. Which was in fact what happened. Almost as though he foresaw that he would not live long, he threw himself into his work without a moment's respite. He often quoted a saying he had from Fr. Leopoldo, "Better live a year or two less and work harder and save one or two more souls".

Threatened with polycystitis, he had himself examined by a specialist in Zürich where he was preaching. He was given no hope of a cure and one or two years to live. Instead of relaxing, he remembered Fr. Leopoldo's words and worked the harder, telling no one of the pains he suffered. A few months before his death, ignoring the advice of the specialists in Padua, he went down to Messina to preach the Lenten sermons in the Cathedral there and then gave a course of Lectures in Palermo. He returned to Padua exhausted but happy. A month later he was dead.

To a colleague who consulted him about getting dispensed from some of his duties, because he thought he had too much to do, he answered without hesitation, "No, no! Work, work! We are called to work for souls; we are called for the salvation of the world."

When the students at Udine wrote to him for his Golden Jubilee, he answered: *Allow an older colleague of yours on the solemn occasion of the fiftieth anniversary of his ordination to say one word: We are born to hard work. The height of happiness is to be able to undertake it. Ask Almighty God that you may die of the hard work of the apostolate.*

He did not, of course, confine himself to exhorting others to work, but bent all his own forces to it with a singlemindedness and constancy that partook of the nature of heroism. Hard work he considered a special gift from God for which he was profoundly and constantly grateful.

I continue to be busy for souls, he wrote to his friend Antonio Settin, *and I thank God that He has granted me this favour.*

CHAPTER VII.

FAITH THE COMFORTER

Our Lord is there also for the poor and will render them justice; they need only avoid evil. As long as one is good, one's sufferings are not in vain.

The world with its storms and injustices and evils comes to an end. God alone is eternal, and He will reward all according to their merits; for this reason it pays to be on good terms with Him.

No one remains in this world for ever. For the short time we are here let us try to do good and to love and help one another.

We must try to bear our misfortunes in silence and without giving them too much importance. If we seek human comfort, we lose a part of the merit. God sees our misfortunes and sorrows and He will recompense us.

Sayings of FR. LEOPOLDO

From his continuous union with Christ in the Eucharist Father Leopoldo had learned one lesson, that mankind has a very great need of consolation. In the difficulties of this life, oppressed by the bloody mystery of suffering, men have an absolute need for an understanding heart, for a word of comfort: they will not shorten the road, but they will give a new impetus to continue the painful way towards God. All this was well understood by Fr. Leopoldo who considered it his duty to bring to torn and troubled hearts the only effective word of comfort, the Word of God in the Blessed Sacrament.

Allow me, Madam, he wrote once, *to speak to you as my faith dictates: I have to serve Our Lord according to the nature of my office, that is to say I must comfort all who come to me. And this is my dearest consolation.*

In fact he had the gift of dissipating storms and restoring calm into people's souls. What he said, the words he used, were always simple, yet the effect was that of a cool hand on a feverish brow, at whose touch the most poignant agony disappeared. Countless tears were shed in his confessional, first tears of sorrow or despair, but turning to tears of joy at an unseen hope or tears of thankful relief that peace seemingly lost forever miraculously returned. It is no exaggeration to say that anyone in Padua with a troubled heart went straight to him for comfort and consolation. Particularly when the second World War broke out, all whose dear ones were absent or in danger came to him. Often he wept with them in their sorrows, but then from his blessed lips would come those few words that only he knew how to say, and peace would descend on the troubled heart.

His words comforted because they were not just human words inspired by faith: one might say that he took the Word from the tabernacle and placed It in the hearts of the afflicted. No other sort of word passed his lips. To people at a distance he wrote the same Word, and they, too, felt the peace that the world cannot give.

He had no time to write during the day—he was always in the confessional—so he had to give up a great part of the night to writing his words of comfort.

I can well understand, he wrote to his friend Antonio Settin in 1911, *how hard and heavy is the cross you now have to bear. I am not going to say, "Be patient!", for I know how easy it is to exhort others to patience and how difficult to put the exhortation into practice. Instead I will write you one simple phrase about what our Faith teaches us on the subject.*

It is a phrase of infinite comfort to suffering mankind, uttered by Christ in clear and unambiguous terms: "Come to me all ye that labour and are burdened and I will refresh you."

No doubt you will say, "That's all very well but where shall I find Him so that I can go and be refreshed?" In the Eucharist, of course. There He is food and drink and the Victim sacrificing Himself for us each time one of His ministers celebrates the Sacred Mysteries of the unbloody sacrifice of the Mass. It is then that Christ the Redeemer, through the medium of His human ministers, offers Himself with infinite and eternal charity for all those who wish to avail themselves of His generosity by attending Mass. The Divine Heart of Christ is there then, available to comfort us any time we want to go to Him.

But attendance at the Sacred Mysteries is not always possible. It does not matter: Christ is Man, but He is also God. He knows our good intentions; in fact they are His gift. Therefore, as we can be united in love with someone who is absent, how much more easily with God Who is near us, nay, within us, as our first cause and last end. From all this you can readily see that the Divine Goodness is always ready to comfort us, that the Sacred Heart always beats for us, and that Our Redeemer endlessly renews His mediation for us while at every moment of time He is being offered to His Father in the Sacrifice of the Mass. You can therefore unite yourself with Our Redeemer by attending Mass, or if you are prevented, by uniting yourself in the spirit of faith and love with the Divine Victim. This is how you can "go to Him." Now, since the Word of God cannot be false, once we have thus fulfilled the condition of going to Him with our troubles, we should be absolutely certain that we shall receive from Him the promised comfort, health and refreshment.

To another person suffering from a great misfortune he wrote in 1933:

I feel I must write to you to bring you the comfort that comes from our Faith. In the Gospel we have Christ's promise: Come to me and I will console you. On the basis of this promise I urge you in your great straits to offer a prayer, a sigh to the Sacred Heart of Jesus Our Redeemer. This Sacred Heart, which was willing during Our Lord's earthly life to undergo the whole range of human sorrows, will comfort and console you and provide for you.

I advise you to go frequently to Holy Communion when you can. When you—and I know I am talking to one who has a deep faith—when you have Jesus in the Eucharist in your heart, open to Him all its bitterness. You will without any doubt feel the truth of the divine promise and then His Providence will look after you.

He felt other people's sorrows and sufferings as much as if they were his own, but his faith always found words of consolation. In 1913 he wrote to a penitent:

You can imagine how sorry I am to hear your sad news. As soon as I heard, moved by my faith as a priest and by the affection I bear you and those dear to you, I knelt before Our Lord in the Blessed Sacrament. I prayed for your family with all my heart and I seemed to hear an inner voice assuring me that even in the great misfortune of the loss of your father, his sons and the whole family will be comforted and that Divine Providence will take special care of them.

With a remarkable and moving human instinct, Fr. Leopoldo had the gift of putting himself in the role of father or brother at the side of the afflicted, understanding just how great the misfortune was to them, so that when he spoke or wrote of comfort they came like a balm from Heaven.

Once more you have suffered a terrible misfortune, and once more I tell you: Have faith, pray and go to Holy Communion. Our Lord, to Whom all future events were known, included you and all others suffering from sorrow or misfortune, when He invited people to come to Him and promised to comfort them. He knew how many and how great are the sufferings of poor mankind, and also how His infinite power can deal with them all. I urge you therefore with all my heart to trust in Him. Divine Pity will move Divine Providence to action when man least expects it.

He did not confine himself to comforting people but also did his best to ensure that their misfortunes served to improve the soul in question by acceptance of them as punishment for past sin and a spur to greater good. *In the midst of all the trials that God sends us, have trust in Him,* he wrote. *He knows what He is doing and if He punishes us for our faults on the one hand, His divine mercy is busy on the other hand preparing us for a more perfect life.*

His own faith in the boundless goodness of the Sacred Heart, living and alive with love for us in the Blessed Sacrament, was such that he never had the slightest doubt that his words would bring comfort and peace. *I have heard you are very unhappy,* he wrote to a woman he knew, *so I am acting for Him Who said "Come to me and I will comfort you," and in His name I tell you that Our Lord Jesus Christ is with you, that His Sacred Heart beats for you. Look! This morning you received Him in Holy Communion. Well, He will make it clear that He is really present in the Sacramental Species and that He rules even those who do not want to obey.*

Or again: *I am writing not only as a friend but also with the authority I received when, quite contrary to my merits, I was ordained priest. Yes, at this very moment Christ, Our God and our Redemeer, is making use of my poor person to give you, who have faith, these words of comfort and consolation. The Heart of Jesus has a special love for you. These are the words: Your faith is great, be it done to you according to your heart's wishes. These are the words I have to say to you in the name of Our Lord Jesus Christ. I feel it is really He Who wants me to say them.*

To another: *In sending to you and your dear ones a word of comfort it is not only I who speak from my heart as a friend but also, in all truth, Christ Who deigns to speak through me who, unworthy though I be, have the great privilege of representing Him as priest and confessor. Thus Christ, through me, fulfils His divine mission of bringing comfort to the afflicted.*

Moved by your faith as a Catholic, you turn to me. I in my turn, renewing my faith in the sacred ministry which I exercise, feel moved to convey to you the necessary words of comfort, and I do this in the absolute certainty of acting in the name of Him Who is the God par excellence *of all comfort and consolation.*

In his enlightened faith Fr. Leopoldo penetrated boldly into the mysteries of God's grace, looking into the future and giving information which humanly speaking he cannot have known, all in order to give comfort to the afflicted. To a woman whose father had not had time to receive the comforts of religion before dying, he wrote: *Let me say something to relieve your sorrow. Before dying, your father asked forgiveness of God; that is, he prepared himself as a Christian for death. It is true that he was not able to receive the Sacraments, but by the grace and mercy of God he was able to ask pardon for everything. In his soul, therefore, faith and charity were at work, and you may be sure that his soul is saved. Pray hard to Our Lord that he may soon be in Heaven.*

In 1938 a man from a village near Padua died suddenly from an apoplectic fit. His son was very upset because not only had his father not had any of the last comforts of the Church but also his life had not been particularly edifying since he frequently blasphemed and never went to Church.

Early one morning the son went to the Capuchin church and approached the sacraments. He prayed earnestly for his father and asked that he might receive through Fr. Leopoldo confirmation that his father's soul had been saved in the way that a suicide's wife had had confirmation from the Curé d'Ars.

When the grief-stricken son recounted the case to Fr. Leopoldo, the latter questioned him about the dead man's life and religion, but the answers were always negative. Finally Fr. Leopoldo asked him if he himself was a frequent communicant, and to this he was able to answer yes.

Fr. Leopoldo remained absorbed in thought for a bit and then, as though inspired and quite certain about what he said, announced that the father, as head of the family, shared in a certain way in the son's Communions and that, by an act of Divine Mercy, he had been able to make an act of perfect contrition before dying, and that he was saved. But Fr. Leopoldo urged the son to continue to pray hard for him.

In another case it was Sister Gemma of the Elisabethine Nuns in Padua whose mother had suddenly died. All her life the Sister had prayed to be allowed to be present at her mother's deathbed to assist her in her last hour, but then suddenly, while her daughter was away in Florence, the mother had been struck by paralysis and died without saying another word. The good Sister was worried to know in what state her mother had so unexpectedly been called to meet her Creator and was also terribly depressed that her life-long prayer had not been granted. Nothing could console her and she was constantly in tears.

Then she went to the Mother House in Padua for a Retreat when someone mentioned to her that Fr. Leopoldo had come to hear confessions. She had never heard of him and had no intention of confessing to him, but finally decided to go, and told him her story. After a long silence:

"Listen! Do you believe that at this moment I, as confessor, represent Jesus Christ?"

"Yes, Father."

"You believe then that it is not I who speak, but Jesus?"

"Yes, Father."

"Good! Then I tell you that you have no need to weep over your mother, nor to pray for her, for she is already in Heaven."

When she had thanked him and was leaving the confessional, he called her back.

"You understand, eh? You needn't weep for your mother, nor even pray for her, for she is already in Heaven and waiting for you."

The following story is related by Signora Giovanna Ferrara from Arzergrande, near Padua.

My son Alfredo was a volunteer Lieutenant in the Frecce Nere *in the Spanish Civil War and as such was in the thick of nearly every battle. He did his best to give us frequent news of himself, usually by telegram.*

In April, 1938, during the Ebro battle, we did not hear for a long time and I was terribly worried because we knew the Frecce Nere *were heavily and constantly engaged. After about three weeks without news, a friend told me how she had placed her son under the protection of Fr. Leopoldo during the Abyssinian War and that he had come back safe.*

I had never met Fr. Leopoldo, but I knew that my son had been to confession to him, so three o'clock that afternoon found me awaiting Fr. Leopoldo who was out but expected back shortly. I was advised to try to catch him before he went to the confessional where a large crowd was waiting for him. This I did, meeting him in the middle of the church.

I told him my trouble and answered a couple of questions. He turned towards the tabernacle and remained silent for a time while I knelt beside him. After a bit, his face lit up and he patted my shoulder, saying, "Have faith!" For a bit longer he concentrated and then, very slowly, "Your son is safe." Once more he fixed his attention on the tabernacle and then patted my shoulder again, saying, "Have faith! Your son is safe." Then he went slowly to the confessional without another word.

I already felt completely free of all worry about my son. Human confirmation came in the form of a telegram despatched that same afternoon.

On 15th November, the feast of St. Leopold, Fr. Leopoldo always said Mass at St. Leopold's altar in one of the side chapels of the Basilica of St. Anthony. In 1938 a Signora Fieschi came to hear his Mass, but she was late—Fr. Leopoldo was already past the *Sanctus*—and the crowd was so great that she could hardly even see the altar from the place she finally found. She was suffering from a spiritual crisis and wanted to receive Holy Communion from the hands of Father Leopoldo, but she knew that Communion was not distributed from the side chapels so she bowed her head in her hands and contented herself with trying to follow the Mass with prayer and meditation.

Suddenly she felt a tap on her shoulder and looked up to see the sacristan who was serving Fr. Leopoldo.

"Are you Signora Fieschi?"

"Yes."

"Then come quickly to the altar. Fr. Leopoldo is waiting to give you Holy Communion."

Full of joy, she did as she was bid. Fr. Leopoldo broke off a piece of the big Host and gave her Holy Communion.

Others approached the altar hoping to receive Communion but Fr. Leopoldo gestured them away and went on with his Mass.

Needless to say, all Signora Fieschi's anxieties and worries disappeared.

* * *

For priests Fr. Leopoldo had an especial tenderness. He knew from experience the difficulties of their apostolate, the bitterness of disillusion and the sharp tooth of ingratitude—the crosses which all priests have to bear. He always did his best to comfort and encourage them, reminding even them of the mysteries of the altar. To one fellow-priest he wrote: *Your letter has made clear to me all your ideas on the subject of zeal for souls and all your difficulties as well. You must continue in your difficult and trying apostolate. Even if you see no results, your work has a value before God. Don't forget that we are Ministers of Christ. And then, for our comfort, we have the Holy Mass and we know that when we celebrate the Sacred Mysteries there occurs that of which St. Paul reminds us, "Christ is always living and interceding for us." We must therefore have perfect confidence that He will infallibly do so for us.*

When he knew that his words of comfort had brought peace to some distressed soul and that God had shown His paternal kindness in relieving human suffering, he rejoiced and thanked God for His goodness, exhorting the person concerned to trust God more and more and to love Him more and more.

Your letter filled me with joy. See how good Our Lord is! He has deigned to make you see the point of His gentle reproof, "O thou of little faith, why didst thou doubt?" When all appeared lost, everything was in fact better than before. Truly the ways of God are ineffable. He humbles us to the dust, mortifies us nearly to extinction, but then exalts us and revivifies us to a much higher degree. When we have learned this lesson, we should always fear and love the Divine Goodness.

There can be no doubt of Fr. Leopoldo's rôle of comforter. There are so many heartfelt and moving letters of thanks and appreciation for comfort, peace restored and difficulties banished that it is out of the question to reproduce more than a small selection.

Fr. Orlini, former General of the Conventual Franciscans: *I recall with the greatest gratitude the comfort I always had from him in the frequent tribulations sent me by the loving wisdom of God.*

Prof. Enrico Rubaltelli of Padua University: *How often in the sad times in my life, in the uncertainties of the troubled years, in the anxieties attendant on a surgeon's work, did I find peace and calm and comfort in the words of Fr. Leopoldo.*

On coming into his small confessional-cell, the man of the world or the man of science, were he a personage or a simple person, felt respect, an atmosphere of confidence and an awakening of distant and hidden feelings, as though closing behind him the door of the cell had suddenly cut off the trying reality and turmoil of everyday life, so that he stood before the man of God bereft of all earthly attachments, as though such attachments would be an offence against the humbleness of the place, the purity of the surroundings and the loving understanding of him who listened.

Then Fr. Leopoldo would come forward as though to greet an expected and wanted guest. Small and humble, full of that calm patience and serenity that completely disarmed one, he welcomed one with words typical of his politeness and humility.

And when he finally spoke his words of comfort, they were balm indeed and consolation for the soul that seemed transformed by them.

Colonel A. Santamato of Rome: *Fr. Leopoldo had the sublime mission of always bringing peace and comfort to troubled hearts and the divine blessing on all who had the good fortune to kneel before him.*

Mgr. Antonio Barzon, Canon of Padua Cathedral: *How great a peace could be obtained there in that little room, tiny and bare, which by its simplicity might have given an impression of emptiness and loss. But he was there, a poor Capuchin, nothing to look at, humble with everyone, gentle and affable, respectful to all because to them he owed the privilege of being able to serve God in this way. Everyone who left that cell did so washed through with peace, the peace of a son of God who has returned to his Father's house. Peace was his gift.*

Signora Lucia Piateri of Verona wrote to him in 1938: *Your words have brought me great peace of mind. May God be as good to you as you have been to me in bringing me this peace.*

Signor Luigi Camposampiero of Padua wrote to him from Spain in 1939:*You are always in my thoughts and I continually thank God for having given me such a confessor. Your words of comfort saved me, body and soul, for without them I should certainly have been moved by the terrible difficulties of my life and the temptations of the devil, to commit suicide. I am tied to you therefore by the strongest links of gratitude and affection.*

Among the innumerable writings placed on Fr. Leopoldo's tomb was the following, of unknown authorship: *Fr. Leopoldo, I met you one day when my mind was oppressed and greatly afflicted. Your words allowed me to find peace in Jesus Christ. Dear Father, elect of God, sent into the world to comfort the afflicted, look after us still, bring us always the word of peace.*

That was it: Fr. Leopoldo, with his kindness, so human, so paternal, was able to implant new feelings in afflicted hearts, knew how to reconcile them to themselves and to God, and to open up for them a more Christian view of life.

CHAPTER VIII.

THE COMMUNION OF SAINTS

St. Francis turned entirely to Christ crucified, clothing himself entirely in His Spirit, exposing himself to the derision of his fellows and the insults of the clergy. His whole life was penance and mortification. He had one ambition: to imitate and to express in himself Christ crucified. God the Father was supremely pleased with this love for His Son, Who was made Man and died for us, and two years before Francis died allowed him to achieve his ambition: his hands and feet were pierced as if by nails and his right side, right up to the heart, as if by a lance. Francis thus appeared among men as the new crucified Christ. This phenomenon—that is, a mortal man representing Our Divine Redeemer crucified for us—was unknown before the great Saint of Assisi.

FR. LEOPOLDO'S Writings

The Communion of Saints whereby the champions of Christ who have gone before us, leaving us the example of their courage in battle, are still close to us and can afford us their protection, was something especially vivid and real to Fr. Leopoldo.

He had his favourite Saints, of course, and at the head of them not unnaturally St. Francis who, as Founder Father, received all his respect and affection. He admired St. Francis not merely as the lover of nature, friend alike of dove and wolf, but while by no means disregarding these aspects of the Saint, he saw him in a much more important rôle, that of the New Christ. He thought of him, in other words, in that supreme quality that made him unique among saints. In this connexion he wrote:

Even before St. Francis, God had spoken to His Church through the saints, making them stand out among their fellows as models of righteousness. However, since God the Father had not revealed His Son in anyone of these as He was later to reveal Him in St. Francis of Assisi, making him a living and faithful representation of the Redeemer of the world (in so far as this was possible for a human being), we cannot but believe that when He speaks to us through this saint, He is speaking more than usually through His very Son.

This should be a great comfort to us since this man who is so near to Christ belongs to us, he is our father and, as such, lives in each one of us, as we live in him as our father and leader.

By the laws of nature and of grace, every man loves himself and what belongs to him: St. Francis therefore loves all his sons, especially when they have recourse to him in faith and humble prayer.

He saw in St. Francis the defender of the Gospel and recognized the necessity of continuing this mission. *What was St. Francis's mission?* (He wrote in the *Bollettino*). *None other than the mission of Our Lord Jesus Christ. As practically everything in his life demonstrates, Francis was chosen to express in himself the Son of God made Man. Christ's mission was to destroy the works of Satan and to give salvation back to the human race. Francis also was chosen for the salvation of souls and to combat Satan: he could say with St. Paul that Christ had posted him in defence of His Gospel.*

Christ's work, of course, is unending: St. Francis's ought also to be, but since he was mortal and had to die, God, Who had chosen him for the task, also provided a solution to this problem.

It is a law of nature that the father lives again in his sons; parents in fact think of their offspring almost as an extension of their own personality and being. Francis also is a father, and his progeny is very numerous and to be found in every corner of the world. He enjoys, therefore, through his spiritual sons perpetual continuity of life and work, embracing all times and all places. From his place in Heaven he can truthfully say, "Through my sons I carry on the work of my Lord; through them I am still at my post in defence of the Gospel."

Now this mission of St. Francis is alive and effective in the measure that the work of his sons is alive and effective. Based on this, we must suppose—nay, we must believe as certain truth, that St. Francis in Heaven is calling upon us to fulfil our mission, which is his mission, which is the mission—of Christ Himself.

God gave St. Francis the task of revivifying the Gospel, not with the clamour and vain splendour of science but rather in sorrow and love. *Anyone,* wrote Fr. Leopoldo, *who thinks about the life and work of St. Francis, sees immediately that he was chosen to renew, so to speak, the work of Our Lord, and to make Him live again amongst us as He did in His own life time, in His poverty, His suffering and even His crucifixion. It is in this way that St. Francis's sons are called upon to preach the Gospel.*

He had recourse to the great Saint with a heart open to love and to the greatest trust, knowing that he would receive through him the greatest graces and blessings. *Our father St. Francis participated in a special way in the work of Redemption, bearing in his body the wounds of Our Lord Jesus Christ. Now there is a community of goods between father and sons, and when we unite ourselves with deep affection to our seraphic father, so we, as his sons, participate in the grace of Christ in which he had so great a share.*

These thoughts were backed by an active devotion to St. Francis: more than anything, he tried to imitate, and to make others imitate, the seraphic founder, knowing that this was the best way of ensuring his protection from his place in Heaven.

St. Joseph, on account of his close relation with the Blessed Virgin, was another object of great veneration. He had the greatest confidence in him, knowing that he would assist him in the last and critical moment of life. His faith obtained from St. Joseph several undoubted miracles which are recounted elsewhere in this book.

Fr. Leopoldo also had a special devotion to St. Ignatius Loyola. He admired greatly the saint's ideas on obedience and had copied out and frequently re-read his famous letter on the subject. For St. Francis Xavier as the Apostle of the Indies he had also a great devotion. In the Capuchin friary in Venice, in the Chapel of St. John the Baptist, there is a statue of St. Francis Xavier dying, placed there in memory of the fact that it was at this altar that he said his first Mass. Fr. Leopoldo went straight there every time he was at the friary in Venice; religious going form Padua to Venice were always asked by him to pay a visit there and to pray for him to his protector.

Sts. Aloysius Gonzaga, Stanislaus Kostka and John Berchmans were also among his patrons, chosen, he said, as models of what he, owing to his physical condition, was unable to achieve.

St. Leopold was, naturally, his special patron, and every year he celebrated the Mass of his feast at his altar in the Basilica of St. Anthony in Padua.

He had many other patrons, among them St. Gregory Barbarigo, the Curé d'Ars, and the Ven. Marco d'Aviano ([6]) for whose beatification he worked zealously, distributing pictures and relics and urging people to invoke his aid.

([1]) Born at Aviano (Udine) in 1631, the Ven. Padre Marco became a Capuchin and devoted himself to preaching, making several tours of Europe and working many miracles. He was Papal Legate to a number of princely courts and was foremost among those whose diplomatic activities led to the great victory of Vienna against the Turks in 1683 which saved Europe from being overrun by the Moslems. He died in Vienna in 1699 and his cause was introduced by Pope St. Pius X.

He himself constantly prayed that God would glorify his Servant with miracles. Two episodes witness the miraculous nature of the response.

The episodes are recounted by Prof. Enrico Rubaltelli of Padua. *In two cases I experienced the efficacy of Fr. Leopoldo's intercession with Padre Marco.*

Until 1938 I hardly knew Fr. Leopoldo personally. I had seen him a couple of times and although I had the greatest regard for his Order I did not patronize his church nor his confessional. When people talked about his piety, holiness and miraculous virtues, I answered that I should believe in them when I had proof. Proof came, clear and indisputable: proof unquestionable, because it was in the sphere of my own professional activities.

The first instance was when my grandson, Marcello Bondesan, fell ill at the age of 15 months. The child was taken ill in December, 1940, with a serious and swiftly developing form of anaemia and consequent fever. The child faded rapidly, losing weight, liveliness and colour, and was sunk in a sort of unawareness of his surroundings. He was attended by Prof. Valentino Angelini who called in Professors Frontali, Bastai and Ferrata in consultation. All agreed that the condition was very serious, particularly in view of the fact that the treatments prescribed had had no effect.

During the crisis of the illness the child's aunt, Lidia Bondesan in Soldà, went to Fr. Leopoldo to ask him to bless the child and pray for his cure. At the time Fr. Leopoldo was unwell, so she wrote her request and received the following answer:

I have understood your request. Inspire your family, your brother and his wife, with faith in Padre Marco d'Aviano. I enclose a picture and a medal for the child. Tomorrow I shall celebrate Mass. I repeat: all have faith and you will receive your favour.

This took place about 10th February, 1941. We prayed as Fr. Leopoldo had told us to and suddenly to everyone's surprise, the child started slowly but surely to gain ground. In a short time he was perfectly cured.

The next incident occurred in May of the same year.

Antonio Geremia, aged 6, of Loreo was operated on by me on 6th May for tonsils and adenoids. The operation was successful and the child was discharged from hospital on the 12th.

On the evening of the 22nd the child was at home and apparently in perfect health when he was attacked by a high fever, with headache, vomiting and loss of consciousness. On the afternoon of the next day he was readmitted to hospital where Prof. Peruzzi and I diagnosed meningitis.

A friend of mine, worried lest people should connect this illness with the recent operation carried out by me, went to Fr. Leopoldo about it. The latter gave him a medal of the Ven. Marco to be placed on the patient and told him to undertake with the Nuns of the hospital a triduum of prayer to Padre Marco. The child, he said, would be cured.

This happened one morning when we had noted an obvious deterioration in the child's condition and considered that death was imminent. When I saw the child that afternoon, not only was he still alive but he had also regained consciousness and the symptoms of meningitis had disappeared.

Formal examination next morning revealed that there was no fever and no signs of the effects of the illness.

Young Geremia was kept in hospital for a few days longer as a safety precaution but was then discharged completely well. He is still in perfect health to this day.

These two incidents prompt me to make a personal confession. I was involved in them personally, as a relation, and professionally. My alternating hope and despair, faith and discouragement, can easily be imagined. One day when my wife was urging me not to lose hope, I said, "If Marcello gets well I too will believe that Fr. Leopoldo is a saint."

The child was cured and from that time I, too, was convinced of the heroic virtue of this humble son of St. Francis and became a regular attendant at his friary. He in turn honoured me with his good will and, if I am not committing a sin of pride, with his friendship.

By ardent prayer Fr. Leopoldo obtained for a young Capuchin recovery from a fatal disease so that he should later be able to forward the cause for the beatification of Padre Marco. The following account was written by Fr. David of Portogruaro, archivist of the Province of Venice.

In 1920 I was in the infirmary of the Friary at Padua. To start with I had pulmonary tuberculosis which was gradually getting worse and worse. Fr. Leopoldo's kindness and reputation for holiness led me to choose him as my extraordinary confessor. My case seemed to arouse his compassion, for he took it very much to heart and during his visits suggested I should turn to Ven. Marco d'Aviano for a cure. Many times he told me that I should not die soon, as was feared, but that I should live to work in the apostolate and further the Cause of Padre Marco. His words inspired me not only with hope but with the certainty that I should recover in spite of the fact that I was steadily getting worse. In the spring of 1923 I was transferred to the infirmary in Venice where I was ill at ease, for my new confessor, in view of my poor and constantly worsening state of health, wanted me to prepare myself for a good death. Fr. Leopoldo, I knew, would not have acted like this. For my part, while in no way rebellious to the will of God, I did not want to hear all this talk of death because Fr. Leopoldo's words were still in my ears and I was waiting for the miracle he had promised me.

The miracle came, though not in the form I had expected. After an operation I was transferred to the Saccasessola Sanatorium where the director, Prof. L. Peloso, interested himself in my case and performed a pneumothorax. After eight months in hospital and ten years of convalescence I was completely cured, thanks to Fr. Leopoldo whose prayers obtained this grace for me from Ven. Marco and whose inspired words sustained me in the long years of sickness. (2)

Fr. Leopoldo's faith was something quite exceptional, as was his ability to inspire faith in others. "Faith!" he would say. "Have faith!"

---

(2) Fr. David finally died of a heart attack in 1960 at the age of sixty after a life of hard work. As was to be expected, he spent a lot of time in furthering the Cause of Padre Marco including doing a great deal of very valuable historical research. He did a lot of other historical research and writing.

and somehow his words would go deep into people's hearts, rousing them from torpor and renewing their lost energy.

Fr. Beniamino of Enego, Fr. Leopoldo's last Fr. Guardian, writes: *Fr. Leopoldo was a man of great faith which he succeeded in communicating to all who approached him.*

In 1934 Dr. Luigi Zanini of Padua wrote to Fr. Leopoldo: *In the midst of all the evils that afflict me, one thing keeps me going—Faith: and it is you who are responsible for keeping it alive with your really God-inspired words.*

CHAPTER IX.

THE ODOUR OF HUMILITY

One afternoon a ray of sunshine penetrated his confessional, lighting up the dancing dust particles. "Look!" he said to the penitent who was with him. "That's how it is when God illuminates souls; it isn't that there are more sins, it's just that God makes them visible to us."

"There's no need to be surprised that things in this world are in disorder: rather we should see that our own house is in order. But we don't need to be afraid. Man reaps what he sows: if he causes tears to be shed, he will shed more. God will demand an account of every tear shed."

All who knew Fr. Leopoldo are unanimous in describing him as the personification of humility. His every word and action were witnesses of this great virtue, yet it all seemed so natural and spontaneous that it was impossible to imagine him otherwise. In fact it was a continual hard struggle of self-denial, of renunciation of the smallest concession to pride. "Giving up material possessions is nothing," he often said. "The real difficulty is giving up oneself by destroying every vestige of pride." This quotation from Gregory the Great may have appeared in the form of comfort and encouragement for his penitents, but it also expressed the painful experience of his own daily struggle to uproot from his soul the last hidden springs of pride.

He had clear and precise ideas on the subject of humility which he expressed as follows. "*Among the sorry legacies we inherited from our first parents on account of their sin is numbered an indomitable spirit of pride and conceit. We all of us feel in our hearts the strongest inclination to expect honour and glory as things due to our excellence and abilities. Unhappy the man who listens to these demands of our sinful nature. If he gives way to this inclination he sins against truth in not recognizing that anything he may have of good in him is the gift of God; and he sins against justice in wishing to appropriate to himself honour and glory which are due to God alone as the first beginning and last end of all good.*

Or again: *Justice, which is Truth, tells us that God alone is the Being* par excellence *and that we, on our own account, are nothing. It tells us, too, that this nothing that we are has nevertheless something purely its own—sin, for sin only exists in the evil will of Man. In the light of this truth, Man is obliged to render due homage to God and to recognize that he himself is worthy of punishment commensurate with his faults.*

Truth above all: the truth that makes us realize that any good in us comes from God and not from any merit of ours. Fr. Leopoldo based his conduct on this concept which he put forward at every appropriate moment when it could give glory to God or encourage others to do so. A friend one day mentioned to him the great amount of good that he was doing for souls in his ministry. Thoroughly embarrassed he said, "That may be true but it has nothing to do with me. For the good which by the grace of God we do manage to achieve we should nevertheless ask forgiveness, for we sow so many tares among the wheat. We are like a rotten cask which will ruin even the best wine that is put into it. Even for what good we do achieve we should repent and ask forgiveness that it was not better."

And indicating the crucifix, "*He* died for souls, not we. We are but poor sinful men, responsible for nothing but sin. Lord, have pity and mercy on us."

His conscience was like a very clear looking-glass which he constantly examined in order to locate the deep roots of pride hidden in the most obscure corners of the soul so as to uproot them mercilessly. His ear had become attuned to the voice of truth and heard it alone, however softly it spoke, to the exclusion of all other voices.

Answering a congratulatory letter from the Community of Udine on the occasion of his golden sacerdotal jubilee, he wrote among other things, *You were good enough to write me a letter of congratulation in which you piled praise upon praise. This evidence of your regard for an elderly colleague is very dear to me and moved me greatly—may it all redound to God's glory. But I have to listen to the voice of conscience, which is the voice of Truth. This voice, which cannot lie, how many things has it to take me up on and reprove me about! And how different it sounds from the human voices which on this occasion are more or less swamping me with praise.*

One day when he was walking with a friend in Padua, a young woman at a window saw him and called in a loud voice to her relations, "Quick! Come and look! The saint-priest is going past."

Fr. Leopoldo, realizing that the words referred to him, grew pale and hurried on, too embarrassed even to answer his friend who was trying desperately to distract his attention by talking of something else. A little further on when they were once more alone, he stopped, crossed his arms on his breast, raised his eyes to Heaven and sighed, "They give me nothing and they take nothing from me. Let us pray Almighty God to forgive me my sins."

After some rather remarkable incident which people attributed to his prayers, a friend of his commented vaguely on the subject and mentioned what people were saying. Fr. Leopoldo became very serious and remained a moment in thought. "Let people say what they like," he said finally, "but it isn't true. God alone is the author of miracles: man doesn't come into it at all. First of all we should thank Almighty God for allowing us to be witnesses of his omnipotence, then we should be embarrassed and afraid, for it has given us a responsibility for which one day we shall have to account. Not for nothing did He say that from those who have received much, much will be demanded." The thought left him confused and fearful.

It was always the same. Every time he heard a word in praise of himself he made a typical firm gesture as though to indicate that the topic was not to be discussed and then changed the subject so lightly that many did not notice the fact. One of his fellow clerics used to joke with him, "Don't forget, Father, that you absolutely must become a great saint and get a high place in Heaven if only so as to not embarrass your neighbours who already believe you a saint. Imagine the disillusionment if at the day of judgment they saw you were no better than the rest of us." These words drew from Fr. Leopoldo no more comment than a hearty laugh.

Given that, in reality, every good in us comes from God and the only thing that is really our own is sin, we must if we are sincere, accept any humiliation and realize that it is not an offence against us but an act of God's Justice which uses this way to cure us of our weaknesses in order to give us a larger measure of mercy in the life to come. In other words such humiliation is effectively not a punishment but a gift.

Fr. Leopoldo, by long and weary practice had made himself so familiar with this concept of perfection that it was almost second nature to him, a concept alas! so far from human standards of wisdom as to be inconceivable. The concept was a part of his life and he bore humiliations not just with resignation but almost with joy. A friend pointing out to him some discourtesy shown him by his fellow clerics received the reply, "They are quite right. I deserve much worse."

The same spirit was displayed in difficult and unaccustomed circumstances. One rainy day he was walking in Padua along a road full of puddles. A car came, and he got into the side of the road to avoid being spattered with mud, but the driver had other ideas and drove close to him, through a puddle, splashing him from head to foot, and drove off laughing. An eye-witness came up in great distress. "Oh, Father, what a mess that ill-mannered lout has made of you!" "Don't you worry about me," replied Fr. Leopoldo, calm and smiling. "It's nothing! I deserve much worse."

On 14th June, 1934, Fr. Leopoldo was in a tram on his way to hear confessions at a convent. When the time came for him to get out there was such a crush that he involuntarily bumped into a youth who, furious, slapped his face. Smiling gently, he said, "Please do the other side now. I should look awfully silly going about with only one red cheek." The wretched youth was so embarrassed that then and there in the middle of the crowd he went on his knees and asked forgiveness. Fr. Leopoldo clapped him on the shoulder. "Nothing at all! Nothing at all! All forgotten now."

Going down one of Padua's side-streets one day, he was surrounded by a group of young street arabs who made fun of him and filled his cowl with stones. The well-known Dr. Angelo Feriani, a penitent of his, turned up at that moment and started to scold the boys in no mean terms. But Fr. Leopoldo calmed him down. "Let them have their fun with me. I'm not much good for anything else."

A famous Professor of Padua University recounts how one day after confession he asked Fr. Leopoldo to come with him for a couple of minutes into the friary garden. He agreed, and in the course of their conversation the Professor let fall some words of praise of the priest. The Fr. Guardian, who was passing by, overheard these words and disapproved of them in terms which the Professor found very humiliating for his friend, and ordered Fr. Leopoldo to return to the confessional. Not only was Fr. Leopoldo not in the least upset, he accepted the rebuke with a smile of quiet satisfaction, took his leave with affability and returned serenely to the confessional.

In the early years of the century the Socialists, imbued with hatred of God and His Church, used to insult priests and friars publicly, using the most obscene language and even throwing stones. One day Fr. Leopoldo and a fellow Capuchin were on their way to the Basilica of St. Giustina to venerate Our Lady of Constantinople when a group of youths accosted them in Prato della Valle and began hurling abuse at them. Unmoved, Fr. Leopoldo turned to his companion and said, "Poor boys, they are the dupes of masters who have led them into error. We must try to save them, at least by praying a lot for them."

Humility, real humility, the humility of heart taught by Jesus, led Fr. Leopoldo to the belief that he was incapable of any good work. Not that he was unaware of the great good he continually wrought for souls by his work in the confessional, he considered it to be entirely God's doing to which he added nothing except a deficiency in zeal and ardour. He knew very well what Saint Vincent de Paul expressed as follows: *The gift of converting souls, and all the other talents in us, are not ours, we are only the vehicles for them... if we see that God does achieve great things through us we ought to be all the more humble in recognizing what miserable instruments God deigns to use.*

Such was Fr. Leopoldo's thought. In this connexion Mgr. Antonio Barzon, Canon of Padua, writes: *Late one evening around Easter I found Fr. Leopoldo very tired and almost unrecognizable from the fatigue of a long day of hard work. He had started hearing confessions in the very early morning and had continued almost without a break until this late hour. I said in a voice between joy and compassion, "How tired you must be, Father... but how happy!" In an unusually lively voice he answered, "Let us thank God, and ask His forgiveness, that He allowed our poverty to come into contact with the riches of His grace."*

This answer showed me a miracle of virtue. I pondered it a number of days, somewhat overcome by the lesson it taught me. His work, carried out to the end of his physical forces, his zeal, everything personal and human about it, he classed as his 'poverty': only God was great and worthy of praise, God Who lavished the treasures of His grace on souls and did not disdain to use the 'poverty' of his ministry as go-between.

Every day Fr. Leopoldo planned to do something really good for the glory of God. On 12th November, 1936 he wrote on a picture of Our Lady: *Now I shall start to do good.*

In Lourdes on pilgrimage he again wrote on a picture of the Madonna: *This morning I said Mass at the Grotto. I have clearly understood that from to-day I must start afresh.*

Signor Luigi Artuso, an infirmarian at Padua, going one evening to give Fr. Leopoldo his regular massage, came upon him at the foot of the infirmary stairs, too weak to go any further. He helped him back to his cell, saying, "But why must you go down to the church, Father, when you can hardly stand?" "Let me do *some* good," he replied, smiling.

The same infirmarian frequently came upon him kneeling on the bare floor of the infirmary cell he occupied. Asked why he was kneeling there instead of getting much-needed rest in bed, he always answered, "I'm doing some good. Up to now I haven't done any."

He considered himself good for nothing, incapable of doing any good. More, he considered himself to be full of faults. He frequently repeated to a friend the words of St. Francis, "If others had received from God the graces I have received, how much better would they have corresponded!" To the infirmarian who asked him how he felt in his sufferings he replied, "Brother, pray God that He will give me the grace to bear my sufferings on account of my sins."

During times of public calamities he humiliated himself so much that he might have been personally responsible for them. At the other end of the scale he accused himself of the smallest lapses, even mere lapses of conventional politeness, considering them to stem from a lack of virtue. "*I am answering your letter a bit late,*" he wrote to a woman correspondent. "*Please be indulgent with me. It is one of my habitual faults.*" Or again, "*I have been a long time answering your letter. I must confess my fault. It is true I am usually pretty busy, but my slowness is also the reason why I fail to observe the proper courtesies.*"

He was so convinced that he was a great sinner that he exclaimed one day almost in tears, "How can I ever justify before God's Judgment all my many sins of omission?" But such was his real humility that this conviction did not lead him into misery and despair: rather, it increased his faith in God's goodness and mercy. He wrote to a penitent, "*It is quite obvious that we must humble ourselves before God and repent of our sins and recognize that we are unworthy, but we must also have confidence in His infinite goodness which covers everything and overcomes everything. Don't be displeased at these words which are addressed in the first place to myself.*"

Fr. Leopoldo was logical. Convinced that he was of no value and quite without merit, he accepted courageously the logical conclusion: that he was not entitled to any consideration. And he acted on this conclusion, considering himself to be the least of his brethren and often saying to a confidant of his how generous everybody was to him and how good they were in putting up with him. He considered himself a dead weight in the Community because he could make no material contribution to his maintenance, and was therefore delighted when some benefactor gave him an offering. "Thank you! Thank you! My superiors will be able to bear with me better now."

This state of mind was responsible for his continuous show of gratitude for the slightest help offered him or for any sign of consideration. His humility and his nobility of mind made his expressions of gratitude quite extraordinarily charming. Perhaps he said no more than just, "Thank you!" but the words were accompanied by a smile that somehow expressed all the gratitude of his heart. People were completely conquered by it.

Br. Gaudenzio, a lay-brother, writes: *I was always greatly struck by Fr. Leopoldo's humility. Shortly after I left the novitiate I passed through Padua where Fr. Leopoldo, in all humility, came to welcome me and ask for my prayers, greeting me as if I were an old friend instead of just a lay-brother who had hardly entered the Order. Later when I was posted to Padua as cook I was almost embarrassed by the way he used to come to me, very humbly and as if he were the newest novice, and ask me to make him a little coffee and bring it to the window of his confessional-cell. Each time he could hardly thank me enough, adding, "The Lord will reward you."*

He never forgot the slightest service. A young religious in the friary at Padua got for him at his request an old chair for the confessional. Not knowing quite how to express his gratitude, Father Leopoldo insisted on his taking a couple of oranges that a well-wisher had given him to help his digestion. A year later he gave him two apples, saying that he had not forgotten the kindness done in getting the chair for him.

His letters, too, are full of this delicate feeling of gratitude. He always makes the distinction between his poor person, unworthy of any consideration, and the greatness of his priestly office for which alone were courtesies and attentions acceptable. Unfortunately space does not permit the reproduction of more than a few of these moving examples.

I am most grateful for the courtesy paid to my poor and humble person. Our Lord, Who is honoured when His ministers are honoured, will know how to repay you.

Thank you for your great faith in my humble and poor person. In honouring His ministers, your intention is to honour God. We know from the Gospel that God's blessing is upon those who honour and bless His ministers.

I am more than grateful for the noble sentiments you express about my small and humble person. May it all be to His glory in Whom is all good and not for the man who is infinitely defective.

Please accept this poor note of mine as a token of the gratitude and affection of the least of God's priests.

Your friendliness and good will are most precious to me. Please continue your consideration for this humble little friar, since you see in him a minister of God.

He would have liked to express his gratitude in tangible form, but since this was impossible, he was lavish with his offers of his spiritual ministry. To an acquaintance in Padua he wrote: *Any time you wish,*

I am ready to serve you in any way I can. I consider it the greatest honour (and this is no polite formula but the honest truth) to be favoured with your trust and good will. Every time you come to see me, therefore, you confer a new favour on your humble friend.

And later, to the same: *One favour I beg of you: if there is any way in which I can be of use to you, do not hesitate to say so. I shall consider myself happy to take every chance I may have to serve you.*

Fr. Leopoldo gave generously of anything he had at his disposal to recompense his benefactors. What he had to offer were his continual sufferings offered to God to obtain favours and blessings, and his prayers, particularly the Holy Sacrifice of the Mass. Nobody knows how many hours of the night he spent praying for his benefactors. Only God knows, for the only witness was the small undying flame of the sanctuary lamp.

To one benefactor he wrote: *The numerous evidences of the great good will which you are kind enough to bear towards my small and humble person, oblige me to try to express my deep gratitude. You know what a poor creature I am, that I can in no way repay your condescension. The only way shown me in my poverty by the Gospel is by prayer, especially the solemn, formal prayer of the celebration of the Sacred Mysteries. During this celebration, in the solemn moments so dear to me, I shall remember you and yours. This at all times, so great is my gratitude to you.*

The continued effort to reach and maintain this true humility of heart created in Fr. Leopoldo a state of mind and feeling which is hard to believe. Around him a whole world was in motion, through his prayers extraordinary things happened, yet everything ended in silence: only, souls were benefited and God was glorified. Nothing was heard, there was no publicity, even in really exceptional circumstances. It seemed as if he were completely unaware of everything, and he could never understand why so many people crowded to his confessional. To a friend who commented on the latter, he answered in all simplicity, "But it's not my fault if they come with so much faith and God, on account of their faith, hears their prayers. How do I come into it?"

The brother infirmarian who for many years was so close to him writes: *He was astonished that professors and other highly educated people came to a poor friar like him for advice: he attributed it all to the grace of God Who deigned to use him as a means of doing good to souls. On account of this humility of his he was so admired and loved that no one who had made his acquaintance ever forgot him.*

It was he himself, moved by humility, who created the atmosphere of silence around him. "We should hide," he said one day, "anything like the semblance of a gift of God in us, so that it cannot be traded upon. Honour and glory to God alone! If it were possible we ought to pass through this life like a shadow, leaving no trace behind, like St. Theresa of Lisieux at whose death the other nuns wondered how the Mother Superior was going to manage the announcement, for they had observed no sign of extraordinary virtue in her."

That was rather how he managed. He exhorted those penitents in whom he had the greatest trust to pray fervently that he should be allowed to do a great deal of good but in such a manner that no one would know about it. There was always a large crowd waiting outside his confessional, but there absolute silence reigned. The only sound was the door opening to let one penitent out and closing behind the next. No noise, no fuss, no expression of enthusiasm. He had chosen the sure road to holiness, the hidden way of humility, and this way he defended by all means in his power.

He did it so well that he passed unobserved in the Community. He was taken for a good, even exemplary, religious, but nothing more. Only those experienced in the ways of sanctity recognized him. This was as he wanted it, and to a friend commenting on it he said, "My son, in order to do good one has to be sly—in a holy sort of way."

Mgr. Gay in *Christian Life and Virtues* writes: *There is a garment of external humility in which the sincerely humble soul clothes the body. There is something self-contained about it, something of reserve and calm, which imparts to the whole countenance and bearing that ineffable beauty, that grace which is expressed by the word Modesty.*

That is a fair description of the appearance of Fr. Leopoldo. In conversation he was calm and reserved, preferring to be asked questions than to take the lead; he never started a discussion but listened carefully to what others said and only spoke when called upon. He never spoke about himself or his experiences. One would have thought that he had never known anyone. Even in confession his manner with penitents was like this, without however in any way lowering the dignity of his office. He spoke of everyone with the greatest respect and always gave pride of place to others. The Mother Superior of a convent records that whenever she had reason to discuss anything with him he always insisted that she be seated while he remained standing, however long the discussion might last. She also recalls that at the time of founding her Sisterhood, whose object is to pray for and offer themselves entirely for priests, Fr. Leopoldo talked to her at great length about the work, showing the greatest admiration for those who joined it and often saying, "I couldn't make the sacrifice you do."

Every evening Fr. Leopoldo went to the Fr. Guardian, or if he were not available to some other priest of the Community, even one of the younger ones, begged forgiveness for the omissions of the day and asked his blessing. Such was the custom among Capuchins of the Venetian Province—but only among the young newly arrived Friars: Fr. Leopoldo continued the practice up to the time of his death.

Little things and big things together by their constancy gave Father Leopoldo an unmistakeable appearance: he was the very type of truly religious humility and as such exercised an irresistible charm. His last Fr. Guardian wrote: *Fr. Leopoldo's manner was completely simple and only different from the others by his external composure, his modesty and his great respect for everyone.*

Humility does not, of course, discount the gifts given by God. That would be a sin against Truth. Rather it recognizes them in order to give glory to God as Our Lady did in the *Magnificat.* So also did Fr. Leopoldo, glorifying God and at the same time asking forgiveness for not having used the gifts as well as He might have expected.

"Notwithstanding all our defects and deficiencies," he said to a penitent, "God has chosen us to hold the balance against the forces of Evil. If we do the task entrusted to us, we shall have our reward."

He had real humility which does not cause despair and inertia, but is a powerful spring to set good works in motion.

CHAPTER X.

LOVE OF GOD

When a man has faith he tries to live according to the Gospel; according to the measure of grace afforded him by God and according to his state of life, he tries to obey all its rules; in honour of Christ he grows under the difficulties and sufferings of human life; he offers himself and sacrifices himself to God the Father, an acceptable and pleasing victim. When the mysteries of the suffering Christ are so enacted in the person of a Christian, then in due season there will be enacted in him the mysteries of Christ triumphant.

FR. LEOPOLDO

Knowledge is the source of love. Enlightened by a most vivid faith, Fr. Leopoldo penetrated deep into the divine mysteries and as a result there was kindled in him the most ardent love of God. And as love mingles and unites two loving hearts into one entity, so Father Leopoldo enjoyed a great degree of union with Our Lord. It would be very difficult to chart the various stages of his journey on the mysterious seas of the love of God, for he jealously guarded the divine secret and it was only a few intimate friends who could glimpse the vehemence of the flame that burned in his soul. Naturally reserved and reluctant to talk about anything to do with himself, he hardly spoke of it to his confessor or spiritual director, mentioning only just enough to be sure of getting the appropriate advice. With other people, not a word. In his own guidance of souls advanced on the road to perfection, he expressed profound judgments on matters of mysticism, but only a few such people realized that he spoke from personal experience, so great was his care to keep hidden what went on in his own soul. But he could not hide everything, for the tongue speaks from the abundance of the heart and we can thus get an inkling of what his true inner life was like.

St. Francis of Assisi was the model he set before himself. In 1908 he wrote: *With St. Francis was born what one might call a particular form of evangelical perfection: the so-called seraphic' spirit, a spirit of special love for God and special detachment from worldly things. St. Francis was perfect in his love of God and perfect in his love of poverty. His sons are called upon to imitate this perfection: that is the grace of the Franciscan vocation.*

In the light of this, he considered the love of God as the supreme object of life and, in comparison with it, everything else worthless. More than once he said to a fellow Capuchin, an intimate friend of his, "Without the burning flame of the love of God our life doesn't make sense, for we are in the ranks of those whose job it is to show the world that one must believe in love for God. Loving God—that's all that matters. The rest is vain illusion."

When one loves someone, one avoids displeasing him in any way. Fr. Leopoldo therefore tried to avoid even the slightest offence against God and found precisely in his love of God the one effective weapon to defeat Satan, the instigator of evil. He wrote: *Satan fears more than anything our charity, which is not just any sort of love but the love of friendship in which two hearts love each other mutually so that each becomes the end of the other and the two become one.*

If this can be true for human beings, how much truer will it be between God and Man since God is an infinitely lovable Being. In fact Our Saviour promised that if we loved Him and kept His commandments, we should be loved by His Father and would come and dwell with Him. When Satan finds us thus united to Christ, he can see that his reign is at an end in us.

We should therefore always seek closer unity with Christ and His Gospel, acting in faith working through charity; then we shall have the grace of Christ abundantly in our souls, then we shall become more and more a source of fear to His enemies and be better able to defend the cause of the Gospel of Christ against Satan who will be humbled and defeated. Holy Scripture tells us that we have only to face the devil and he will flee.

For his part, Fr. Leopoldo never voluntarily committed any offence against God, and this was quite obvious to all who had any contact with him.

We reproduce here various notes on this aspect of Fr. Leopoldo's life written by people who lived a long time with him.

Fr. Leopoldo was ardent in his love of God. For my part, I am convinced that he never committed any deliberate fault.

Fr. Leopoldo had a burning love of God. God was the main subject of everything he said. I am convinced that he never committed a mortal sin nor even a deliberate venial sin.

I am convinced that Fr. Leopoldo never fell into mortal sin nor committed any deliberate venial sin; he had an absolute horror, which impressed me deeply, of the slightest offence against God.

Personally I consider it out of the question that Fr. Leopoldo ever committed a mortal sin or deliberate venial sin. This has always been my firm conviction from the time he was still a young student.

Every moment of the day Fr. Leopoldo was burning with love of God, and I am convinced that he kept his baptismal innocence. I never knew him commit a deliberate venial sin.

I am convinced that Fr. Leopoldo never fell into serious sin. Talking to me one day of my spiritual affairs, he said, "By the grace of God I know that I have never committed a serious sin." The calm certainty with which he uttered these words left one in no doubt as to the accuracy of this inner conviction of his.

I am convinced that he never fell even into deliberate venial sin.

With the utmost diligence he avoided anything remotely resembling a fault, and if he thought he had in any way erred he repented immediately, asked God's pardon and some punishment in expiation. A close friend of his found him one day in the confessional in a state of great sorrow. Asked why, Fr. Leopoldo exclaimed with a deep sigh, "What can you expect? One must await the consequence of one's action. Just now I gave way to impatience and I'm waiting for the punishment that God will quite justly send me."

Mgr. Canon Barzon writes: *Fr. Leopoldo was ardent in his love of God. One day an expression escaped him—an expression which I should have attributed to excess of zeal—but he immediately pulled himself up and publicly demanded God's pardon if there had been anything less than good in it.*

His conscience was so delicate that he was in constant fear of offending God and went to confession daily and sometimes oftener. It may seem that he overdid it, or suffered from scruples, were it not that his humble submission to his confessor bore witness to a rectitude and purity of spirit that could not tolerate the slightest shadow in the flame of his love of God: it had to be immediately got rid of by penitence and sacramental absolution.

If he heard anything recounted against God or against his neighbour, his expression and attitude were immediately eloquent of the pain it gave him. In the confessional, where he had to listen so often to horrible sins and the constant trampling of God's goodness in the mud, he suffered agonies. His soul, like that of Jesus in the garden under the weight of the sins of the whole world, was racked with the most anguishing torture. The physical exhaustion of day-long sessions in the confessional, the sufferings to which his ailments subjected him, these were nothing to the one overwhelming agony of the offences against God poured out by the penitents, often with infuriating indifference. Often he seemed so exhausted that he aroused the pity of all who saw him.

Sometimes, with clear indications of divine approbation, he intervened to prevent sin.

In a village near Padua there was a dance-club which for a number of years was a source of scandal on account of the sinful entertainment offered. The Parish Priest had done everything possible to persuade those responsible to give up an enterprise that was causing so much evil in the parish and surrounding villages, but in vain. The misguided people, their sole interest in the profits, remained unmoved.

In 1925 Fr. Leopoldo, aware of the scandal caused by the club, sent for one of the men of the village. "Go at once to the head of the club," he said, "and tell him to give up his sorry enterprise immediately. If he doesn't, God has decided to destroy his house, and all will perish in the ruins."

The man went off bravely to pass on the message, and the head of the club, knowing that Fr. Leopoldo did not speak idly, withdrew from the enterprise and would have nothing more to do with it. Some of the members, however, got together with the landlord of the local inn and organized a substitute. Unhappy people! They should have known better. The new head of the club died suddenly a few days later, then the innkeeper's son and then one of his grandsons. Then finally it was decided to dissolve the club and the wooden platform used for dancing was taken apart and divided between the members who used the wood for making pigsties. But then the pigs all died: they were replaced, but the replacements died too. Finally they saw the hand of God in all this and the wood was burned.

* * *

Love not only tries to avoid anything that might displease the loved one, it also tries to demonstrate itself in constant consideration for and union with the loved one. Fr. Leopoldo thus wanted always to be in close touch with God in both thought and deed. He often said, "We work with our bodies here on earth, but our souls should always be in the presence of God. We can say, then, that we should always be both on earth and in heaven." The vow he had made, and which he frequently renewed, for the redemption of the Eastern people was (as we shall see later) to keep his thoughts constantly in the presence of God. It was a vow demanding a really heroic effort, but he observed it scrupulously. Should he for no more than a couple of minutes cease to think of God, then he immediately confessed it with lively sorrow.

A Paduan writes: *It often happened when I was talking to him that he would suddenly look at the clock, become very sad and say, "Oh, dear me! Where have my thoughts been wandering? Wait for me a moment." And he would rush to the tabernacle to ask forgiveness because for a couple of minutes his thoughts had not been centred on God.*

He thought about God and loved to talk about Him. In fact no other subject really interested him. People who had much to do with him knew what subjects to discuss, otherwise without anyone's noticing it he would gradually steer the conversation round to the one subject which filled his mind and heart. Fr. Bernardino of Cittadella writes: *Fr. Leopoldo lived continuously in the presence of God. It was obvious that his thoughts were always on God and the great truths of the Faith, which were the favourite subjects of his (always brief) conversations.*

And Mgr. Giacinto Ambrosi, who lived a lot with him: *I can say with absolute certainty that I never saw, even for an instant, his attention distracted from his one interest in life: God, the Church, Souls. He was always either praying—and with what fervour, devotion and recollection—or was about his favourite duty of hearing confessions, or studying his favourite authors St. Augustine and St. Thomas, or talking of God or of Church matters. Even during recreation, if he took part, it was necessary to keep the conversation on God or religion, for it was quite clear that nothing else interested him.*

Fr. Alfonso Orlini, former Father General of the Conventual Franciscans, writes: *Of one thing I am firmly convinced, and it is that the venerable Father lived continually in the presence of God, and that whatever matter was in hand he applied to it the high principles of those who see the light of God.*

From this arose the fact that although he was no speaker and suffered in addition from defective articulation, his enthusiasm was easily stirred and he spoke fluently about the things of God and defended with animation the interests of the Church.

And Signora Caterina d'Ambrosio: *In our venerated Fr. Leopoldo the presence of God could be strongly felt, so strongly that one could not remain standing in his presence: some force made one go on one's knees even if one had not come to receive absolution at his hands.*

* * *

True love does not stop at words but includes deeds, particularly bearing pain and suffering for the beloved. It is the same with the love of God: unless we make sacrifices for Him, it is pure illusion.

Fr. Leopoldo often said, "The love of Jesus is a fire fed by the fuel of sacrifice and love of the Cross: without this fuel, it dies."

He gave witness to this in his domination of his own strong and impetuous character, a struggle which lasted, one can say, throughout his life. That he succeeded completely is witnessed by his meekness with everybody, so that one had no idea that he was ever tempted to any stronger feeling. In his speech on the occasion of

Fr. Leopoldo's sacerdotal golden jubilee Mgr. Guido Bellincini said, "If it were not that it is a virtue on your part, Fr. Leopoldo, we should be inclined to say that you have betrayed the blood of your compatriot St. Jerome who, conscious of the tendency of his fiery blood, accused himself to God in the following terms, 'Forgive me, Lord! I'm a Dalmatian.' We should be inclined to say, in contradiction to St. Jerome, that the people of Dalmatia are the gentlest in the world, so gentle and friendly and patient are you always, like a doctor, ready to answer any call, always ready to lend a sympathetic ear to our confidences, always as serene and imperturbable as a saint."

But Fr. Leopoldo did not belie St. Jerome's phrase, for the struggle to overcome his tendency to outbursts of indignation was an heroic one.

He suffered acutely if people made disparaging remarks about his lack of inches, for instance, and in early days his face would reveal momentarily the hurt to his soul, but later even this was overcome and his only reaction was an amiable smile.

Mgr. Cuccarollo writes: *People who had only occasional dealings with Fr. Leopoldo got the impression that his temperament was all sweetness and light, they found him so gentle and so full of charity and readiness to sacrifice himself for others, but his intimates knew that he was by nature volatile, forceful and irascible. One realized that he had to use great force to control himself. In the heat of discussion one could sometimes see from his face the effort he was making to bite back the words of indignation that rushed to his lips; he would finally change the subject saying, "I'm so sorry, but blood isn't water, you know, and I have Dalmatian blood."*

* * *

In the hard daily struggle he took no account of blood and tears, for he wanted to give Jesus proof of his love, becoming like Him meek and humble of heart.

Fr. Leopoldo fought not only to dominate his impetuous character but also by mortification to subject the body to the spirit. He was of such a frail and small build that he seemed physically no more than a pocket edition, but ignoring this, he looked upon his poor bundle of human flesh, labouring constantly under various ailments, as his sworn enemy and expected it to be ready to make any sacrifice that might be demanded by a soul intent on the highest degree of perfection. In 1903 when he was at Bassano del Grappa, the Master of Novices had to have the floor and the choirstalls washed to get rid of the bloodstains where he had used the discipline. Later he was physically unable to undergo the prescribed discipline and this upset him greatly. Each year at the canonical visitation of the Father Provincial he accused himself of this as of a fault and asked forgiveness for it.

He mortified himself in eating. He ate so little that people were astonished that he was able to stand up and carry out his exacting duties on so little nourishment. It was almost a permanent Lent with him: he pratically never took wine or sweet things or fruit. If on occasion he could not get out of drinking wine, he never took more than two fingers. If on occasions he ate an orange to ease his digestion, it was done only under obedience. When benefactors gave him delicacies, he never ate them himself but brought them to the Fr. Guardian so that they could be given to the sick brethren. Outside the friary he would never, in spite of the insistence of his benefactors, take anything to eat or drink. At table he ate what was put before him; and never was a complaint heard about the quality or the cooking. All this was done without the least ostentation, even with an attempt to hide or camouflage any refusal so that people thought he had already eaten, or that his health did not permit the food in question. Father Alfonso Orlini again writes: *A thing that always greatly impressed me and others was Fr. Leopoldo's wonderful spirit of mortification. When he came to hear confessions at the Basilica (of St. Anthony), he often stayed for a meal with us and everyone wondered at the small amount of food he took and admired the way he dodged the insistence of others with vague excuses about his health.*

He had also promised God never to leave the friary for recreational reasons but only in line of duty. He would never take a couple of days holiday even in the overwhelming summer heat. One summer a priest invited him to spend a short time with him in a house in the hills and was most pressing in his invitation. Fr. Leopoldo said, "All I need is the exercise I get going to the Jesuits' school to hear confessions. My poor little legs can't cope with anything more. Thank God I can occupy myself and do some work: I must make the most of the opportunity to do so."

There came a time, however, when the doctor ordered him on account of his stomach trouble to take certain small amounts of food outside normal meal times and to go out for a walk for at least half an hour every day.

To Father Leopoldo this seemed to be exaggerated coddling and contrary to the spirit of mortification, so he wrote to his Spiritual Director and received the following reply: *I tell you plainly that the decision made that you should take this slight relief and these foodstuffs you may accept with a clear conscience in spite of your promises. Further, as your Spiritual Director, I think I had better order you to do so, not under pain of even venial sin but as a meritorious action whose reward will be proportionate to your obedience to him whom you have chosen to direct your soul. Do it to please Our Lord and you will be helping the salvation of souls in the ministry to which God has called you.*

He obeyed.

He mortified himself in the matter of sleep. For most of his life he slept only five hours a night. He confided to a friend, "Five hours is enough for me. I never go to bed after luncheon, but if I feel really tired I take a bit of a rest in a chair." Privation of sleep is one of the worst torments, for the human organism really needs sleep, sometimes even more than it needs food. Fr. Leopoldo chose this mortification because, as he said, he could not do greater penances and, perhaps more so, because he could do it without being noticed. It must have been real physical agony after the exhausting sessions in the confessional. In the evenings he could be seen kneeling in the infirmary chapel saying his office and sometimes he was so heavy with sleep that his head would fall forward and the breviary slip from his hands. Immediately he would pull himself up and start again. If a fellow priest suggested he should go to bed he answered with a smile, "One more moment. Just one more moment!"

Gradually the others would withdraw to their cells to retire, but he remained. When he had completed reading the office, he stayed on to pray, putting out the light so that no one should see him.

The slightest concession on this point, however much demanded by extreme tiredness, was regarded as a failure. One suffocating summer day one of his penitents arrived at three in the afternoon and not finding him in the confessional, went up to his cell in the infirmary. He found Fr. Leopoldo in bed with fever and vomiting. The latter was upset and said, "Please don't be scandalized at finding me in bed at this hour. Today I just couldn't go on."

He mortified himself in bearing the cold. His poor physique suffered terribly from the cold but he never asked for any heating in the confessional which was damp and never got the sun. One freezing winter day, a friend finding him there stiff with cold, asked why he didn't have a small stove put in.

"Do you think," he answered, "that when so many poor people suffer from the cold, I would have the face to warm myself at a stove? What could I say to them when they come to confession?"

Towards the end of his life a group of priests, penitents of his, moved by pity, planned to provide him with a small stove and to buy him the wood for it. They asked his superiors about it, but it was not so easy. Friaries don't have heating. What would the rest of the Community say? But Fr. Leopoldo, reduced to a pitiful state of health, almost transparent he was so thin, really needed the stove and finally, after careful consideration, permission was given. Thanking his benefactors, he said, "I didn't ask for this, but you have done me a great charity, for in this cold I really could not carry on."

One way of showing his love of God was in bearing patiently the pains and trials He saw fit to send him. First among this was his physical inferiority: nature had been really miserly with him. His family were by no means giants, but he, the last of twelve children, was a mere scrap. According to his identity card his height was four feet five inches; he was by no means handsome, his articulation was faulty and he walked awkwardly. The armchair in the confessional-cell engulfed him so that he was scarcely to be seen. Everything combined to give him the sort of physical inferiority complex which inevitably reacts on the mind, making the subject hypersensitive, seeking offence yet always fearing to meet persons who would be assumed to be mocking. Society, alas! does not accept the ugly duckling, but tends to despise and avoid it or at best to put up with it with ostentatious pity. The duckling suffers indescribable psychological tortures which allow no respite, and which give rise to a hatred for everybody.

Fr. Leopoldo, however, was able to face this situation and master it, in the first instance, by patience and resignation to the will of God: later he came to love it for the opportunity it gave him for humility. With simple candour he said, "Physically I am negligible, even ridiculous." And he had plently of occasion to suffer from the fact. Some of his fellow friars called him, even in public, the "Pocket Edition." The Servant of God, Cardinal Lafontaine, Patriarch of Venice, welcoming Fr. Leopoldo to the Villa Fietta where he had come to hear the confessions of the Bishops of the Province of Venice assembled for a Retreat, said laughingly, "Here's our two penn'orth of Fr. Leopoldo!" It was said, of course, in a fatherly and brotherly way, a token of confidence and affection. People said things like that because they knew he would not take offence. Nevertheless they served as sharp reminders, unnecessary though they were, that physically he was not like other men. Frequently if he went outside the friary on his own he would be besieged by street urchins who filled his cowl with stones.

At the beginning of this century anticlericalism had reached such proportions that it was scarcely possible for a religious to appear in public without setting off a riot of mockery. One day Fr. Leopoldo found himself passing in front of the Café Pedrocchi where a crowd of university students was lounging. Such a small priest was an obvious target for their insults and derision and worse, and it was with some difficulty that he got away from these irresponsible youths. Back at the friary, he stayed a long time before the tabernacle praying for his tormentors. Later he often recalled the incident with an appreciative chuckle.

The thing that upset him most was his defective articulation. However hard he tried to pronounce each word properly, they came pouring out in a rush. It was an embarrassment for anyone in conversation with him, but much more so for himself.

He could never preach nor read aloud. But his work kept him in constant contact with people of every sort and kind—a continuous martyrdom. His fellows used to say he should overcome this fault because it aroused people's pity, and who knows what efforts he made to speak clearly. It embarrassed some people who thereupon pretended not to notice, but others laughed at it. And he knew he was being pitied or laughed at.

Even at Mass it was agony. He made such a careful preparation and then, at the very altar, he had to come to grips with these blessed words. He felt terribly humiliated by it and when anyone served his Mass for the first time, when they got back to the sacristy he apologized if he had not pronounced the words properly, as if it were a culpable thing on his part. God had however made it possible for him to pronounce with absolute clarity the words of the Consecration and those of Absolution. When in 1934 he had the privilege of going to Lourdes, he confided in a friend that he was particularly glad to go in order to ask Our Lady to remove or at least alleviate his difficulties of speech. Instead, with the passage of time this particular cross grew heavier.

It was certainly no small thing that by continuous effort Father Leopoldo had so effectively overcome the psychological effect of his physical deficiencies that they became an essential part of his charm. Probably no one not suffering from the same disadvantages can appreciate the magnitude of the victory. Only the Love of God could have brought him so far.

Virtually throughout his life he bore with a variety of infirmities. His frail constitution could not put up much resistance against disease, so that illness of one sort or another, often serious, was his constant companion. It is difficult to account for his arriving at the respectable age of 76. He had eye trouble and was almost constantly under treatment for that. Arthritis racked him and had contorted his feet and his hands. One after another all his teeth had to be pulled. His stomach gave him constant trouble: he ate like a bird, but digestion was often accompanied by pains and cramps. Abscesses and infections were commonplace. Commoner still were fevers that burned up his already frail body.

Under the goad of all this suffering he appeared calm and resigned. No word of complaint against God, but rather praise because, to his way of thinking, it gave him the possibility of expiating his faults in this world. "The Lord God wishes it so," he would say, "then—so be it!" Then, so as not to appear as a victim or martyr, he always added, "But I'm much better! Much better!"

There was nothing of pose about his patience. When some penitent expressed a desire to suffer for Our Lord and asked him to pray that God would grant him the grace to undergo great sufferings for His sake, he answered with fatherly kindness, "No, no, my son! You talk like that because you are well. It's a nice idea, but no more. Let us leave that sort of thing to those souls specially called to it by God. For us poor sinners it is enough that we bear with what God is pleased to send us. Let us pray simply that He will give us patience to bear with what we have."

True to his own teaching, he bore his own tribulations with exemplary patience. A lay brother who was for some time infirmarian at Padua writes: *When in my job as infirmarian I had to give him painful treatments, sometimes an exclamation of pain escaped him. He immediately asked pardon, "Forgive me, Brother, and don't be scandalized. It is just the flesh rebelling, though the spirit remains always ready to praise the Lord."*

Another lay brother: *In 1933 Fr. Leopoldo had a poisoned finger. When the doctor had to lance the finger he wanted me to be there to hold it steady. The operation was done without anaesthetic and poor Fr. Leopoldo suffered agonies. He did not complain, but raised his eyes to Heaven and uttered pious ejaculations. The doctor was not very expert, which increased the suffering, and did not want to continue the operation, but Fr. Leopoldo said, "Go on, doctor! Cut away. Don't worry about me." Three of four such painful incisions were made. I could not understand how he was able to bear it without crying out, for his whole frail body was contracted with pain.*

During his last illness, the infirmarian, noticing how he was trembling under the agony of the tumour in the oesophagus, said, "Poor Father, how you must be suffering!"

"Yes, I really am suffering, but it is all for God. He willed it so: His will be done."

His patience under suffering during his last illness astonished all who came into contact with him, particularly the specialists. One Professor writes: *Fr. Leopoldo was always patient during his illness. Particularly during the last stages of his disease (tumour in the oesophagus) he showed a fortitude in bearing and dominating the pain that impressed me as truly heroic.* Another writes: *I never heard Father Leopoldo complain of his ills although he suffered greatly. In particular the tumour in the oesophagus must have caused atrocious agonies.*

Fr. Leopoldo's patience and fortitude in bearing his manifold physical sufferings had their counterpart in the courage with which he faced the spiritual trials by which God wished to prepare him for mystical union with Himself.

This we shall read about later.

Chapter XI.

LOVE OF HIS NEIGHBOUR

Not a saying this time, but a gesture. It often happened that a penitent under the weight of his particular cross would say, "Father, I can't go on." He didn't say anything, just raised his hand a little higher to indicate the crucifix that hung before the penitent—the crucifix, balm for all hurts and the answer to all Whys.

The link between love of God and love of one's neighbour is indissoluble. The ardour of the one is the measure of the intensity of the other. In the heart of Fr. Leopoldo his burning love for God had also kindled a great love of his neighbour.

He often said, "The yardstick by which we measure others will one day be used to measure us. This truth from the Gospel makes me tremble every time I think of it, for I do not know how well I apply its lessons in practice. We must treat all people well, for however well we treat them it can never be well enough. We must use charity towards all if we are one day to have charity from God. Charity! Charity! Only with and through charity are we on the right footing with God, with our neighbour and with ourselves."

Charity towards all his fellow men, always in relation to God, produced in Fr. Leopoldo such noble feelings, such generous and deeply human acts, such sacrifices as touched the heights of heroism. Charity made friend and brother of all who had dealings with him and it was so genuinely expressed that each thought that it was for him alone. He was in fact of noble birth, but nobler still in mind and heart. From his mother, Caroline Zarević, daughter of Elena Bujović countess Perasto, he inherited an exquisite delicacy of touch and a calm gentleness that was shown in his every action and in his readiness to follow the wishes of others and put his services at the disposal of others. He said once himself, "My Mother was a Countess and, as well as gentleness of mind and education, was of extraordinary piety. Anything good about me I owe entirely to her."

Never an out of place action, never a gesture that could even remotely hurt or humiliate anyone; always respect and delicacy even when dealing with the coarsest people imaginable. In fact, if it were possible, he was gentler and more affectionate and considerate with the poor and ignorant and suffering, as a mother has special ways with a child favoured by her because less favoured by nature. Poor people, used to quite different treatment, understood him and experienced feelings of a gentleness seldom encountered in their rough lives, and expressed it in speaking of him in their dialect in terms which can perhaps be expressed "'E ain't 'alf bad, the old 'un!"

Respect for people means also respect for their actions. With Fr. Leopoldo one did not have to bother about what he might say in one's absence. If he had something to say about a fellow religious and felt obliged in charity to speak his mind, he called him aside so that no one else knew about it; but a word of criticism about anyone not present was unheard of. In serious matters of public knowledge when it was impossible to say anything good about someone, he would interrupt the conversation to say, "Let us pray that God will intervene."

Mgr. Cuccarollo, who knew him so well, writes on this point: *Never did one hear from his lips an unfavourable judgment or criticism of a fellow religious, for charity is the substance of the religious life and he was never so rash as to judge anyone.* And Fr. Angelo of Fidenza OFM Cap: *He really loved his neighbour for God's sake. I never heard one uncharitable word from his lips. In fact he always spoke well of people, even when others thought otherwise.*

He had a great tenderness for the poor. He was in no position to give them any material help, but he tried to come to their assistance in every possible way. He recommended them to the good offices of the rich, or to his superiors. Sometimes, with permission, he would himself go into the kitchens and beg the brother cook to provide something for some unfortunate. Fr. Odorico writes: *He had great pity on the poor and tried to help them as best he could, begging alms for them from his richer penitents. He occasionally received offerings for this purpose which, with permission, he distributed to the needy.*

Fr. Bernardino of Cittadella, OFM Cap, writes: *Fr. Leopoldo really loved his neighbour. In conversation he often expressed his profound sympathy for the poor and deplored the hardness of some of the rich.*

Another noble trait in Fr. Leopoldo was that, what he could do for the poor, he did with secrecy and discretion so that they should not be humiliated.

For the sick, one can say without exaggeration that he gave his life.

In the friary at Padua in his day there was the infirmary for the old and sick members of the community and he seemed unable to keep away from them. According to one lay brother: *Fr. Leopoldo had great sympathy for the old and infirm members of the Community. Every day, and sometimes more than once, he used to come to the infirmary to comfort them. When, in the absence of the Fr. Guardian and Fr. Vicar, he as the senior priest was temporarily in charge of the friary, he gave himself no rest but was always with the sick. When I said that he really need not go to such trouble as the sick were well cared for, he replied that the Superior should make any sacrifice to ensure that the sick got everything they needed or desired.* For their part, the sick looked forward to his visit as though he were an angel from God.

For the sick outside the friary he was also very diligent and made every effort to visit them when asked for, regardless of personal sacrifice. In the summer he often visited them in the suffocatingly hot hours of the early afternoon, since later he would be busy in the confessional. In particular cases he went as far as other towns in the Veneto, or even further afield, to help some unfortunate on his deathbed.

Sometimes he even obtained cures for his sick.

The following story is told by Alberto Bedin. *In 1933 I fell seriously ill and in a short time was close to death. On the morning of 31st July I was dying and the doctor said I could not last beyond the afternoon. In my room was a mass of people waiting to assist at my death, including the Parish Priest who had not left me all day.*

My relations, knowing that I was a great friend of Fr. Leopoldo's, had the idea of fetching him to my bedside and at about three o'clock in the afternoon drove to Padua to fetch him.

When he came into the room, he said to those present, "Have faith!"

Then he sent everyone out of the room, including the Parish Priest, and remained alone with me. I was not aware of what was happening, but I suddenly felt blows on my face and then saw Fr. Leopoldo near me. Suddenly he began to kiss my face. Then he opened the door and called the others in. "Have faith! Come and help me pray. The man is mine now."

Then, with the assistance of the Parish Priest, he administered Extreme Unction—and I was cured.

At four o'clock the doctor arrived expecting to find me already in eternity but he found me instead sitting on my bed laughing and talking with those who had come to see me die.

For his part, Fr. Leopoldo went off in confusion. "It was faith in the Holy Oils," he said. "Faith in the Holy Oils worked a miracle."

* * *

He loved his neighbour and constantly exhorted everyone to charity. A lay brother recounts that he was constantly preaching charity to them. "If you don't love your neighbour," he said, "you'll never get to Heaven."

To a Mother Superior he often said, "Always use charity towards your Nuns and educate them in the school of charity and love. Teach them to do everything for the love of Jesus. No harshness. They have a lot to answer for who abuse their authority to treat harshly and with little charity the souls God has confided to them. One day they will see that they have achieved no good and they will reap as they have sown."

He once reproved a priest for having refused someone absolution, giving as his reason, "Charity ought to move the priest to arouse in the penitent the sentiments necessary for absolution."

A Capuchin priest writes: *One day I confessed to Fr. Leopoldo that I had made fun of an old man on account of some natural defect. I can still remember his reaction. His head, normally bent forward in an attitude of kindly attention, came upright, his eyes shot fire, he rose to his feet becoming almost tall, and threatening me with his forefinger, proceeding to reprove me harshly. Astonished, I hurriedly examined my conscience again to see if there were some graver fault to call down this tirade, but I found nothing. Seeing me confused, he became gentle again and continued his correction more calmly.*

To lay penitents who were well off he recommended charity and almsgiving as a sure way of earning God's blessing. Antonio Bergamasco of Padua writes: *I often went to confession to Fr. Leopoldo and, every time, he advised a small offering for the poor. He always thanked me effusively and once said, "You do a lot of good being charitable to the poor. Remember them always and you may be sure that faith, and charity towards the needy, will obtain great graces for you from God." This exhortation he repeated on several occasions. I tried always to put it into practice and I must say that in difficult circumstances in my life Providence has looked after me in an almost miraculous fashion.*

He loved everyone, including those who had offended him, whom his generosity in forgiveness won over and bound to him with bonds of real affection.

When the material means at his disposal were insufficient to succour the needy, he had recourse to God. He reminded Our Lord of His promise made to those who turned to Him in their troubles and had no doubts about divine help for the unfortunate. In fact the divine Goodness could not resist such love and reacted in ways that had all the appearances of the miraculous.

One day in 1932 Signora Innocenza Maria Venturini of Padua came to Fr. Leopoldo in terrible straits. She had five lire (then about a shilling) left in the world, and this she offered him for the poor. Deeply moved by this gesture, he said, "Have faith, Madam. God will multiply this sum a hundredfold."

When she got home, a friend of hers, without being asked, offered to lend her 1,000 lire and the next day she was repaid a loan which she had long ago written off since the debtor had repeatedly pleaded inability to pay.

A similar event is narrated by another Paduan: *In 1928 I was ill and reduced to great poverty. Needing some medicine, I managed to borrow 40 lire and went off to buy it. Passing by the Basilica of Saint Anthony, I was going to drop in and say a prayer when I met on the doorstep a poor woman with two small children, crying bitterly.*

I asked what was the matter.

Apparently her husband had abandoned her and the children and she had come from Portogruaro, where they lived, to Padua to try to trace the husband who had fled there with another woman.

"It's more than twenty-four hours since we ate," she ended, "and I have nothing left."

Terribly moved by this story I gave her the 40 lire I had borrowed and then took her to the Rector of the Basilica, Fr. Lamberto Perroni, who also consoled her and gave her generous help.

But now I found myself in a fix. I needed the medicine but had parted with the money. Thinking I had perhaps sinned against prudence, I went and told Fr. Leopoldo the whole story.

He was almost as upset as I was, but finally he said, "Have faith! God has accepted your charity: He will multiply it. Have faith."

I went away considerably cheered, and almost immediately Fr. Leopoldo's words came true. The same evening I was in church praying before the Blessed Sacrament when a lady I knew came up to me, pressed forty lire into my hand and said that in addition she would let me off entirely the sum of four hundred lire that I owed her.

This story comes from a village near Padua.

In 1927 a very poor harvest had left me in great difficulties. I had already weighed the grain and it was terribly little.

I went to Fr. Leopoldo and told him of my trouble. He listened carefully and then said, "Pay careful attention to what I am going to say. God will multiply the grain for you. Believe this and you will be able to verify it physically. But not a word to anyone, understand?"

I found I believed him and went home happy. A few days later I weighed the grain again and found to my astonishment and fear that there was almost a ton more than I had previously weighed. I say to my fear, for it is a frightening thing for a sinful man to come face to face with divine intervention.

As soon as I could, I went and told Fr. Leopoldo, who was delighted. Then, suddenly serious, said, "Let us humble ourselves before God, for we are the real authors of nothing but sin. Sin is the only thing we can call our own."

* * *

In spite of his own entirely different way of life, Fr. Leopoldo understood perfectly well the tragedy of poor families, often with many children, when the father was out of work. In his day there did not exist the social security measures that nowadays help to some extent in cases of extreme distress. He would be unhappy about such people, but always had recourse with boundless trust to the Father of us all. His prayers were responsible for countless families being relieved and God thereby glorified.

* * *

In 1916 Pietro Zanardi was in straits from lack of work. He had five children under fifteen and not a crust to give them. He tried everywhere to get work, but all doors were closed to him. Finally he became desperate and his mind began to betray him: his worry was too much and he could no longer bear the cries of his famished children asking for bread. He considered ending it all by drowning himself.

Providence, however, took a hand and made him go and see Fr. Leopoldo. Early one morning he found the good priest in the confessional cell and poured out his story, ending with a declaration of his decision to drown himself.

Fr. Leopoldo listened seriously to the whole sad story, but when it came to the part about drowning, he laughed, "Oh no, my friend! Let the river flow on in peace. Have faith! I promise you, not I myself but in God's name, you will soon find work."

"In fact," he went on after a pause, "you will find work before you get home. God will never abandon you. Have faith!"

The poor Zanardi was so struck by these words that the temptation to suicide vanished and faith was renewed. He thanked Fr. Leopoldo fervently and started for home.

He had hardly started when an acquaintance met him and said, "I've just been to your house to look for you, and I'm very pleased to have run into you like this because my boss needs you. Come with me now."

Zanardi went and got a job with very good pay. When he got home he embraced his wife and children and recounted to them how Fr. Leopoldo had saved them, not only materially, but from the danger of suicide and damnation.

Giovanni Armellini recounts the following story.

After an unbroken series of misfortunes, illnesses and money losses, my poor family, consisting of my wife and seven children, was in need of a great and difficult favour, to wit that in the midst of a serious unemployment crisis I should find a suitable permanent job in my own town, near my family.

At the beginning of December, 1933 I put the story to Fr. Leopoldo, not disguising my discouragement and despair. He listened attentively, thought for a long time, and then said, "My dear Sir, you must not lose heart. Let us pray together in faith and you can be sure your prayers will be answered before the end of the year."

We prayed together in my family and what he had foretold came true, for on 21st December I got exactly the job I needed.

However, a new trial was awaiting me. A great financial upheaval as good as put me on the street. The shock affected my health to the extent that my life was feared for. My family seemed on the point of losing its ancient patrimony. On top of this, false statements impugning my commercial honesty were being made.

Fr. Leopoldo, who was aware of the whole truth of the matter, was constantly having to console my distracted wife. "Have faith in Providence," he said. "God knows all about it: let Him do what is necessary. You and your children will be on the edge of an abyss, but you won't fall. I assure you of this in the name of God."

There were some very critical moments. Often it seemed that complete catastrophe was about to overtake us, but we prayed with faith and heard Mass every day as Fr. Leopoldo had told us to, and after a bit everything came out all right as he had predicted.

* * *

Fr. Leopoldo could not resist a mother's sorrow. He wept with them and sent such heartfelt prayers to Heaven that grace and consolation were the immediate result.

In 1932 Signora Elisa Fiorazzo Salerni was threatened with great tragedy. Her only son had a mental affliction such that Prof. Borgherini decided that he would have to be put in a mental hospital.

The poor mother, distracted by this tragedy, made worse by the fact that the son was her sole support, did not know where to turn. A providential inspiration sent her to Fr. Leopoldo.

The good priest was greatly moved by her misfortune and remained for a long time in thought. Then suddenly his face lit up and he said happily, "You can be at peace, Madam. In today's Gospel we read about the widow of Naim. You, too, are a widow with an only son. Jesus must have pity on you too. Have faith! Your son will be cured."

In fact when she got home she found her son perfectly quiet and normal, and from that day on he suffered no more mental disturbances in spite of long hours of difficult brainwork in an office.

Signora Capato of Adria had a son of twenty who in 1940 was afflicted by epilepsy and suffered very frequent attacks. All known treatments were tried in vain. The mother went on foot to Padua to invoke the aid of St. Anthony. Arrived on the outskirts of the city pretty exhausted, she stopped for a rest. Another woman, seeing her state, enquired what was wrong and, when she had heard, suggested she should go to Fr. Leopoldo who would tell her if her son could be cured. She went accordingly to S. Croce and told Fr. Leopoldo about her misfortune. "Dear Lady," he said, "don't you know that epilepsy is incurable?"

Taken aback, the poor woman began to weep. Fr. Leopoldo was silent a while, then he smiled. "Have faith!" he said. "Your son will get better. He will be cured. No doubt about it!"

She went home consoled. Her son felt suddenly much better. But after eleven months he had another attack. The terrified mother went back to Fr. Leopoldo who, without waiting for her to speak, said, "It was the devil, but you will see that from now on he will have no further power over your son. Go now, and have faith!"

From then on there were no further attacks.

* * *

The sick were a special object of Fr. Leopoldo's charity.

Moved by their sufferings, he stormed Heaven with prayer until his petitions were heard. "In these cases," he said, "you have to be importunate, like the man who importuned his friend in the middle of the night until he had to get up and give him what he asked."

A whole volume would be necessary to recount all the instances of his help for the sick. Two cases will have to suffice.

In 1939 Signora Anna Gazzi of Stellata Po was suffering from a tumour requiring a serious operation. All the arrangements had been made for her to enter hospital, but first she wanted to go to Padua to hear what Fr. Leopoldo had to say about it.

As soon as he had heard her story, he said, "You don't need to have the operation. Go home and you'll be cured."

Encouraged by this, she told him about her husband who had to leave his employment that day.

"You needn't bother about that either," he said. "Your husband will be taken on again by the same firm."

Happy in the belief that all would come true as foretold, she went home. The pain started lessening immediately and in due course the doctor was able to certify that there was no trace of a tumour.

The evening of her return from Padua there came a note from the firm where her husband worked, withdrawing his notice and asking him to return.

The next incident is recounted by Signora Maria Zanirati, also of Stellata Po.

For three years my daughter had been suffering from spinal arthritis and, in spite of all the treatment afforded her, was steadily getting worse. She could not undertake even the lightest work and finally lost all power of movement. A specialist who saw her pronounced a cure virtually impossible.

In 1939 I dreamed that I should go to Padua to see Fr. Leopoldo, and I went the very next morning. As soon as I was in his presence I felt a boundless trust arise in my heart and the firm belief that all my wishes would be fulfilled. In tears, I told Fr. Leopoldo my story. He was greatly moved and remained for a time in thought before saying, "Your wish will be granted in the course of the day. Rest assured that your daughter will be cured, but you must go to Holy Communion every Sunday."

I took heart and told him of another worry. One of my sisters was in dire financial straits on account of family misfortunes. "Don't worry about that," he said at once. "Your sister's circumstances will change. Providence will not forget her."

I was deeply moved by so much kindness, but I was still not quite happy. There was something else worrying me but had not the courage to mention it. The good priest saw my state of mind and encouraged me to tell him everything. So I told him about a nephew who had been wounded in the Spanish war and had a bullet lodged near his heart. It could not be extracted but gave him constant pain and could cause his death at any moment.

Fr. Leopoldo remained thoughtful for a long time, then very gently said, "No, Madam. That, I'm afraid, not."

I thanked him from my heart for the favours obtained and went into the church to thank God for His goodness. After about ten minutes Fr. Leopoldo appeared in a doorway and beckoned me. "Madam," he said happily, "that too will be granted. Your nephew will get better."

All came true as he had foretold. When I got home I found my daughter doing the washing and from that day on she had no more illness. Three days later my sister wrote that an unforseen piece of good fortune had solved her problems, and my nephew told me his pains had disappeared and he was able to get on with his work as before.

* * *

Faced with unfortunates suffering under social injustice, Fr. Leopoldo was fired with holy zeal and, in his faith, was able to comfort them with the thought of Divine Justice that would one day put everything in its place. To a victim of unjust oppression he wrote: *Above human wills, and above human malice and evil, there is One Who controls human affairs and Who is the supreme Judge from whom there is no appeal. He has told us that as we do to others, so it shall be done to us. So, have faith in the justice of God and you will not be disappointed.*

In cases where immediate measures were necessary, he knew how to obtain justice for the oppressed from God.

In 1937 about fifteen peasant families in a village near Padua found themselves in a sorry plight, for the landlord was determined to take from them the fields they rented. One of the people concerned went to Fr. Leopoldo for help. He listened to the story with indignation and then said, "Tell them all to have faith. What you fear will not happen. Your landlord may dispose of the land, but God disposes everything. Have faith!"

So it was. For all his efforts, the landlord could not get possesion, and the families concerned continued to be able to earn an honest living.

In 1940 a peasant from a village near Padua was sent by his landlady to Fr. Leopoldo to ask for a blessing on her granary in order to get rid of the mice which were infesting it in plague proportions and ruining the wheat. The peasant added that she would not give him a certain quantity of grain due to him.

Fr. Leopoldo grew indignant. "Tell her to give you your grain," he said, "for until she has carried out her duties the mice will not leave her granary. Tell her I said so."

At first the lady would not hear of it. Finally, terrified by the damage the mice were doing, she gave the peasant his grain and the mice disappeared.

In 1941 a peasant near Padua was in sad straits. A neighbour of his was trying to have him evicted from his house so that he could take over his fields to add to his own. With this end in view, he was constantly slandering him to the landlord. The wretched peasant was in despair, expecting to find himself and his five children on the street at any moment.

Full of pity and righteous indignation when he heard this story, Fr. Leopoldo said, "Woe to him who tries to harm you! Have faith! Before you and your children are deprived of house and fields, it will happen to him."

And so it happened. The landlord would not believe the slanderous inventions recounted him and one fine day removed the slanderer from his house and land.

In 1934 a man from the neighbourhood of Padua found himself in critical circumstances. He had let a house belonging to him to another man on condition that he did not sublet it. The tenant however did sublet it, without saying a word to the owner, who in the course of an argument said that the tenant had not acted as a man of honour. Whereupon the tenant flew into a rage and threatened an action for defamation. The thing was serious, for the tenant's lawyer called on the owner and said that the damages would probably be in the region of 20,000 lire.

His own lawyer first of all assured him that he had nothing to fear and he would win any action. Later he changed his mind and advised him to settle out of court for 20,000 lire, saying that if it went to court he would get the worst of it.

In the meantime the case had become quite a sensation and everyone was awaiting the outcome.

The owner of the house, however, had no intention of submitting to an injustice, so he went and sought Fr. Leopoldo's advice.

Fr. Leopoldo became quite excited. "Not a penny should you give him! Have faith, and it will all come out all right. In fact—That's it! From this moment no one will mention the matter again. Just have faith."

Miraculous! Neither the plaintiff nor either lawyer made any further move.

A year later the owner of the house amused himself asking his friends why they had not followed up the case that had so interested them at the time. They were all astonished to realize that they had completely forgotten it. More remarkable still, his own mother who originally had hardly stopped talking about the case, never referred to it after his visit to Fr. Leopoldo and when he reminded her at the end of the year she appeared to come out of a dream and could not understand how she had come to forget it.

* * *

Fr. Leopoldo's charity had no limits. He was moved by any human troubles and obtained from God favours that are scarcely credible, on one occasion just to save someone from public humiliation.

Early on 12th December, 1928 Signorina Anna Giovanelli, a school teacher, came to Fr. Leopoldo in tears. "In this morning's *Gazzettino* there is a report of the conviction of a very close relation of mine. I have to take the 'bus to school, as I do every day, and on the 'bus there will be ten of my colleagues who buy the *Gazzettino* every morning, and read and comment on the news during the journey. They are bound to read and comment on this item. I can't bear the shame of it." And she wept again.

Fr. Leopoldo was sorry for her. He remained a short time absorbed in prayer and then said, "Go to your school in peace. No one will say anything."

Thinking that these were only words of kindness and consolation, the young woman could not make up her mind to go, but continued to weep. Fr. Leopoldo repeated with quiet conviction, "Go on! I promise you no one will say anything. In fact, no one in the 'bus will read the paper."

She went. There were her colleagues waiting for the 'bus, right in front of a news stand, but not one of them bought a paper. They all seemed rather serious and pensive. During the journey the driver, surprised not to hear the usual chatter, exclaimed, "What's got into you all to day? Are you all suddenly dumb?" Even on the return journey no one had a paper.

Fr. Leopold was right. Neither that day nor the next nor at any time was the slightest reference made to the incident.

In Padua in 1934 an unmarried woman was living with her brother, keeping house for him and making all the necessary household purchases. Unfortunately he was one of those men (alas! not rare) who expected everything to be just so, but when his sister asked for the necessary money, flew into a rage and cursed and blasphemed.

Frightened to ask for money, the sister sometimes bought food on credit. At the end of one month she found she had a bill of 500 lire and did not know what to do. Mention it to her brother, she dared not. Take the money surreptitiously? Yes, but suppose he noticed?

In tears, she consulted Fr. Leopoldo who told her to take the money from her brother's note case.

Back at home, she found 5,000 lire in her brother's savings, took 500 lire and paid the bill.

Then she began to be frightened. He could not fail to notice that 500 lire were missing. Then what?

She went back to Fr. Leopoldo the same day and explained what was worrying her now.

"Don't worry! Have faith! I'll deal with the matter."

She did not quite understand what he was driving at, but his words had the effect of calming her completely, and she went back home.

Once there, she thought she would just check upon the amount left, and to her astonishment and joy the full 5000 lire was there.

She fell on her knees on the spot to thank God, and the next day went to thank Fr. Leopoldo. He blessed her with a smile. "Always have faith in God," he said.

* * *

When it was a question of innocent children suffering, he could hardly express his feelings. Nevertheless he knew how to comfort distracted parents and very often obtained miraculous cures.

In January, 1942 the child Luigino Masiero was attacked by a high fever. The doctor could find no cause for it, but suspected typhus or meningitis. By the 7th January the child was so much worse, with a temperature of 105° F, that they thought the end had come.

The child's father went to see Fr. Leopoldo, but he was ill in bed. However, he sent him a medal and a scrap of paper on which was written, "Have faith! The child will get better."

The father returned home contented and placed the medal on the child's chest, whereupon the fever left him and he was cured.

Another cure is recounted by a grandmother from Padua.

In 1936 one of my grandsons had a serious form of bronchial pneumonia and his life was despaired of. His mother was in despair and wept continuously. I went to Fr. Leopoldo and asked him to pray for the child.

"Be calm, Madam," he said as soon as he heard my story. "Go and hear Mass at the Basilica of St. Anthony and then go and see your grandson. When you come into the room the fever will disappear and he will be cured."

I did as he told me and immediately after Mass rushed round to see my grandson. As Fr. Leopoldo had said, I had no sooner set foot in his room than the fever disappeared and in a short time he was perfectly well.

This case is recounted by the lawyer Agostino Soldà of Monselice.

In 1939 my three-year-old son Sergio got pneumonia, with a very high temperature.

Next day I drove to Padua and demanded Fr. Leopoldo's help.

"Be calm!" he said. "He'll get better. Come and let me know as soon as he does."

Full of confidence, I returned home and went straight to the sick-room where I found Sergio sleeping peacefully. At eight the doctor came and was surprised to find the child breathing regularly. With our permission he woke the child and examined him thoroughly. He found no trace of fever nor of pneumonia. He left us, muttering, "I don't understand... There's nothing there any more."

However, we understood well enough. Fr. Leopoldo had worked a miracle for us.

In 1936 Signora Ester Bettella's nine-year-old son was ill with pernicious anaemia. Everything that medical science could suggest was tried, but in vain. The illness grew steadily worse. The distracted mother took the child to Fr. Leopoldo and implored his aid. After praying a bit, Fr. Leopoldo approached the boy and placed a hand on his head. "There's nothing wrong with him," he said. "Nothing. Just have faith!"

From that moment the child showed no further signs of illness and grew up strong and healthy.

Giulio Boaretto of Cartura, near Padua, had reached the age of eleven completely dumb. All possible treatments had been tried without success. In July, 1930 his parents took him to Fr. Leopoldo to be blessed.

The good priest was deeply moved by the tragedy of his condition and prayed for a long time. Then he blessed the child, saying, "Go in peace, my son, in two days you will speak."

Two days later the boy began to speak perfectly.

* * *

When Fr. Leopoldo knew that God was demanding the greater sacrifice, he did all he could to prepare the people concerned to accept God's will and managed to obtain for them the grace of resignation.

On 14th June, 1937 a man from a village near Padua was in the town and bought a picture of the Sacred Heart which he took to Fr. Leopoldo to have blessed.

Happy to see this picture, Fr. Leopoldo blessed it, looking at it again and again and asking its owner to set it by the window where he could see it better. Then he took it in his hands and contemplated it in silence. This went on for minutes on end. Finally, upset, he turned to the amazed man and said, "Listen, Sir. In this life we all have to suffer and now the Sacred Heart wishes to associate you with His sufferings. Accept the trial which He will send you. Go in peace: I shall pray for you."

The man went off, uneasy and not knowing what to make of these words. He was just approaching his house when his brother ran out to meet him with the terrible news that while he was in Padua their mother had had a stroke and died.

One day a mother brought her sick child to Fr. Leopoldo to be blessed. He prayed a long time over the child and blessed it lovingly. Then he turned to the anxiously waiting mother. "Madam, we must always be ready to do God's will," he said slowly. "He arranges things for our good. This child is destined for Heaven, the world is too ugly a place for him."

A few days later the child died, but the mother found great comfort in her sorrow in the prophetic words of Fr. Leopoldo.

Brotherly love, evangelical charity in the full sense of the words, was for Fr. Leopoldo something about which there could be no question, something that was to be shown to everyone, good, bad or indifferent. In fact if any preference was shown, it was towards those who least deserved it. The following account by Fr. Raimondo of Herne shows clearly the depth of love borne by Fr. Leopoldo towards a fellow religious who had grievously hurt him.

I saw the most exquisite charity at its best on the occasion when a lay brother left the friary. For a variety of reasons which I will not judge, the brother was expelled from the friary in a somewhat abrupt manner. He left under protest and thoroughly envenomed. At the time I was living in a sort of annex to the friary and it was there that the brother was sent to await the necessary dispensation from Rome.

When I went to the friary I met Fr. Leopoldo who had just come out of hospital. He called me into his confessional and adjured me in God's name to make "the unfortunate fellow" welcome and to beg the Superior of the house to treat him well so that at least he should not lose his faith. In tears, he repeated several times, "His faith must be saved!" Then, haltingly on account of his emotion, he said, "Tell the poor fellow I'll pray for him. Tell him I'll remember him in my Mass tomorrow—in fact... in fact I'll say my Mass entirely for him, and he will always have my blessing. Tell him that Fr. Leopoldo will always be his friend."

I was moved myself by so much charity. He spoke more like a mother speaking of an errant child. Fr. Leopoldo knew better than anyone his guilt and that he deserved expulsion, but for him the important thing was that a member of the family was leaving his father's house to return to the dangers of the world, and in comparison with this, all other considerations paled into insignificance.

* * *

For Fr. Leopoldo there was only one rule—charity. To relieve human suffering, he often offered himself to God as a victim for his neighbour.

Somebody once asked him how it was that saints confronted with a sick person could say with such certainty that he would be cured. On what were their words based?

"They say," he answered, "that one of St. John Bosco's priests once commented how happy he must be to be able to work miracles. To which he replied, "My son, if you knew what miracles cost, you'd pray God never to give you the gift! That's the answer to your question.' When Saints find themselves faced with some unfortunate who asks them for a miracle, they place themselves between God and the person concerned and ask God to send the punishment or trial to them in place of the other. Given the union they have with God, they know by a sort of supernatural intuition whether God accepts the substitution, and if so, can announce the miracle with certainty. But God takes them at their word and they have to take what was coming to the person for whom the miracle was worked.

In this way the saints resemble Our Divine Redeemer Who interposed Himself between mankind and His Father, expiating Himself the sins of the world."

It was the same with Fr. Leopoldo himself.

Countless times did he offer himself as victim in order to obtain a cure, a comfort for the afflicted, the conversion of a sinner or an abundance of grace for souls destined for great things.

And God took him at his word. Miracles multiplied around him, people were converted, everyone left his confessional comforted and full of joy, but he had to pay dearly for it.

As a local newspaper put it, *Fr. Leopoldo did not want the sick to suffer. He wanted to bear our burdens himself. "Put it all on my shoulders and don't worry," he would say, smiling as he saw peace of mind gradually taking possession of the person before him.*

Chapter XII.

EVERYTHING FOR SOULS!

"Fr. Leopoldo," someone once remarked to him, "you have heard so much that nothing can surprise you now."

"On the contrary, my son, I am constantly astonished by the way people put their immortal souls in jeopardy for the most frivolous and futile reasons."

Fr. Leopoldo really loved his neighbour, suffering with him, forgiving him, consoling him and trying in every way to help him; for he considered him a part of himself. But the real fire of his love was directed towards the *souls* of his fellow humans. Beneath the respectable garments of the rich as under the stinking rags of the down-and-out he saw the immortal image of God, even when it was degraded by sin. To snatch these souls from Satan and bring them safe to God he sacrificed his whole life, working without surcease to the limit of his strength.

When the Capuchin church in Padua was destroyed during the terrible air-raid of 14th May, 1944, a small cell beside it remained untouched amid the rubble. It was no more than a few square feet in area, cut off from air and light by the surrounding buildings, freezing in winter and suffocating in summer. This was Fr. Leopoldo's calvary where for nearly forty years he remained a voluntary prisoner for the salvation of the souls who came in an uninterrupted stream to see him. The agonies he suffered in this daily imprisonment can scarcely be imagined. Always there, for ten, twelve or even fifteen hours a day, never thinking of rest or relief, always suffering. And all because his love of souls was greater than any desire to escape, and because from the bare walls of the cell looked down the figure of Christ nailed to the Cross for the salvation of these souls. Seeing the Crucifix, he would repeat to himself, "I shall remain too, till I can do no more, even unto death, for souls are of more value than my poor life."

Penitent followed penitent, came in, confessed, and left; but he remained, motionless in his small armchair. Slowly the hours passed, and became days, months and years. The seasons came and went, but he was always there. For nearly forty years.

An incredible life, but for him it was *the* life and he could not conceive the possibility even of another sort of existence.

"Father," a colleague asked him, "how do you manage to hear confessions for so long?"

"Well, you see—it's my life!"

"But your health is not all that good, Father. You should think of having a break."

"Oh, no, please! That would be my death!"

Almost prophetic words, for when he did finally have to give up hearing confessions death was not long in following.

He never cried halt: never sent anyone away on account of irritating insistence or an inopportune time. If he did leave the confessional for a moment and the bell announced the arrival of another penitent, he was back like a shot, pleased to see the newcomer. "Here I am, Sir! Here I am!"

It might happen ten times or a hundred, he was always the same. Right up to a late hour at night, perhaps when he was already in bed, a member of the Community might knock at his door and ask for confession. Without the slightest sign of impatience he would get up and welcome the visitor, "Here I am! At your service!"

Had it been possible he would have remained day and night in the confessional, forgetting food and rest alike. "How can one leave so many poor penitents just to go and get corporal nourishment?" he asked, his voice heavy with sadness.

He held that a priest should sacrifice himself, even to death, for souls, and he was miserable to think that some ministers of God did not see things in this light but thought more of their own convenience than of the salvation of souls.

Holy Saturday, 1933. Fr. Leopoldo had been hearing confessions without a break since the early hours of the morning. It was now ten o'clock at night and there were still many waiting outside the confessional. The Father Guardian sent Brother Gaudenzio to say that Father Leopoldo should stop hearing confessions and go and have his supper and not go back afterwards.

Fr. Leopoldo, miserable though he was at the idea of leaving unconfessed people who had waited so long, nevertheless obeyed immediately. He went to supper, but he couldn't swallow anything. He sent for the Brother. "Go to Fr. Guardian and beg him for the love of God to allow me to go back to the confessional."

When Brother Gaudenzio came back with the permission, his face lit up with joy. "Thank you! Thank you!" he said, and rushed off back to the confessional without giving another thought to food.

At this time, incidentally, he was suffering agonies from a whitlow.

* * *

As a matter of conventual routine the church was closed in the early hours of the afternoon, and at a fixed time in the evening. This was real torture to Fr. Leopoldo who wanted confession to be available to all throughout the day and until late at night, but it was a matter of obedience and he accepted it.

He often said to a friend, "Pray for me that God may enlighten my superiors so that they will give me greater opportunities to exercise my ministry: they are too good to me and pay too much attention to my health."

Fr. Cesario of Rovigo writes: *When I went as Guardian to Padua in 1931 and Fr. Leopoldo came to pay his respects to me, I asked him to carry on as before his apostolate of the confessional. I added that in the evenings when the church was shut, if anyone asked for him he might let them in by the friary door. He was overjoyed at this permission and it was wonderful to see him, late in the evening, waiting by the door and, when he heard anyone approaching, opening it and welcoming them. "Come in! Come in! Here I am!"*

Among Fr. Leopoldo's penitents was an Army officer stationed in Trieste. Wherever he had to go through Padua, he wrote to his beloved Fr. Leopoldo in advance to be certain of being able to see him in the short time between trains. Often this was late at night, but Fr. Leopoldo was always waiting for him at the door. On one occasion it was two in the morning, and winter. The officer hesitated to knock, thinking it hardly possible that the old priest would still be up, but he did, and the door opened immediately to reveal Fr. Leopoldo, shivering with the cold but delighted as ever to see him.

Though he suffered a great deal, he did his best to hide his infirmities from his superiors lest they should order him to rest.

A friend found him once in the confessional shaking with fever. "Oh, Father, do have some regard for your health! For the love of God, go to bed."

"We are born to labour: we'll get our rest in Heaven. Gentlemen with a cold can go to bed, but we poor chaps have got to go on working even with a fever. Anyhow, how could I possibly go off to rest with all those people waiting outside for my assistance? Another thing, if my superiors knew I had a temperature, who knows how long they might forbid me to hear confessions. I give you the job of obtaining by your prayers strength for me to cope with my burdens. Pray to Our Lady—tell her to show herself a mother."

He prayed, and made those of his penitents in his confidence pray, that God would send him many souls to help, particularly 'big fish'.

He received willingly all who came to him, writes an acquaintance, *and accepted with real enthusiasm the suggestion I occasionally made to send him someone who had particular need of his mercy. "Bring him along!" he would say happily. And before we parted he would repeat, "It's understood, then. I shall be waiting for this soul."*

And when these souls, moved by grace, came to him, he welcomed them joyfully and if after they were reconciled to God they wept, as often happened, tears of joy and relief, his tears were mingled with theirs and he would embrace them.

The following story is related by a Paduan.

For more than twenty years I had not been to confession. On the eve of my wedding I decided to go to Fr. Leopoldo, for I had heard that he was so good with everyone. He greeted me with great kindness, as if I had been an old friend. After my confession he stood up, took both my hands in his and thanked me profusely. I was astonished and a bit disconcerted, and he must have seen this on my face, for he ex-

plained with a smile, "I am thanking you with all my heart for giving me the grace of being the first to hear, after such a long time, your expression of penitence in confession."

The salvation of souls was his favourite topic with those who understood this great ideal, this wonderful work for the glory of God.

A Mother Superior writes: *I frequently conversed with Fr. Leopoldo. A normal subject was the value of souls redeemed by the Precious Blood and the need he had of help to fulfil properly his ministry in the confessional for the benefit of these 'treasures'. He adjured me always to pray a lot for him.*

He insisted also that my prayers should be that his Superior would not on health grounds forbid him to hear confessions. He often repeated, "I must do everything for souls, everything. I must and will die in harness. Please pray that I may die in harness."

His love for souls was such that he would gladly have suffered martyrdom for their salvation. A Monsignore from Padua writes: *One day when there was a great mass of people waiting outside his confessional, seeing that he was in pain and knowing what a labour it would be, I said almost in pity, "Father, if people who confess God before men are martyrs, so are those who confess men before God."*

He smiled at me, and then sighed and said, "Please God I could be a martyr for the salvation of souls."

Knowing all this, one can imagine what an agony it was for him in his last illness not to be able to hear confessions. His physical and moral suffering were nothing beside this deprivation.

If he saw a soul slipping away from him and had any doubt about its salvation, his distress knew no bounds.

An ex-Navy NCO had not for many years approached the sacraments. The anticlerical atmosphere in which he had lived had quenched the flame of faith and substituted a hatred of priests. Retired and already getting on in years, he persisted in this attitude, to the scandal of many people. His relations did everything they could to bring him back to God, and finally induced him to go and see Fr. Leopoldo.

He went, mainly so as to be rid of the importunities of his children, but he did not go to confession, merely airing his anti-religious and anticlerical prejudices. Fr. Leopoldo said nothing, waiting for him to work out the evil in his heart.

Finally he said, "Father, I have no intention of going to confession, but if I may I will tell you something that torments me, giving me no peace."

"Carry on, Sir."

"Well—I had a friend. He is dead now and I prevented the priest from seeing him, although his family wanted it. In fact we had, during his life, several times promised each other, even sworn to it, to prevent a priest approaching the other's death bed."

Fr. Leopoldo sprang to his feet. His eyes filled with tears which overflowed and ran down his cheeks and beard.

"My son! My son! What have you done! What did you know of the life to come? I weep for your great crime. You should weep too. Let us weep together..."

Shocked, the old sinner did not know what to do or say, but finally he, too, wept. All doubts and prejudices dissolved as if by magic. He confessed amid tears the sins of his life away from God and was completely changed and converted.

From then on he lived an exemplary life and died an edifying death. What is more, his conversion led many friends of his back to God.

* * *

Finally here is a judgment by Mgr. Giacinto Ambrosi OFM Cap, Archbishop of Gorizia:

He was always ready to receive his numerous penitents at any time of the day or night, and always with his habitual kindness.

Never a sign, I won't say of impatience, but even of tiredness. His fellow priests might be impatient on his behalf when they saw him besieged by penitents who gave him no quarter; but he himself, never. His happiest days were when he had heard the most confessions: any time he was less happy it was because he thought he had not heard enough.

The greatest miracle Fr. Leopoldo worked was with his own life, giving every moment of it to the glory of God and sacrificing himself with real heroism in the hard and exhausting work of the confessional.

Certainly the Church has known others who applied as much devotion and fervour to the confessional as did Fr. Leopoldo, but I cannot believe that any gave more, for I cannot believe that in this delicate and difficult work it were possible to do more or better than he did.

Could Fr. Leopoldo have done more to show his love of souls?

CHAPTER XIII.

PRAYER

Every one of the Faithful, in order to be a true follower of Christ, must defend the Gospel, particularly by his own example, for the Faithful should be the light of the world. He must also defend it by prayer and by Christian acceptance of the daily sacrifices that life brings.

FR. LEOPOLDO

10 - *Fr. Leopoldo of Castelnovo*

God has bound up his promises to us with prayer. He has made it quite clear that we can have anything from Him, but only through prayer. Although God gives us everything for nothing, we must still merit it by prayer. Here, of course, we are in the realms of mystery... Never mind! Let us pray."

These words, which Fr. Leopoldo so often repeated, are an accurate reflexion of his ideas on prayer and of the programme of his own spiritual life, which can be expressed in that one word, prayer. And he really did pray. Whenever he was not engaged in the confessional or in study, he devoted the time to prayer. Everyone saw it: all who knew him are unanimous: his life was one unending prayer. In the confessional, if even for a few moments there was no penitent, he would get up from his chair and kneel on the floor to pray. In the early afternoon while the others rested, he was in church praying. If he had to leave the friary on his own, he walked with his eyes on the ground and prayed . Even walking about inside the friary, he prayed. He prolonged his evening prayer till well into the night. Many times at midnight or later the Brother Infirmarian would come upon him in the chapel or in his cell, on his knees with the light out so that no one should notice.

Mgr. Luca Pasetto, OFM Cap, Patriarch of Alexandria, writes: *When I was Guardian at Thiene I often used to come back about midnight after a late preaching engagement and I always found Father Leopoldo, on his knees on the floor, praying before the tabernacle.*

His lips were always in motion, forming some invocation or ejaculation in praise of God.

He prayed for himself, asking God to enlighten him so that he might know Him better and unite himself to Him in conformity with the Divine Will; he asked to know himself better so as to recognize his own insignificance; he asked for an increase in the desire for perfection, burning away all impurities in its ardour. To these ends also he asked for the prayer of good people he knew. *"Pray to the Divine Love of the Sacred Heart that I may become His perfect servant,"* he wrote to one lady.

He prayed that his health might be good enough for him to remain at work in the confessional until his death. For this too he was always asking for the prayers of others. "Pray to God for me that He will give me back my health for the benefit of souls." "Ask the Sacred Heart in His infinite love to give me health so that I may serve Him as confessor."

He prayed for others. Always in pain himself, he understood the sufferings of others and begged God to alleviate them.

"I am learning to my cost to pray for others." Or, "I am trying, as the saying is, to put myself in your shoes, so I am praying for you as I pray for myself when I know the hour of trial is at hand." "I was very sorry to hear about the terrible condition of your family. I prayed immediately, and pray continuously that God will not allow them to suffer so much."

In extreme cases he would spend a whole night in prayer to obtain a favour for some unfortunate person. Domenico Lanza of Padua writes: *I know for certain, for he himself confided it to me, that in special circumstances when he wished to obtain some exceptional favour from God, he spent whole nights in prayer.*

And God heard the fervent prayer and accepted the sacrifice of this innocent soul.

On 14th November, 1934, an unhappy mother came and told Father Leopoldo about her misfortunes. A widow with numerous children, her elder sons were out of work and she had no money for the rent. She had received notice of eviction the following day and her furniture was to be sequestrated to satisfy her creditors.

What would happen to her and her children without house or furniture on the threshold of winter?

Father Leopoldo, deeply moved, did his best to comfort her and promised to pray that God would have pity on them. Only, they must pray too, with faith. No idle words, these.

After an exhausting day in the confessional, he went down to the church after the rest of the community had gone to bed and spent the night in prayer prostrate before the tabernacle.

Such love could not be gainsaid. The answer came at once.

The very next day the *Questura* went to evict the widow and to confiscate her furniture, but their truck would not start and nothing was done. Soon afterwards the sons got jobs and paid off the debts and then they moved to a better house.

Particularly in cases where young people were too early threatened by the difficulties of life was Fr. Leopoldo's paternal heart moved to even more intense prayer.

The following incident is described by Fr. Pancrazio of Campese, OFM Cap.

In 1903 when still a student I fell seriously ill with peritonitis and enteritis. The long duration of the illness, combined with various painful complications, had reduced me to such a state of exhaustion that all hope for a cure was abandoned. I was told one day that my doctors had given up hope and that I had at most a month to live.

That evening Fr. Leopoldo came as usual to visit me. I told him what I had been told and indicated that I was resigned to God's will in this matter. He listened carefully and then, drawing himself up, said very firmly, "No. You won't die. I shall pray for you. You've got to get well, see? You have a lot of work to do. Understand? You mustn't fear death in the near future. Don't worry, I'll see to it."

"But Father," I insisted, "I am quite happy to die."

"No, no! You mustn't say that! You must get better so that you can do some good. You understand, eh?"

"I understand," I said, more to keep him happy than anything, for I didn't put much faith in what he had said. A little later I had an operation. All winter I was ill, but in the spring I began to pick up. In June I was examined by Prof. G. Zancan who was astounded by my state of health and said, "When I took on your case I had no hope of curing you. Now I find myself faced with an unexpected, half-

miraculous, cure. The finger of God is upon you, otherwise there could have been no cure."

Since then my health has been excellent and I can now work hard and hope to be able to do the good for which Fr. Leopoldo counted on me.

Fr. Leopoldo had such great faith in the efficacy of prayer as a means of relieving human suffering that he never had any doubt about its results which often took visible and marvellous form.

In January 1927 a man from a village near Padua was the subject of false accusations by his enemies. The day before the case was due to be heard he went to ask Fr. Leopoldo's help and the latter encouraged him to hope for a successful outcome and added, "I shall pray, and you should go now to the Basilica of St. Anthony and tell him: 'My confessor, Fr. Leopoldo, sent me for you to free me from this calumny!' The Saint will hear you and all will go well. Just have faith!"

All did go well. In court his innocence became evident and his accusers were suitably punished.

* * *

He prayed for others in expiation of the sins of his penitents.

One evening, towards midnight, the Brother Infirmarian found him in the infirmary chapel praying intently before the tabernacle.

"Dear Father, why are you still here? You are so tired. Do go and get some rest."

"I can't. You see, I'm doing penance for people whose confessions I've heard. I give them light penances, but then I have to make it up myself."

He prayed with all his heart and soul and tried to put into practice the words of Christ that we should pray without ceasing: when not engaged in vocal prayer he directed all his actions to God so that they too became prayers. What degree of mystical union he had reached in prayer we shall, as already noted, never know for certain. It is certain that in prayer he did not experience those known precise external manifestations of mysticism. However, God in His communication with souls is not obliged to follow the text-books on the subject. One thing we do know for certain: in his prayer Fr. Leopoldo did not stop at minor external practices and conventional pious forms, but plunged deep into the contemplation of God and His attributes. Even his conversation was pretty well confined to the great theological truths.

A variety of circumstances, however, showed clearly that there was something exceptional about his prayer: that mysterious absorption before pronouncing words foretelling the future or announcing a miracle; the deep recollection in prayer, so as to be totally unaware of what was going on around him and to need almost violence to recall him to material reality; his radiant, almost transfigured face, particularly after the Consecration of the Mass; his eyes, at times luminous as two suns. All these points bore witness to the closeness of his union with God.

He himself in a few phrases that escaped his lips gave clearly to understand that after the Consecration he often had direct contact with God so that he was in no doubt that he was in God and God in him. One day when he was talking to a penitent about the goodness of God in showing Himself to souls and uniting them to him, a sob escaped him, he spread his arms, raised his eyes to Heaven and said, "But why are these things for me? A miserable creature like me! Please ask God to be merciful to me." On a picture of the Sacred Heart he wrote: *Divine Love of the Sacred Heart, who deigns to show me signs of infinite Love, have pity in me.*

One positive, verified fact, however, opens a window on the mystery of the intimate relations between God and the soul of Fr. Leopoldo, and that is his periods of spiritual aridity.

They took concrete forms that made them appear, not natural trials or the trials that God sends to fervent souls to further them on the road to perfection, but on account of their great bitterness and the wonderful effects produced on his soul, real mystical trials.

They were very frequent and such as to cause him real agony. He was suddenly attacked by the most violent temptations.

His faith wavered: what had seemed clear and certain and precise was swamped in a wave of uncertainty: everything seemed to tumble about him like a house in an earthquake. In particular the eternity of Hell confused his mind: "How can God," urged a mysterious, almost audible voice, "punish eternally a sin committed in a moment of time? Is it just? Above all, is it merciful? Well, then..." It was agony for him. His faculties were numbed and incapable of reply, as if his brain were in a sort of mental straitjacket.

Even after the attack had passed, if someone mentioned this frightening truth, he paled as if still suffering from a terrifying nightmare and said, "Let it be! I don't think of it. It makes my head spin. God is our Father—that's enough. He alone knows how to do what is good."

Everything that he had done, everything that he was doing, seemed mistaken; it seemed impossible to continue with his work since he had ruined so many souls and lost his own; he was sick, discouraged and afraid. From the depths of his disturbed mind arose angry feelings of revolt against his continual suffering and his physical inferiority. If at these times he was in any way humiliated, the incident became disproportionately serious and almost unbearable. The angels of darkness came and tormented his senses with horrible temptations and disturbed his mind with revolting thoughts and vivid fantasies. It was an agony worse than death. Hemmed in on all sides, he no longer knew what to do, whom to consult, so that he appeared to others confused, disfigured and almost imbecile. At times it was so bad that people wondered about his mental stability. Then he had recourse to his confessor, two or three times a day; and in the middle of the night he would go, trembling, and knock at the door of his cell in order to get some comfort. But here he was repulsed, for the confessor, probably not fully understanding God's design for this penitent, sent him away with harsh words loud enough to be heard by others. He did not insist but withdrew and spent the rest of the night in tears.

At such times he was assailed by vague terrors and trembled like a leaf. He was like a tree in a storm. At times he wanted a confidant of his to come and see him several times a day and to stay with him and keep him company because, he said, he was so afraid.

He had recourse to his Spiritual Director, who replied at once. Following are extracts from some of the latter's replies.

Be calm, and do always what I have told you. Walk with a clear conscience and in time of difficulty imagine that I am at your side repeating my decisions. Don't let anything disturb your spirit, but always rejoice in the Lord, for you have every right to rejoice. Walk swiftly in the way you have been shown; and walk in security, for it is the way to Heaven. Believe absolutely in my words, for they are not my words but those of Our Lord Jesus Christ Who loves you greatly.

On another occasion:

I urge you to be calm and to regulate your conduct, as you always have done, by what I have said. Calm, absolute calm in all things. You have every right to peace and tranquility and if at times you do not enjoy them, this you must attribute to the inscrutable ways of the Lord Who, as always, lays a heavy hand on those He loves. Never forget what the Archangel Raphael said to Tobias, that to become acceptable to the Lord he must be proved by temptation. This is what is happening to you.

Courage, therefore, and complete trust in God, our kind and loving Father; kind and loving because He is our Father.

You know as well as I do, and better, that the strength of a soul lies in being able to say with all one's heart the words of the suffering Christ, "Father, Thy will be done." Herein is everything, all the greatness and perfection of a soul.

Again:

You must not let sadness take hold of you. When Our Lord hides Himself, think of the desolation of sadness of Jesus in the garden and unite your sorrows with those of our Divine Master. It means sacrifice, but the comfort and reward are great.

In the midst of all these trials, faith in his Spiritual Director as the mouthpiece of God remained firm and these letters, which he treasured and often re-read, were balm to his tortured soul.

In God's good time the storm passed, yet it was not a storm that left ruin and desolation behind it, but the Hand of God bearing nothing but good. His spirit having touched rock bottom, his humility was increased; his love of God because less demanding, desiring no consolation but only the Will of the Beloved. After one of these experiences he wrote: *Until now I have been pushed into every kind of unfaithfulness towards my God, but from now on I wish to love my God with a pure love as my Father and my All, my Jesus as my Spouse, the Blessed Virgin as my most gentle mother and the angels and saints as my friends and brothers. I wish the victim already offered for sacrifice to be consumed by the fires of the purest love.*

His trust was increased and his absolute faith in God's goodness. He wrote: *I count on receiving everything from the love of Our Lord Jesus Christ for us, from his Divine Heart.*

In order to sustain him during his long struggle for perfection, God allowed him, after trials, spiritual consolations which can be understood only by those who have experienced them.

His soul flooded with supernatural joy, he wrote once: *Our physical and moral sufferings are in no way commensurate with the joys we shall one day experience in Heaven, nor even with those which from time to time our Heavenly Father in His supreme goodness allows us as a foretaste here on earth.*

The trials came to an end, but the experience remained and was used by Fr. Leopoldo to enlighten and direct other souls. He wrote to a penitent: *In moments of spiritual aridity we—I as well as you—have the opportunity to understand to some extent what Our Lord must have suffered when from His blessed lips came the words, "My God! My God! Why hast Thou forsaken me?" This is a trial reserved for His chosen ones; nevertheless He is always there, behind the scenes, watching to see how we come out of it.*

In order not to be discouraged we must bear in mind that God's gifts to us are always in proportion to the trials he sends us. We are called to Mount Tabor, but formed on Mount Calvary.

How wise are the counsels of God! Only in Heaven shall we fully understand His designs for souls.

We do, however, know this for certain that when God pulls on the bridle, whether directly or indirectly, he does so with a Father's hand with infinite kindness. We must try to understand this fatherly hand on the rein taking care of us with infinite love.

As previously noted, he was most reserved in talking about such matters and only did so with souls who needed it and could understand it. *If possible,* he wrote, *we should go through the trials without giving any external sign, knowing that with joy our Heavenly Father prepares us for the trial and with the trial renders us worthy of greater graces.*

That is in fact how he acted when it was left to his own decision. He spoke to his confessor, to his spiritual director and perhaps to some intimate friend and that was all. After that, absolute silence. It is worth remembering, too, that even during the hardest and bitterest trials he continued his ministry in the confessional as though nothing were happening.

* * *

Fr. Leopoldo prayed, and urged others to pray. By word of mouth or by letter, this was his constant exhortation to souls under his direction: Pray. *According to divinely established order and in the ordinary course of Divine Providence, all good must come to us through prayer,* he wrote.

He taught them how to pray, emphasizing particularly the need for humility in one's demands, for God listens only to the humble. *He urged prayer,* writes one acquaintance, *as an infallible means of obtaining divine grace, and placed great emphasis on the need for humility since we cannot demand anything of God by right.* A propos of Christ's words about insistence in prayer, he was never tired of repeating that one should pray uninterruptedly until the prayer has been answered, if it be in conformity with God's designs for us.

Allow me, he wrote, *in the affection of my friendship for you, and in my faith as a minister of the Gospel, to exhort you to pray and to ask untiringly for the favour you need with all the intensity of your soul.*

To another: *I can understand your sorrow that you have not yet received the favour for which you have so insistently prayed. Our poor human nature resents it, but our faith tells us quite clearly always to pray and have confidence. Every day, therefore, pray to Our Lady the moral source of all good, and then pray to Ven. Fr. Marco d'Aviano to intercede with Our Lady. Scripture teaches us to pray so that we, as the saying is, take Heaven by storm.*

He also gave great importance to communal prayer, for this, he said, God could not resist. He wrote to a nun: *The Gospel says, Whenever two or more are gathered together in my Name, I am in the midst of them and if they ask for anything in my Name it shall be given them! So—you must inspire complete confidence in your pupils and make them pray together with faith and you will see that Divine Providence will meet you.*

So much love of prayer, transmitted by Fr. Leopoldo to his penitents, constituted an inexhaustible source of good for their souls, for from his words and example they learned to walk on the true road to salvation.

Chapter XIV.

THE CONFESSOR

Asked if poor workers constrained by necessity to accept unjust conditions of work could do anything to realize their rights, he answered, "The fruits of the fields are the fruits of the capital contributed by the owner and of the work contributed by the labourer. Capital means money, but labour means sweat and blood and life. Which is more valuable, money or life?" "Life, of course!" "Well then, you understand me..."

In those days workers' rights were far from being recognized. Fr. Leopoldo, so far as his office allowed, was a pioneer in this field.

One of the most wonderful effects of the Redemption is the Sacrament of Penance. Divine power given to man, whereby the priest becomes God since he absolves or condemns, a function that belongs to God alone.

All priests have this divine, power, but sometimes God sends us an exceptional minister of His pardon so that His mercy shall be more abundantly evident.

Fr. Leopoldo was undoubtedly one of these.

He exerted an extraordinary influence on souls.

People had only to see him, or just hear his name, to be moved to approach him and lay bare their consciences.

Even when he was still a young priest hardly at the beginning of his ministry, whenever he stopped at a friary penitents immediately began to flock to his confessional. At Padua the movement assumed really exceptional proportions. A crowd gathered by the door of his confessional and waited hours and hours in their eagerness to kneel before him and hear the words of absolution from his lips, confident that they would receive enlightened advice and sure guidance.

It was not only the poorer people who flocked to him, but people from every stratum of society. University professors, students, professional men, industrial and commercial magnates, and high-ranking army officers mingled with peasants and labourers patiently awaiting their turn. Noticeable among them were priests, secular and regular, and many prelates of the Church. It seemed that Fr. Leopoldo was the ideal confessor for priests, so many came to him. At the annual Retreat for priests in Padua, Vicenza and other cities, Fr. Leopoldo was much in demand and practically all the retreatants went to him to confession. The Bishops of the Province of Venice, too, when they met for episcopal conferences and retreats at Paderno del Grappa, insisted on having Fr. Leopoldo with them.

He was often called to people's sick beds, sometimes to the most distant places in Italy, and he always brought salvation. Many who would not normally have allowed a priest near them were profoundly moved by the mere sight of him and made their peace with God.

Why all this? It was the result of a variety of causes which defy analysis since they disappear into the realms of the mystery of God's grace. Human reasons are inadequate to explain a phenomenon of such wide range. Fr. Leopoldo's contribution, however, was to put everything he could into his work, starting from a sound doctrinal foundation.

Hearing confessions is not, as many probably believe, an easy matter. The confessor is a judge who deals with matters of supreme importance which affect the fate of souls, not for a matter of months or years as in the case of a civil judge, but for all eternity. It is a question of absolution or eternal damnation, no less. The first thing a confessor needs, therefore, is a sound knowledge of Divine Law and the extremely complicated mechanism of human responsibility. Not for nothing does the Church insist on sufficient knowledge before conferring this power, with its terrible responsibility, on her priests.

Fr. Leopoldo took this aspect of it very seriously and prepared himself for his work by studying with great care dogmatic and mystical theology, ascetics, moral theology and canon law, not only during the period preceding ordination but throughout his life. For dogma his favourite writers were, as already noted, St. Augustine and St. Thomas, and for morals St. Alphonsus and other modern authors: their works he kept handy in the confessional so that he could readily consult them. He gave the greatest importance to Papal letters and encyclicals, for in them, he was wont to say, was to be found the safe way through the greatest moral complexities. This did not mean that he was a prodigy of learning in these matters, but that he had a firm background against which he could face with calm any problem however difficult. If he was in any doubt, he had no hesitation in seeking the opinion of someone he considered more competent. This firm doctrinal background was recognized by persons really learned in that field.

In this connexion, Fr. Alfonso Orlini, former Father General of the Conventual Franciscans writes: *My discussions with Fr. Leopoldo were often continued at length outside the confessional and touched on theological and social questions, exchanging confidences about the ministry. They were of the greatest interest to me and gave me a clear idea of his rare wisdom.*

Often he put forward most complicated questions of conscience, sometimes requiring reference to the Holy Office. They were expressed in general terms as purely theoretical cases, but I imagined they were real questions he had come across in his ministry. At times I had to ask for time, not feeling able to give an immediate answer, but I must admit that he always had an answer already and that it was always most satisfactory.

A thing that astonished me was how, tied up all day in the confessional, he managed to be au courant *with controversial questions, not only theological but also philosophical, and to bring out their salient points and give very accurate opinions about them. Privately I often wondered if he did not have the gift of infused knowledge.*

When in my work, which lay principally among people of culture, I realized that a convert had a certain dislike of coming to me to confession, perhaps because we were personal friends or professional colleagues, I always sent him to Fr. Leopoldo. I realized then that this holy Capuchin succeeded in winning these souls who needed special and expert handling and in making up for my previous deficiencies. For that reason, while still admiring it and praising God for it, I no longer wondered at the influence he exercised on souls, and precisely on those souls most difficult to set in the way of perfection, the souls of the learned.

Mgr. Antonio Bettanini, Professor at Padua University: *I was a penitent of Fr. Leopoldo's for thirty-three years. I had many opportunities of getting to know him well, particularly as he was kind enough to discuss a variety of subjects with me.*

I always had the feeling that I was dealing with a saint. His sanctity shone out through his life of prayer, through the advice he gave in confession, advice always based on sound theology, a field in which one knew he was at home, not from the study of books so much as from prolonged thought and meditation. His deep knowledge of souls and the finesse of his psychology meant that his judgments were sure and his penitents satisfied and at peace.

Anyone who said he was too generous and easy-going merely displayed his own ignorance of the things of God and of moral theology which Fr. Leopoldo knew inside out and applied in the light of supernatural principles.

Mgr. Giacinto Ambrosi, Archbishop of Gorizia: *Fr. Leopoldo studied theological matters closely and in the solution of moral problems, besides showing himself up-to-date in all questions, showed perfect balance in his decisions and never presumed to say that a moral proposition was probably right unless he was quite certain of his judgment.*

* * *

Fr. Leopoldo, however, realized that book-learning would have been of no value to him if God's grace had not transformed it into wisdom. He therefore prayed constantly for the gift of wisdom in order to be able to direct souls in confession, asking also for the intercession of of the saints, particularly the Curé d'Ars and St. Catherine of Alexandria, famous for her wisdom. Every year on her feast he went to the church dedicated to her and, asking to be left alone, placed her relic on his head and begged her earnestly to obtain for him from God the wisdom so necessary for his ministry.

Heavenly wisdom, which no human master can teach, was vouchsafed him together with a fine grasp of essentials. He did not lose himself in details but went straight for the main principles, seeing everything in terms of the love of God and one's neighbour. Fr. Leopoldo's wisdom had all the characteristics of the Gift of Wisdom. Mgr. Giacomo Dal Sasso, Professor of Philosophy at the Padua Seminary, writes in this connexion: *Divine Wisdom found a chosen abode in the soul of Fr. Leopoldo, which it enriched with its splendours and graces.*

* * *

To the gift of wisdom God had added the power to read the hearts of others, a marvellous gift which makes a lasting impression on anyone upon whom it is exercised, reducing him to a feeling of nothingness. Our security, in fact, rests largely on the impenetrability of our conscience to human eyes; but if one finds oneself face to face with someone who can tear aside the veil and read deep into the remotest corners of one's heart, one feels lost and filled with fear.

In common with the Curé d'Ars, St. Joseph Cafasso and many others, Fr. Leopoldo had this gift of reading the deepest secrets of one's conscience. Witnesses are many and incontrovertible.

Fr. Alfonso Orlini: *Certainly Fr. Leopoldo could read one's heart. I have heard him refer to incidents and acts in my life which humanly speaking he cannot have known.*

Mgr. Giacinto Ambrosi: *A practice of Fr. Leopoldo that surprised people was that sometimes he would not allow the penitent to explain himself properly, nor even to confess the sin even though the penitent thought it necessary. For my part, I should say that, whether on account of long association with penitents, or his acute intelligence, but certainly also on account of his diligence and habit of self-examination, Fr. Leopoldo had acquired an exceptional insight into souls. One must not discount the possibility that he was specially endowed with the gift of knowing the secrets of hearts. There are many incidents to witness that he frequently did read the hearts of others.*

Prof. Angelo Zambaldo, of Tregnago: *Fr. Leopoldo read consciences clearly. I remarked this on several occasions when I went to him to confession with no more than small faults to confess and, before I had opened my mouth, he said, "You don't need confession: go straight to Holy Communion." When, however, I had real need to make my peace with God, he allowed me to unburden my conscience. I have always been astounded by this.*

Giuseppe Bolzonella, of Padua, had being going to Fr. Leopoldo for confession for some time. One morning in 1939 he went as usual to confess. He had just knelt down but had said nothing at all when Fr. Leopoldo, who seemed quite abstracted and had not even looked at him, began to tell him everything he had done, down to the last detail.

"But, Father," he said when the priest had finished, "that is what I am supposed to be telling you!"

Fr. Leopoldo shook himself, looked at him and smiled. "Never mind!" he said amiably. "Just forget about it."

* * *

Many of the Elizabethine Sisters of the Mother House in Padua agree that Fr. Leopoldo knew of their spiritual needs before they had mentioned them and that he often would not allow them to accuse themselves of their faults, and it was clear that he knew what they were because his subsequent words were always to the point.

The mother of one of the nuns was ill once and the nun had asked permission to visit her and been refused. Miserable, she told Fr. Leopoldo of her disappointment. "Don't worry," he smiled. "Go back to Rev. Mother. She has already changed her mind."

And so it was. As soon as the Superior saw the nun, she called her and told her to go and spend some days with her mother.

* * *

Fr. Raimondo of Herne, OFM. Cap, writes: *One day when I was at the friary at Padua a young friend of mine came to see me and we spent some time walking up and down the cloister in conversation. At one point Fr. Leopoldo passed close to us, glanced at my friend and went on.*

"Who's that little friar?" asked my friend as soon as he was out of earshot.

"What! Don't you know? That's Fr. Leopoldo. But what's the matter? You seem all upset."

"Didn't you see how he looked at me?"

"Much as he looks at anyone, I should have said."

"No, no! He looked at me in a special manner. You only saw a glance, but he saw right into my conscience; he saw my whole life."

I tried to pick up the conversation again where Fr. Leopoldo's pas-

sage had interrupted it, but my friend was paying no attention. Every now and then he murmured, "That priest read my conscience."

A bit impressed in spite of myself, I said that the only way to give himself peace was to go to confession to "that priest."

"I will," he said, "right now, for I shall never forget that look as long as I live."

Next day I questioned Fr. Leopoldo in the hope of learning or guessing what happened, but he only smiled sweetly and changed the subject.

A Catholic paper printed the following after Fr. Leopoldo's death: *We feel a great need to know ourselves and it was this need that made Fr. Leopoldo so much sought after. We felt that he could see into our innermost selves and know us and help us to know ourselves.*

It is not for me to say whether this was intuition or direct enlightenment, but the fact remains that being with him was like being under a powerful searchlight that penetrated our darkest corners.

How many spiritual problems did he resolve with his tired calm voice and his habitual, "You see..." And you did see, because he saw and heard and lived your own personal drama.

* * *

In 1934 a Paduan who had been many years estranged from God came with some friends to Fr. Leopoldo. They were making their Easter confession and he only accompanied them to avoid their further insistence, for he had no intention of going to confession but stood at the end of the queue so that when they had all confessed and gone he could slip away without their suspecting that he had not confessed.

He reckoned without Fr. Leopoldo, however, for as soon as the first penitent had finished, the priest came to the door and addressed him. "You, Sir, come on in now. I've been waiting for you, you know."

Taken aback, he did as he was bid, but once inside the confessional did not know what to say, for he had made no preparation. Fr. Leopoldo spoke for him. "You didn't want to come, did you? But God wanted you to come. Don't worry! I'll tell you what to confess." And he told him everything "... and this, and that. Right?" A stammered yes. "And now you are sorry, aren't you? And you will lead a good Christian life from now on?"

This time a firm and heartfelt yes.

"Well, then, God forgives you everything. And I thank you for bringing me so much joy, but I expect to see you again. You'll come, won't you, and we'll be good friends."

It was a completely changed man that left the confessional. When his friends asked how it had gone, he answered, "That's no ordinary man: he's a saint."

He returned often to Fr. Leopoldo and they became, as he said, good friends.

In April, 1939 Fr. Leopoldo had been for some hours hearing the confessions of the Elizabethine Sisters in the chapel of their Mother House in Padua when, without being sent for by anyone, he left the confessional saying to the next penitent, "I'm sorry to make you wait, Sister, but there is someone in the parlour who needs me."

At that moment someone had arrived seeking him. He had come from a great distance and, not finding him at the friary, had been redirected there.

A cleric came to confession. He was on the point of being ordained and before such an important event wanted to make a general confession. Fr. Leopoldo was against it. "No need. You have no need to make a general confession. I tell you this in God's Name."

The young man was not satisfied, but went to another priest and made a general confession. Thereafter he did not come to Fr. Leopoldo any more.

Some twenty years later, having the cure of souls and being faced with a difficult problem, he went to Fr. Leopoldo for advice. Fr. Leopoldo looked at him and smiled. "We know each other, don't we? You were the young cleric who wouldn't believe me and went and made a general confession to another priest. But I don't mind telling you again, that confession was quite unnecessary."

Returning to the friary on foot one day, he was passed by a cyclist quite near the church. The cyclist had not set foot in a church for a good forty years, despised the church and the clergy and boasted that he didn't believe in God.

Fr. Leopoldo, who had never seen him before, stared at him so that he stopped.

"Do you want something, Father, that you look at me like that?"

"I want you to come into church with me now."

After a moment's perplexity: "All right! I'll come!"

They went into the church and Fr. Leopoldo led him to his confessional and later sent him away at peace with himself and with God. From then on he lived a good Christian life and never tired of telling his friends how Fr. Leopoldo's look had penetrated like a sword into his soul, rendering him powerless to resist the invitation to reform.

A Capuchin priest went to Fr. Leopoldo and asked to make a general confession before his Solemn Profession; he had been preparing for it all during the retreat. He had hardly opened his mouth before Fr. Leopoldo interrupted him, "That's enough. I understand everything. You don't need to say any more."

The other insisted, begging to be allowed to go on for his own peace of mind.

"In that case, so that you shall have peace of mind, I'll tell you all you have done."

He then proceeded to spend twenty minutes telling him in the greatest detail all the faults of which he was going to accuse himself, plus a few others which in spite of his careful examination of conscience he had forgotten.

"There, you see! It wasn't necessary for you to accuse yourself, because I knew everything. Learn to believe what your confessor tells you."

Umberto Petit of Padua: *I had not been to confession for many years when on Holy Saturday, 1934 I felt the need to return to the Church. My reluctance to go and kneel once more before a priest was great, but an almost irresistible force was urging me to this step. I passed a number of churches before finally entering the Capuchin Church at S. Croce. There was a crowd of people waiting for confession and, after waiting a bit, I was thinking of going away, almost glad to have a more or less plausible excuse for not going to confession. I was on the point of leaving when from a door by the altar came a small, bent old friar, walking with a limp. He came to me and said, "You have come for confession. Come with me or you will go away without confessing."*

I followed him into a small room near the altar. Soon I had made my confession and was back in church, calmer and happier than I had been in my life. Later I went home, wondering to myself how the little priest could have known what I was thinking and planning to do. Next day when I went back to the same church I ceased to wonder, for I learned that it was Fr. Leopoldo and I had already heard him spoken of as a saint and one able to read people's consciences.

In 1937 Signora Maria Gotti of Padua brought a young woman who was in serious difficulties to Fr. Leopoldo for his blessing. The latter was in a hurry, for she had a train to catch. There was the usual crowd waiting outside the confessional-cell and they asked if she might go in ahead, but the people would not hear of it. Discouraged, they were just about to leave because they could not afford the time to wait, when Fr. Leopoldo suddenly appeared in the door of the confessional and said to them, "Come on in first." He took them in, blessed them and sent them away with words of comfort.

* * *

As well as the gift of reading hearts, Fr. Leopoldo had received the gift of Counsel which, with that of Prudence, allowed him by supernatural intuition to know immediately and with certainty what course to follow, particularly in difficult cases.

High-ranking prelates asked his opinion on difficult situations arising in their dioceses, Parish Priests submitted to him complicated cases occurring in their parish work, fathers referred their often agonizing family problems, and even commercial magnates sought guidance and light from him.

Fr. Leopoldo listened carefully, entered into himself, asked God for light, sometimes going and praying before the tabernacle or at the Lady Altar, and then with the greatest clarity and certainty gave the advice requested. His advice was always prudent, hopeful and instinct with profound wisdom. In the half-light of his tiny room everything seemed to change when he spoke: difficulties dissolved and new and safe courses were set for consciences previously in doubt.

Prof. Enrico Rubaltelli writes again: *Where Fr. Leopoldo shone was when faced with a soul oppressed by moral or material difficulties, or by a difficult decision in a matter affecting personal spiritual welfare or that of the family. He would pause for a moment in recollected silence, seeming to commune with God, and then he would explain the appropriate solution or the action to be taken. The answers were so realistically conceived and so lucidly given that they seemed obvious and the only possible solution, and people were often astonished that they had not seen it for themselves.*

Or Fr. Alfonso Orlini again: *In all his advice he showed himself prudent and at the same time absolutely sure, so that I was always happy to follow his directions which were afterwards confirmed by events as being the only correct course to follow. Often I was restrained from actions or courses which, I had to admit afterwards, would have harmed me spiritually rather than helped as intended.*

In tracing the ways of piety to be followed, he could always stick to a safe path without straying into exaggeration, a fault that is inevitably fatal. His advice was always a model of balance.

Answering a letter from the Servant of God Guido Negri, he wrote: *The more noble the cause with which we are dealing, the greater are the difficulties, the more fearsome are the enemies we encounter, and the greater is our need to observe prudence.*

The thing that frightens me most with young people is enthusiasm.

True, enthusiasm as such is good, but of its nature it tends to excess and can so easily overflow into excess, thus becoming less than good, for all forms of excess are wrong.

You must therefore carry on in your generous course. God wants you as His apostle so, as far as is possible for mankind, divine wisdom and grace must guide your steps.

Now, here are the answers to your questions.

I. The desire you express to imitate Our Divine Redeemer in His sufferings is certainly a signal gift from God, but this desire must be subject to obedience, therefore you must accept my advice. As far as mortification is concerned, it is enough that, except where convention demands otherwise, you take no food or drink between meals.

II. As far as physical mortifications such as hair-shirts etc. are concerned, I absolutely forbid them.

III. As far as appearances are concerned, you will dress as is expected of someone in your station.

Mgr. Antonio Bettanini, Professor at Padua University, writes: *He was always prudent in his advice and admonition. When I asked him how I should comport myself among my lay colleagues at the University, he advised me not to be provocatively religious, but to behave discreetly, adding that the wearing of priestly garb with dignity was in itself an apostolate.*

To religious Superiors he advised kindness and moderation in giving orders and making regulations. Fr. Venceslao of S. Martino di Lupari writes: *When I was Fr. Leopoldo's Provincial, knowing how much affection I had for him, he trusted me and would often say, "Father Provincial, if I may... try not to load the conscience of the Communities with regulations that are not really necessary... You see, regulations made by Superiors have to be kept, and if they are not really necessary they are just a trap for the weaker brethren. Forgive me, please, for mentioning it..."*

To the rank and file he recommended faith in their Superiors and absolute frankness with them, relying always on God's grace. To a nun he once wrote: *Try to explain the whole thing to your Mother General; that is, give her the facts as they are. In the second place, as a good religious whose greatest comfort is prayer, pray and encourage your pupils to pray.*

Where his prudence was most evident was in the advice he gave about the choice of a state of life, particularly in the choice of the religious or priestly state.

Signorina Maria Prearo: *Sometime in 1926, when I was finding it very difficult to decide what I should do with my life, an eminent priest told me to see Fr. Leopoldo. He received me with great kindness and I was moved, or rather astonished, to find that he was familiar with all my life to date, including things that I had no intention of telling him. He told me straightaway that the life of the cloister, which I was considering, was not for me but that he would tell me definitely in a year's time what I should do.*

For a whole year I tried at various times to get to see him. In the meantime unsuspected events were gradually leading me towards the path which in the first interview Fr. Leopoldo had hinted at. When at last at the end of a year I was able to see him again, he told me with certainty what I was to do in the way of humble parish mission work and in helping abandoned children. Thereafter he advised me with great wisdom and supported me in the difficult trials I had to meet. Father Leopoldo was in truth an enlightened and prudent counsellor. One felt that God spoke through him.

The Salesian priest Fr. Eugenio Pila: *For some time before my ordination to the priesthood I was tormented by a spiritual crisis. Confused and uncertain on the subject of my vocation, I had considered leaving the seminary and returning home. Before reaching a decision I consulted Fr. Leopoldo. He listened carefully and then said categorically, "You are called by God to the priesthood, but since your bent is not for preaching or work among the people, to become a secular priest would be to place your eternal salvation in jeopardy, for you would fall into inaction and a priest cannot be saved unless he works hard for souls. You will therefore become a Salesian. Following the example of their holy founder, the Salesians are workers* par excellence *and you will partake of all their merits." He then brought me before the tabernacle and, indicating the Blessed Sacrament, said as though inspired, "That's understood then? You do as I said, believing that that is what God wants for your eternal salvation and for the salvation of the souls for which you will work among the Salesians." I took his advice and now on the 25th anniversary of my ordination and the 20th anniversary of my profession I am bound to thank God for the great grace He accorded me in inspiring Fr. Leopoldo to advise me to join the Salesians where I have found my peace.*

Another Salesian, Fr. Antonio Barbacci: *I was for many years a penitent of Fr. Leopoldo's and had occasion to observe how God had favoured him with special gifts in foretelling the future, and one day I confided my anxieties to him. He leaped to his feet and took from a small table a picture of St. John Bosco and gave it to me saying: "Pray to this saint." He did not say anything else but for me this was a sudden flash of understanding which led me to become a son of St. John Bosco. I had already been ordained several years when I again came across a picture of the Ven. Marco d'Aviano which Father Leopoldo had sent me many years before I had mentioned to him my intention of becoming a priest. Among the affectionate phrases he had written thereon was 'dear colleague.' He had seen quite clearly into my future!*

Fr. Adelmo of Arezzo, OFM Cap: *In 1919-20 I was in Padua as an infantry subaltern. I used to go to the Capuchin Friary and there was introduced to Fr. Leopoldo. In the crisis of vocation I was undergoing he helped me courageously and brought peace back to my soul. He told me firmly, "God wants you to be a priest in our Order and you will teach the young people of our Province." His words came true, for I had scarcely finished my studies in 1927 when I was assigned to teaching our young people in which office I remained until 1946.*

The gift of Counsel was of assistance to him not only in guiding others but also in governing himself, for certain occasions of evil arise even in the exercise of the most holy offices. He wrote: *I, who hear so many confessions, must be on my guard lest the evil of others attaches itself to me. With some people the utmost caution is necessary to avoid the risk of losing one's faith. So often one finds oneself between the hammer and the anvil and does not know to escape or which way to turn. In such circumstances I say, "God will see to it: He will preserve me from evil."*

Fortitude was another gift of God's to Fr. Leopoldo. Fortitude which gives to the will the impulse and strength to bear any pain and to achieve great things for the glory of God. We have already seen the courage with which he bore his continual illnesses and the voluntary mortifications, in particular the long years of the terrible cross of the confessional. The same fortitude was apparent in everything he did.

He once said, "When I hear confessions and give advice, I feel the full weight of my office and I cannot betray my conscience. As a priest and minister of God, when I have my stole on I fear no one. Truth first and above everything !" In fact he never looked at people in the face but said boldly what had to be said regardless whether it might be displeasing to his interlocutor or to others. He would raise his eyes to the crucifix and say, "It was He Who gave us the example of fearing no man and even giving one's life for Truth."

He did have certain difficulties with people whose *amour propre* was stung by his advice, but he bore them all courageously and never withdrew anything that he had said before God.

On one occasion, for example, a great lady came to consult him about a very serious matter. Wanting to see her daughter married, she had advertised in the papers and in due course the girl married. The marriage was not a success and now she wanted to obtain a decree of nullity. When he had heard the case, Fr. Leopoldo turned to her indignantly, "You did a pretty shabby bit of trading with your daughter, Madam. I can't put it any other way."

Hurt and humiliated by this frank answer, the woman tried to get back at Father Leopoldo by reporting a travesty of his words to an ecclesiastical tribunal, but the truth came out and everyone admired Fr. Leopoldo's forthrightness.

One day a man came to confession. He had many grave sins to confess, but they would all have been cancelled by the infinite mercy of God if he had admitted his fault and asked for pardon. Instead of this he insisted on defending his sin. Gently Fr. Leopoldo tried to show him where he was wrong, but it was no use. So, in defence of God's justice against this miserable sinner, he rose to his feet and pointed to the door. "I cannot give you absolution on those conditions. Go! Go away! You have put yourself among the accurst of God." The wretched fellow wanted to argue the point, but Fr. Leopoldo just stood there pointing to the door. Finally before Fr. Leopoldo's menacing attitude the man broke down and asked on his knees for mercy, promising to amend his ways. At this Fr. Leopoldo became his usual gentle self and raised the man up saying, "Now we are once more brothers." He gave him absolution and sent him away consoled. From then on he lived a good Christian life.

It was he himself who, at Fr. Leopoldo's funeral, recounted with tears the story of this encounter.

At Treviso a nobleman was nearing the end of his life. For a long time he had not been to church. Some good people managed to persuade relatives to call Fr. Leopoldo. They came by car to collect him, but when they got to the sick man's house they tried to persuade him to bless him from behind the door so that the patient should not see him and suffer shock. But Fr. Leopoldo had not come there in order to indulge in any hole-and-corner stuff, and he gave them to understand that the sick man had need of something better than that before appearing before God. He insisted as much as he could, but when it was apparent that they would not heed him, he raised his voice and said to those sorry individuals, "Enough of this farce! One cannot play the fool with God. You are responsible for that poor soul."

He had to leave without achieving anything, and when he thought about it afterwards he always wept for grief.

A priest came to ask his advice. He had written, he said, a long book in which he had finally clearly explained the mystery of the Holy Trinity, no less! "A mystery explained is a mystery denied," exclaimed Fr. Leopoldo. "Burn your manuscript at once!" He would not hear any more and sent the unfortunate cleric on his way.

To complete the picture of Fr. Leopoldo as a wonderful judge of souls one must add to his fortitude an exceptional mildness. He often recalled what St. Francis of Sales wrote: *You must try never to allow yourself to become angry, for it is much easier to hold oneself completely in check than to regain one's calm once one is angry. If a sudden flash of anger takes you by surprise, get hold of yourself at once, praying God to help you.* These words could be a description of his life.

This virtue of his is perhaps best described by quoting from Mgr. Guido Bellincini's address on the occasion of Fr. Leopoldo's golden sacerdotal jubilee. *One must say that on man who is compounded of the senses, the external aspects of a character exercise an especial fascination. Among these qualities gentleness holds a very high place; gentleness, the enchanting quality of velvet softness that allows a soul to adapt itself to exterior pressure, to round off sharp corners and deaden sharp blows, whose aim and object seems to be to adapt itself to the good and convenience of others. Think of someone unceasingly devoting himself to the service of others; think of someone who for fifty years, all day and every day, always smiling and welcoming, remained shut up in a small room something like a punishment cell aggravated by the monotonous mumbling of human miseries at his side; realize then that from this man a burst of irritation, a movement of impatience, a sign of distaste, the slightest alteration in his subdued voice were unknown. There you have in great part the secret whereby Fr. Leopoldo gained the confidence of so many souls. He is the living embodiment of Our Lord's words, "Blessed are the meek for they shall inherit the earth."*

Prof. Jacopo Tivaroni of Genoa University: *The first time I went to Fr. Leopoldo to confession the kindness and gentleness with which he listened to me made me wonder if he were not lax and shirking his duty. Soon afterwards, however, I realized my mistake. Father Leopoldo had in him something of that gentleness that Christ showed towards repentant sinners, and it is surely from this divine example that he derived his kindness and indulgence. That is what I thought then and still think after having had him as confessor up to the time of his death, a period of eighteen years running.*

Prof. Enrico Rubaltelli: *Throughout the years, whatever the time of day, whether there were crowds or not, in health and in his long sickness, I found Fr. Leopoldo always the same. He was always calm, serene and humble, humble with that truly Franciscan humility which astonished me anew every time, humility which confused people who came to him for advice, comfort or pardon because they were blessed and thanked and sent away not as people who had come to ask for something but as if they had come to give and had given generously.*

* * *

To his gentleness Fr. Leopoldo added generosity in forgiveness, a generosity that at first sight might have appeared to be laxity of moral principles, but which was, in fact, understanding of human frailty and faith in the inexhaustible treasure of grace. It was not acquiescence in or indifference to the faults, but forbearance for the sinner so that he should not despair of his ability to reform and get himself back on a sound footing. Not a dealer in cut-price absolution, but the generous dispenser of the Blood of Christ shed for the salvation of sinners. The basis of his generosity was the divine mercy.

Mgr. Giacinto Ambrosi, a confidant of Fr. Leopoldo's, writes: *The generosity with which he treated even hardened sinners, a generosity which seemed excessive to some, may have given an odd impression. But I think that to get a clear valuation of his kindness and generosity in forgiveness one would have to be informed, as he was, with the infinite kindness and mercy of God. In any case one has only to think how measured and precise he was in everything in order to discount the possibility of any lightness in this matter.*

Mgr. Antonio Bettanini: *The phrase, "God's mercy is greater than any expectation," was often on his lips. One day I told him how perplexed I was by the generosity with which he gave absolution. He thought for a bit and then replied, "If I regret one thing, it is having had, admittedly only very rarely, to refuse absolution."*

Fr. Leopoldo had learned from Jesus Himself the way one must treat souls and often said to people who wondered at his generosity, "Look, He (indicating the crucifix) gave us the example. It wasn't we who died for souls, but He who shed His precious Blood. We must therefore deal with souls as He taught us by His example."

Then, almost joking, he would add, "If Our Lord were to reprove me for being too generous, I could tell Him it was His own fault for giving me the bad example of dying on the Cross out of love for souls."

Just before he died he was able to say, "I have been hearing confessions for more than fifty years and my conscience doesn't reprove me with having always given absolution. Rather I am sorry about the three or four times I couldn't. Perhaps I didn't do all that I should have done to move the sinner to penitence."

Mgr. Canon Antonio Barzon writes: *Fr. Leopoldo was my confessor and spiritual father for more than twenty years. Anything that my soul has achieved of good I owe to him and his boundless kindness. Sometimes I allowed myself to say in a tone of filial confidence, "But Father, you are being too kind to me ... you'll have to account for it to Our Lord. Aren't you afraid that God will demand an account of our generosity?"*

"You just do as I say," he answered, adding immediately, "If there is anything I ought to repent of it is that I didn't interpret God's infinite goodness in this way right from the start."

And I did as I was told because I felt that his authority was that of a father acting in God's name, and because his words penetrated my soul, illuminating everything...

Souls overwhelmed by so much kindness and mercy found themselves anew, set themselves once more on the right road and understood that so great a love must be met with love.

* * *

To be a confessor was Fr. Leopoldo's vocation, a vocation he had known about while still a boy. The following story in his own words was told to a nun in Padua.

"When I was about eight years old I committed a fault which didn't seem serious at the time, and I still don't think it was serious. My sister reproved me and then took me to the Parish Priest for correction and punishment. I confessed my fault, and the priest, after a severe scolding, set me to kneel in the middle of the church. I was very upset and asked myself why it was necessary to treat a child so harshly for a minor offence. I made up my mind that when I was grown up I should become a friar and a confessor and be very merciful and kind to sinners."

After he was ordained, seeing that it was impossible to go as he had wished into the eastern mission field, he recognized even more clearly the vocation to which God had called him and for which He had prepared him with so many gifts, and embraced it accordingly with the greatest enthusiasm. When his colleague Mgr. Vigilio Dalla Zuanna wondered aloud how he could bear so many hours in the confessional, he replied, "Since God has not given me the gift of words for preaching, I want to dedicate myself to bringing souls to Him in the confessional."

* * *

Let us try now to get an idea of the method used by Fr. Leopoldo in confession. It can be no more than an attempt, since he had an entirely personal way of hearing confessions which was derived largely from his special gifts and signal virtues. He did not think in terms of method, but acted as his mind and his heart, full of God, dictated. To follow his example one would have to have his soul. On many occasions great sinners coming into his cell shed tears of repentance at the mere sight of him: they were already converted. Methods of hearing confession hardly come into it: rather, a whole life in close union with God was the preparaton for such miracles of grace.

However, something can be said about his methods.

He had, above all things, a very great opinion of the Sacrament of Penance. He would never subscribe to the idea that confession is a job for those who are unable or incapable of other forms of ministry. For him it was *the* Sacrament, in which alone one could come into direct contact with souls, convert them and guide them on the road to perfection up to the highest degree of union with God. Only in the confessional can the priest blend his soul with that of the penitent, moulding the latter and giving it a really Christian character. All other aspects of the apostolate, however "showy" they may be, if they do not lead to this intimate union, are useless, are flashes in the pan. This was one of the basic concepts of Fr. Leopoldo: the apostolate to which he was called was, therefore, a sublime one. For him, going into his confessional was a far more important thing than the entry of judge and jury into court to decide on a matter of life and death concerning the accused. For this reason it distressed him greatly to see priests popping in and out of their confessionals as though it were a matter of small moment. "The greatest grace God can give us", he told a priest once, "is that of finding a real confessor and spiritual director. How few priests have this gift! Any priest can hear confessions, but there's all the difference between just hearing confessions and guiding souls in the way of perfection."

It was a task that he himself approached with trepidation.

* * *

To be a good confessor one must first of all gain the confidence of the penitent. In this Fr. Leopoldo succeeded wonderfully. His very person, so small as to be scarcely visible in the semi-darkness of the cell, his features calm and radiating kindness, his eyes full of serenity, his measured and paternal gestures, all combined to awake confidence in all who approached. Often he would get up and go to meet the penitent as if he were greeting an old and expected friend. Nothing he did or said could in any way humiliate the visitor and cause him to close his heart. He paid attention to everything, knowing that confidence is built on a variety of imponderables which may often appear insignificant.

His greeting, "Si accomodi, Signore" cannot be translated into English since it can mean "Won't you come in?" or "Won't you sit down?" or almost anything indicating that one should be at ease. This variety of interpretation led to an odd little incident indicative of his care not to embarrass people. The story is told by Giovanni Chivato of Padua.

It was many years since I had been to confession when I finally made up my mind and went to Fr. Leopoldo. As I came into the confessional, he got up from his seat and came to greet me as if I were a friend he was expecting. "Si accomodi, Signore! Si accomodi!" he said. In my confusion I sat down in his chair and he, without saying anything, knelt beside me and heard my confession. It was only at the end that I realized what I had done and started trying to apologize. He smiled. "Nonsense! Nothing at all! Go in peace."

This act of kindness on his part made a profound impression on me for the delicacy with which he avoided any comment that might have embarrassed me. Needless to say he had won me completely.

If the welcoming atmosphere was not enough and the penitent remained mute or hesitant. whether from fear or shame, then Father Leopoldo would encourage him with fatherly and human words that could not be resisted. Occasionally he would come down to the same level. "Don't worry.... You know, even I, a regular priest, am not all that good. If the good Lord hadn't a firm hand on the bridle, I should be doing worse things than other people... So, don't be afraid." And this was said with such genuine humility and in such a brotherly way that the penitent was moved to open his heart. As the penitent gradually laid bare his troubles—and they could be few or all the ills that flesh is heir to— so Fr. Leopoldo took shape, so to speak, becoming the father with his gentle dominion and supreme power. It was now that his work began.

Fr. Leopoldo did not confine himself to just listening to what was said to him: he wanted to go deeper. What the penitent says shows only a small part of his soul. So much remains unspoken because it is hidden away in the depths and so identified with his nature, character and way of life that even if he did half-see it he would be unable, with the best will in the world, to give it expression. In this mysterious domain Fr. Leopoldo could penetrate with a sure touch. Sometimes it would be a flash of revelation dispersing the shadows, but most often his insight was due to experience, the fruit of long years of patient and intelligent observation. This observation was so discreet that the penitent was unaware of it, but nothing escaped Fr. Leopoldo — dress, expression of eyes and face, tone of voice... He had learned to read the interior from outward signs, and he did it with certainty. He was thus able to fill out what the penitent told him and to reveal to him secrets of his own soul of which he was probably not aware. The soul was laid bare and saw itself as it had never done before. But the process was so gentle and carried out with such consummate tact that not even the most sensitive person was ashamed but only amazed to find himself in such new country. A sudden impulse would make him confide himself entirely to the care of the confessor who could see where none other had seen before and to allow his gentle hand to treat the spiritual wounds revealed.

Not only did he lay bare these wounds, he also made each penitent aware of his responsibility in the matter. He abhorred the modern tendency to diminish personal responsibility for one's faults, especially the theory based on the unavoidability of sexual phenomena. Physical constitution, illness, upbringing and milieu were all factors given the greatest consideration, and he kept himself up-to-date with serious studies in this field, but he would not hear of the abolition of all blame. Responsibility varies in an infinite number of degrees between individuals, but each has some and must recognize it. In this matter he was intransigent. He had a very clear picture of the mercy, compassion and forgiveness of our Lord, but the principle of personal responsibility was not to be disputed. If he came up against difficulties in this matter with a penitent, he would use all his skill and knowledge to make the point, but if this did not work and the penitent's mind would not bow to the evidence and arguments set forth, then the kind and merciful father gave place to the judge dealing severely with the wickedness of one who tried to condone his errors with captious reasoning in order to disguise his malice and his love of sin. Sometimes on such occasions this change of front was enough to break down the apparently unbreakable resistance. If not, he sent the unhappy, for the moment irredeemable, person away and followed him with his tears.

Such cases were very rare, perhaps three or four in his fifty years of ministry, and he did not abandon them but offered his prayers and sufferings for them till the end.

Once the difficulties were cleared up and the way opened for the working of grace, Fr. Leopoldo began the work of dressing the open wounds, like the Good Samaritan, with the oil and wine of compassion, never adding humiliation to the already suffering souls. "Why should we humiliate any more," he asked, "souls which have come to prostrate themselves at our feet. Are they not humbled enough? Did Jesus humiliate the publican, the woman taken in adultery, the Magdalene?" It was not just that he did not humble them further, he treated them with great respect, all of them without distinction were they nobles, professors, workmen, peasants or shaky old women. What he saw was a soul red with the Blood which Christ shed for its salvation. He held himself unworthy to approach them at the moment the mystery of divine grace was working in them, and excused himself to them and before God if in any way his comportment might have fallen short of what was required by so great a mystery.

So much skill and so much virtue naturally disposed the penitent to listen with a receptive mind to the instruction and exhortations which followed. What he said was not just a routine affair, the same for everyone; he said what was needed by each individual soul in a manner easily understood by the person in question, using dialect and popular phrases if they would help. This was a point he considered very important. "In the confessional," he told a fellow-priest one day, "we must not put on a show of culture or talk over the head of the penitent of the moment or we shall only succeed in spoiling the work of God that is in progress in him. It is God Who does the work: we should remain in the background, confining ourselves to assisting this divine intervention in the mysterious ways of salvation and sanctification."

What he did say was carefully thought out, measured and brief. No superfluous phrases: just what was necessary. The result was that you did not get the impression of being before a teacher bludgeoning you with knowledge, but of being with a man at once father, brother and friend.

Again Mgr. Canon Barzon writes: *He listened, made suggestions, gave absolution: not many words, a proverb, a glance at the crucifix, a sigh perhaps. Normally that was all. Yet no one left his confessional, his spiritual embrace, without feeling renewed, without new hope in his heart.*

And Mgr. Bellincini: *Fr. Leopoldo did not spend much time in exhortation. Carefully weighed advice, a wise phrase, perhaps even only one word: it was enough, and it showed how his studies and knowledge translated themselves into practical wisdom. This wisdom was also based on his great experience but more than that on the special, gift of God to his beloved priest.*

To which Filippo Conconi, a Paduan lawyer, adds: *The words used by Fr. Leopoldo in the confessional expressed profound truths, but they were so simply used that they appeared banal unless one thought about them quietly afterwards. It seemed that in his instruction, advice and admonition he said only the most ordinary things, but underneath them there was a wealth of culture.*

Signora Caterina D'Ambrosio, of Padua, writes: *Great was the power of Fr. Leopoldo's word. It illuminated and conquered one, made one better, more pious, more fervent in one's duties and in the acceptance of sacrifices. To be with him was like experiencing a moment of Heaven; all earthly cares fell away. A single phrase from him was more enlightening than years of personal effort: a word from him was worth more than a whole course of sermons.*

One left his confessional feeling always reborn to a new life with one's soul full of new strength.

One day I went to him on behalf of a friend and at her request. She was involved in a liaison which she wanted to give up but lacked the strength to do so. After making some suggestions, Fr. Leopoldo added, "But where the heart is involved only God can loose the tie." From this apparently casual remark I realized that the case was for the moment hopeless, and in fact it was so.

He corrected, instructed and guided souls. He had learned the lesson that a confessor should not be a dictator imposing his own ideas but, as he often said, simply an instrument of the grace of God, which alone can accomplish its miracles. With this in mind he studied all the good points in his penitents and never attempted to put them on any other road but that on which God had already set them. It was a wise course, and gave each soul a feeling of individuality and responsibility. His penitents recognized this and were grateful. Witness a Monsignore from Padua: *Fr. Leopoldo was very prudent, and this was particularly noticeable in his relations with penitents and in his spiritual direction. His method was not to induce others to submit to his particular way of seeing things, but rather to adapt himself as far as possible to others in order to help them to work according to their individual capabilities.*

Naturally this system could not be applied to everyone, and when the occasion demanded, he could impose his authority with great firmness and certainty.

Many people are so unsure of themselves, so timid or so wavering that they need a firm and resolute hand. With such there can be no discussion, for that would only add to their uncertainty. The confessor must give orders, impose his own ideas and allow of no self-recrimination. Only thus do they get the support they need and the necessary strength to walk in the way of righteousness. This psychological phenomenon was well known to Fr. Leopoldo, who was able by word and gesture to impose his will, word and gesture that perhaps he alone could use because his faith knew that God was with him.

There are plenty of witnesses to this.

Prof. Angelo Zambaldo of Tregnago: *Fr. Leopoldo was clearly prudent, and equally clearly his prudence derived from his faith and the grace of God. When giving advice or admonishing, he could if necessary speak with all the authority of God's minister and was undoubtedly enlightened by the wisdom of the Lord.*

Giovanni Armellini of Padua: *Before coming to a decision or giving advice, Fr. Leopoldo retired into private prayer, but thereafter he was precise and decisive. He would allow no discussion, but said, "Have faith! do this and... that's enough!" On one occasion I was in desperate straits and I explained the whole sorry story to him. He interrupted to ask, "Do you believe in the Gospel?" When I said I did, he reminded me of the incident where the apostles thought they were going to sink, and Jesus reproved them for their little faith. "Just cling to Our Lord," he ended, "and that will be enough." He sent me away almost brusquely, but I left him a changed man and was able to overcome the crisis that threatened to overwhelm me.*

Many Elizabethine Nuns of the Mother House in Padua confirm how with a few words he was able to restore peace to troubled souls, assuring them that it was not he who spoke in his own name but Christ speaking through him. At these words all doubts and scruples vanished and peace was restored.

Fr. Pietro Zambon of Padua: *On 17th September, 1923 I was in Padua making a retreat with the Jesuits. For some time I had been tormented by uncertainties and had not been able to find peace. The day before I had confessed to one of the Jesuits but it had not helped, for I was still in a turmoil. That day Fr. Leopoldo came to the house and I had the idea of going to him for confession, although I did not know him at all. When I knelt before him, he made the Sign of the Cross over me and, without allowing me to open my mouth, said, "Before God you are in the right. Your confessor says so; that is, God says so through His minister. Understand?" I was too astonished and confused to say anything, but all my doubts and worries disappeared and I was at peace.*

Kindness or firmness as the case demanded, but always the soul in question benefited and often real conversions resulted. One significant incident follows in the words of Riccardo Carini of Padua.

One day I was with a number of others waiting in the narrow passage leading to Fr. Leopoldo's confessional when suddenly a powerfully built peasant came blustering in and said in a loud voice, "It's forty years since I've been to confession, but now I must go or my landlady will take away the land I rent. Be so kind as to let me go in immediately, for I haven't time to waste on this sort of thing." We let him go in first. After nearly half an hour he came out a changed man and went off weeping like a child.

What had happened in Fr. Leopoldo's little room? Certainly the grace of God had touched that sinner's heart and transformed him. From then on the peasant, to my certain knowledge, often came back to Fr. Leopoldo.

* * *

The crown of Fr. Leopoldo's work in the confessional was, of course, absolution: absolution which he gave so generously that, as we have seen, it appeared exaggerated to some. But he paid no attention to such criticism, being guided by higher principles: he looked to the Divine Mercy of God Who was prepared to shed every drop of His blood on the cross so that sinners might have forgiveness.

With his exceptional enlightenment, he saw the fault in question not as a single isolated event but in the framework of the whole life of the penitent. Experience had taught him that spiritual illnesses are not like physical ones where often surgical intervention can remove the source of illness and leave the patient healthy. Spiritual illness is not so localized; it spreads its tentacles into every corner of the spirit and the cure demands not only a skilful doctor but long and difficult treatment.

Sin precipitates man into a deep abyss, and in order to get out of it and back on to the way of virtue he has a long and steep path beset with difficulties. For this he needs a guide with a firm but gentle hand to support him. Fr. Leopoldo was this guide, but so masterly was his touch that many were not aware of the extent to which God's grace was working in them through him.

His work for souls showed an extraordinary breadth of vision and great-heartedness that could only have come from God and which were beyond the understanding of the narrow-minded.

"Your great-heartedness, Fr. Leopoldo," wrote Mgr. Canon Bellincini, "is not laxity of moral principle but an understanding of human frailty and faith in the inexhaustible treasure of grace: it is not acquiescence in or indifference to faults, but forbearance so that the sinner shall not despair of his ability to reform and reestablish himself on a sound footing."

"How frail human nature is!" Father Leopoldo often exclaimed. "Original sin caused a terrible wound! And how greatly do we need the infinite mercy of God!"

Or again: "God has given us all different talents, so we cannot expect the same perfection in everyone. Perhaps in His eyes one who has received few gifts and who manages with great labour to achieve a little good has more merit than one who with greater gifts achieves more good but with less trouble. For this reason we must be very merciful in our judgment of souls and must follow their efforts with charity and zeal."

To the Mistress of Novices of the Salesians in Padua he said once, "When people write the lives of the Saints, they usually write one long lie. They should write everything about them: their repugnance, their difficulties, the struggles they had to keep themselves holy, even their falls and faults. Instead, far too often they write only about their virtues, as though they were impeccable and free from the effects of original sin. Only Our Blessed Lady had that privilege."

"Tell your Novices," he went on emphatically, "so that they will be able to continue in the way of perfection without losing heart on account of their faults."

* * *

An outstanding characteristic of Fr. Leopoldo's work was the almost miraculous way he followed up his penitents. He felt them almost as a part of himself. He prayed for them and awaited their return. When saying good-bye to a newcomer, he always added, "Come back again. I shall be expecting you."

Thereafter he forgot nobody, which was really astonishing. Hundreds and thousands of people came to him and poured out their troubles, asked his advice, or explained their personal circumstances or those of their family, yet he remembered everybody and everything.

People unable to see him for eight to ten years or more were astounded when they did come back: Fr. Leopoldo, sunk in his armchair was apparently half-asleep, but no sooner had they opened their mouths than he would say, "We know each other, don't we? And how did that affair work out?"

Father Alfonso Orlini recalls that he was one day in the refectory with Fr. Leopoldo. *At one moment he turned to me and said, "It is 25 years today since you first came to confession to me." I could not understand how he could remember such a detail when one thinks of the thousands of souls he followed up.*

Fr. Raimondo, a Capuchin: *As a student in Padua I used to go to Fr. Leopoldo to confession. At first it seemed that he gave me absolution without taking any interest in my spiritual welfare, saying a word or two perhaps in order to say something. Later I realized that he took a very lively interest, but he did it so wisely and with such a delicate touch that at first it appeared to be lack of interest. In fact it succeeded in gaining my confidence.*

Then I was surprised at certain imprudent criticisms of his way of hearing confessions, for I had found in him what I had sought in vain in other more esteemed spiritual directors.

In time I understood even better how he knew and loved and followed up his penitents, who in turn felt themselves bound to him by indissoluble bonds and accorded him the fullest measure of confidence.

A priest from Genoa: *In 1935 I was in Padua as an Army Chaplain. An absolute newcomer to the city, I asked the Bishop to suggest a confessor. He sent me to Fr. Leopoldo who welcomed me kindly, but his words to me were so measured that I was not really satisfied. He did not seem to take any interest in my soul. For some time I did not go back to him. Then one day the Bishop asked how I had found Fr. Leopoldo, and I told him.*

"Go back to him," the Bishop insisted. "I am sure he is suffering on your account."

"I can't believe that. With all the penitents he has, he has no time to think about me."

"You don't know Fr. Leopoldo. Go back to him. You will be glad."

Mostly in order to please the Bishop I did go back. Fr. Leopoldo leaped from his chair and knelt before me.

"Forgive me, please", he said, "if I was not able to understand your soul." Two great tears rolled down his cheeks. "Please forgive me, I'm a wretched sort of fellow."

I did not quite know what to do, but knelt too and embraced him. Only then did I realize what sort of man this Fr. Leopoldo was who knew my soul better than I did myself.

* * *

Fr. Leopoldo kept up with his penitents not only when they continued to come to him but also with distant ones by letter. These letters have a particular value for us, for they show quite clearly that he did not confine himself to pious exhortation but tried by every means to build up in them a solid Christian conscience which would serve in his absence to guide them on the path of virtue.

To one woman he wrote: *You are right to have followed the Parish Priest's advice, for the priest is master and guide of the faithful. Go to him in all your difficulties and through him God will guide you on the right road. Carry on always in this belief and in this Christian sentiment and you will always have a clear conscience.*

To another: *I have understood your meaning. What you have done and the intention with which you did it was all that was necessary. Now you must leave everything to the infinite mercy of Our Lord, whose Heart is constantly offered in sacrifice for us. Be at peace, therefore, and do not try anything else. I repeat: The infinite love of Our Lord will do everything.*

He was against his penitents losing themselves in a welter of pious practices, tying themselves up with promises about unimportant things. Instead, he urged them to frequent the Sacraments, the source of all grace and the foundation of a Christian life. *As for the prayers and obligations you have imposed upon yourself in order to obtain the desired grave* (he wrote to yet another woman), *I absolve you from all these petty obligations: continue to pray as best you can, but without tying yourself down with special promises: more to the point, frequent the Sacraments, that is Confession and Holy Communion, as much as you can and try to hear Mass every day.*

He prevented any straying from genuine piety and therefore wanted attention fixed on God and not on himself. *You complain that you cannot fully open your mind to me. Don't worry about that. It is not the man who provides the grace but the infinite mercy of God. Your mind is quite clear to the divine wisdom which is the author of every good thought and right desire. The good begun will be completed by the help of grace.*

There were two virtues especially which he tried to cultivate in the lives of his penitents, charity and an apostolic zeal. *Holy Writ says we must pray one for another that we may be saved. Everyone therefore has a mission.*

Just as in the material life God gives wealth to one man so that he may have honest enjoyment of it and share it with others, so in the supernatural world of grace He gives one person more light and more grace so that he may himself benefit from it and then share it with others. Anyone whose conscience tells him he has received more graces than others should be correspondingly generous-hearted towards others.

For souls called to exceptional vocations he had a very special interest and care. He was always asking for prayer for them so that he himself might be able to guide them safely on the road to sanctity.

I shall tell you what is in my mind. I have to do with a soul which seems to be called to achieve great things in its walk of life. It is necessary that Our Lord allows the completion of the good work already begun. At present this matter is, after your soul, very much in my heart. I beg you to pray with the utmost fervour.

* * *

The foregoing, and much else besides, can be said about Father Leopoldo's method of hearing confessions, but they are merely external things, outside himself, symptoms if you like of the real method which was love. He saw Christ in his penitents and loved them as father, brother and friend. Moved by this love, in order to do them good, he was able to find means that one cannot really describe, let alone catalogue. Can one teach a mother what to do in order to love her child?

Fr. Leopoldo really did love his penitents.

This was an entirely individual aspect of his relations with them, and was something beautiful, human and very moving. He himself summed it up in the one word *friendship*. Under his unimpressive exterior beat a heart of a nobility and generosity that is given only to those closely united to God who is Love itself. People who came to him, particularly those who came regularly, were not clients but friends. He never forgot Jesus' word to his disciples, "You are my friends," but wanted to relive in himself something of this infinite love. He built up around him a sort of family in which he was not the head, the master or the leader, but a brother, a confidant and a friend of all the others.

In his family he did not think of himself as a person whose friendship was a benefit or privilege for others. On the contrary, the friendship was a gift from them, a grace granted him by God in spite of his not deserving it. This unusual way of looking at it resulted in an exceptional generosity and magnanimity which bound others to him with unbreakable ties of affection.

From his earliest years he had had this capacity for affection. When at sixteen he was in the Seminary at Udine, a friend came from Castelnovo to visit him. Hardly had the friend gone when he seized pen and paper and wrote to him: *Having already left the world and mother and father, brothers and sisters, relations, everything to follow our Beloved Lord Jesus Christ, having been on pilgrimage in distant places, and having been received in charity into the refuge of our Father St. Francis, I was granted the favour of embracing you today, my dear friend, and of giving you after such a long time the kiss of peace. I have known you a long time and we had many happy days together, but God separated us here on earth in order to unite us again finally in Heaven.*

As he grew older, so his capacity for friendship increased, taking more concrete form and inspired by the highest religious principles. In 1906 he wrote to Luigi Bordignon: *What you say about yourself concerning me that, you will always remember me, is very gratifying: it is also true in reverse. Man is by nature a gregarious animal, needing the companionship of his fellows, since no one can be sufficient unto himself. Religion sanctifies this natural tendency in commanding us to love all men, but particularly those to whom we are bound by special relationships.*

As already said, his humility made him feel unworthy of the friendship of his penitents which he regarded as a favour accorded him by grace and was therefore full of simple gratitude. *Since God has granted me the signal favour of your acquaintance, your friendship will always be dear to me.*

Or: *Please maintain your friendship for me, which I consider a favour from Heaven and for which I am most grateful to you.*

I had the privilege of making your acquaintance on the Lourdes pilgrimage. The evidences of your esteem and affection will always be important to me and I shall always treasure the photograph of that group including yourself and your wife and my poor self. Please maintain your friendship for me, which I regard as a gift from God.

I know how fond you are of me. For me it is a gift from Heaven. The Sacred Heart with all its generosity of affection is with you. Our Lady too. I bless you both.

I am immensely grateful for the feelings you entertain for me. Twice you came to Padua to see me, but I was not worthy to have the pleasure of your visit. I had to resign myself to the dispositions of Providence, but I hope that God will once more allow me the great consolation of spending a few moments in the company of one so dear to me.

He shared in his friends' sufferings and did what he could with the means at his disposal to comfort them. In 1913 he wrote to Emilio Sabbadin: *True friends recognize each other as such in misfortune. In my position I can only help my friends by spiritual means. These means, that is prayer and consolation, I use with all my heart in an attempt to do good, to console and comfort you and your dear ones. You know me well enough to realize that I am sincere in this. Allow me in this time of terrible trouble and sorrow to embrace you as a friend and, if you permit it, as a beloved brother.*

Sometimes God rewarded so great an affection for penitents-become-friends with supernatural intervention. A friend from Padua relates the following story.

Beset by sorrows and injustices, bewildered and overwhelmed by events that had got beyond my control, I lost my health and strength. My mind became so darkened that I procured a weapon and tried, alas, to end it all. At that moment, however, Fr. Leopoldo appeared clearly before me and disarmed me.

Faithful friends of mine had gone to warn him of my mad attempt but before they spoke he said, "You have come to tell me about our friend, haven't you? God didn't allow it. I have his soul in my hand. Stand by him and help him."

He was very sensible of any sign of affection from his friends and returned it with fervent prayer. *I am most grateful for your affection and esteem. Such solemn and dear tokens as naming your son Leopoldo after me are more than I have had from my relations. I am most grateful. I confess I don't think I am worthy of such affection and esteem. Justice demands that I refer everything to God and to the saint whose name I unworthily bear. In thanks for your kindness, then, I shall pray to St. Leopoldo that he will keep a kindly eye on his young namesake.*

In 1905 when he was transferred from Bassano del Grappa to Capodistria, the friends he had made at Bassano could not get over his departure and wrote to him frequently. To one of them he replied:

Although it is now nearly nine months since I left Bassano, many people cherish an affection for my poor person still and demonstrate it in various ways. I thank them all, and you in particular, for their friendship. You cannot imagine how dear it is to me. In whatever corner of the globe I may find myself, I shall remember you always.

You said my departure left a void among you. One thing I am certain of, that I left there a number of good friends, but I have the consolation of knowing that I can, in the charity of Christ, still do them some good by my prayers.

When a friend of his got over some difficulties, he shared whole-heartedly in his joy. To Luigi Bordignon, recovered from a serious illness, he wrote: *Thank you for remembering to give me news of your health. I thank God from the bottom of my heart for having heard my prayers. I wanted nothing so much as that He should give me back so dear a friend. Now that I have been granted this favour, I am happy. I must end this letter, but not the affection I feel for you, for you are always present in my thoughts.*

But he always carried his friendships to a higher level so that they should have their more important effect of leading to the love of God.

In the name of the great and holy friendship between us, I exhort you to nourish a tender love for the Sacred Heart and for Mary. It is a wonderful thing to serve our Lord. I know, because I have been given the privilege of doing so. I exhort you, therefore, to frequent the Sacraments whenever you can. Don't take this suggestion amiss, but cherish these words of mine.

To Antonio Settin: *I value your friendship for many reasons, but especially because of your love for our Redeemer and God. In Jesus and Mary I renew my affection for you, in them I shall always love my very dear friend.*

When his brother Tommaso died, he wrote to their friend Andrea Corner: *We three, my poor brother and you and I, have always been rather more than just good friends although life has taken us on very different ways. The friendship which has always united us is not the sort that dies. Based on our common faith and hope, it will continue to the end of our days to reach its perfection in Heaven.*

So much was expressed in letters. It may be that even in translation the continental style of them comes through as somewhat unreserved and even gushing. The same is perhaps true of various attempts by his friends to describe his friendliness in his relations with them as man to man. In memory they may be carried away by their emotions: in any case most of his penitents belonged to a people that is more demonstrative than those for whom this translation is primarily intended and who do not suffer from any Anglo-Saxon inhibitions about expressing their emotions. The fact remains, however, that he loved his penitents and they loved him—in their thousands.

This perhaps was the secret that transformed confession from a painful necessity to a positive joy for his penitents. He did not appear as a judge but rather as a father, a brother or a friend. The joy was the joy of the angels of God upon a repentant sinner.

CHAPTER XV.

THE GIFT OF PROPHECY

Anyone who gives thought to the immense ruin caused by the bad press, first of all in the moral order and then, of necessity, in all other spheres of human life, must join in the mourning of the prophet Jeremiah over the ruin of Jerusalem. In this sphere our enemies can be our teachers; from them we can learn how to use the press for the salvation of Christians as cleverly as they use it for their ruin.

FR. LEOPOLDO

Another gift which God sometimes grants His servants—in order to make known the degree of intimate union with Him to which they have attained—is the gift of prophecy. This was among the gifts granted Fr. Leopoldo.

To a penitent who asked him how it was that saints can predict the future, he explained it by the following simile. "It is very simple really. Suppose we are at the foot of a high mountain, can we see what there is in the other side of it? Of course not; the mountain is in the way. But if we start climbing, our field of view gets wider and wider until, at the top, we can even see what is on the other side. The mountain is perfection, is God: the higher we mount, the wider our vision becomes, the more new things are revealed to us. When we have reached union with God—the summit, that is—then nothing is hidden from our eyes. But this is the privilege of saints. For us poor sinners, it is enough that God is merciful to us."

In fact Fr. Leopoldo had gone a long way up the mountain and his eye could penetrate the veil of the future as many incidents testify.

Mgr. Sebastiano Cuccarollo writes: *When I was Parish Priest at Tomba in Adria I used often to visit Fr. Leopoldo at Padua. One day he said to me "Our Lord has a much heavier cross for you." I gave no particular thought to these words and forgot them, but when eight years later I was made a Bishop I remembered them and they seemed to me to have been truly prophetic.*

Fr. Alfonso Orlini: *When I was elected Provincial of the Province of Venice, I went straight to see Fr. Leopoldo. He congratulated me and then said, "You know, you won't be long in that job. You will be elected Father General."*

At the time I did not pay much attention to this, taking it to be no more than politeness, but in less than three months I was elected Minister-General. I think this was a real case of prophecy.

The Archbishop of Gorizia: *Fr. Leopoldo often told his penitents with the utmost simplicity what was going to happen to them. I myself experienced it.*

At times the meaning of his prophecies was not clear until after the event. Witness the story related by the foundress of an Institute of nuns.

I came to know Fr. Leopoldo in 1913 when I accompanied my mother to go to confession to him. Afterwards he asked me to come into the sacristy where he told me with great solemnity tempered with joy that Our Lord had great plans for me.

This left me somewhat confused, for I had at that time not even thought of the work I was later to undertake. In fact I was almost afraid, for the man who had spoken had the reputation of being a saint. For some time I stayed away from him. It was not until my work was prospering in spite of many difficulties that I grasped the significance of his words.

In 1935 Cesare Friso of Albignasego was very ill. Stones originating in the kidneys had settled in an extremely dangerous position. After a careful examination it was decided that an operation was urgently necessary if the kidneys were not to be irreparably harmed.

Fr. Leopoldo, consulted on the matter, said, "Have faith! No operation is necessary. The stones will come away of their own accord. Have faith!"

The specialists had stated that without an operation the kidneys would be ruined in three months. Instead, eight years passed. Every now and then the patient returned to Fr. Leopoldo, who repeated his verdict and urged him to have faith. In 1940 the patient complained that he was always being told to have faith, but that he had now lost it completely.

"Oh, well," replied Fr. Leopoldo, "I'll have it for you. In any case, until 1943 there's time."

"What do you mean, Father, until 1943 there's time?"

Fr. Leopoldo in confusion tried to make him forget the phrase and urged him once more to have faith.

In fact in August, 1943 the stones did come away and subsequent radiography revealed the kidneys in perfect condition. No further disturbances were ever felt.

Sometimes the prophecies were much more precise.

Fr. Cesario of Rovigo, OFM Cap, writes: *After many years in the Army, I returned to my friary in 1919. My contemporaries who had not been in the Army were already ordained. Naturally I was also very anxious to reach this much-desired goal. After the first two years of Theology, my Superiors applied twice to Rome for a dispensation so that I might be ordained sooner than Canon Law normally allows. Each time the request had been refused. The Father Provincial, on a visit to Padua, told me quite clearly that there was no hope and I should have to wait another year.*

In October I was still in Padua. One evening I was in Choir examining my conscience before going to bed, when Fr. Leopoldo, who was also there, got up and came to me. "Courage!" he said. "You will be ordained this year."

I was amazed. I thought it impossible. Rome had twice said No, and the year was drawing to a close. We should soon see who was right.

In the meantime I went to the friary in Venice. The great news came in the middle of November. Contrary to all expectation, permission for my ordination arrived from Rome. Cardinal La Fontaine was kind enough to accede to the request of my superiors and to confer all the Orders on me, holding an ordination for me alone on 17th December.

I understood then that Fr. Leopoldo, enlightened by God, could read the future.

Signorina Anita Santon, of Padua, after long years of acute suffering had to undergo two serious operations as a result of which she suffered from colitis and cystitis. Treatments of various sorts were tried over a long period, but all proved useless. The professor in charge of the case said she would never be cured since the ailments had now taken a chronic form.

Exhausted by the sufferings she had been undergoing for nearly fifteen years, Signorina Santon realized that human science could do no more for her. Only God could help. She went to Fr. Leopoldo and told him all her troubles.

"Have faith!" he said at once. "You will get better."

"But, Father, how can I possibly get over so many ills?"

"If you have faith, you will do so."

She went away consoled and certain that her ailments would disappear but days passed, months passed, a whole year went by and she grew steadily worse.

In September, 1941 she went back to Fr. Leopoldo.

"Father, I can't go on. I can't eat, I can't sleep and life is impossible. It would be better to die."

"But didn't I tell you that if you have faith you will be cured?" he asked gently. "I'll repeat it again: Have faith and you will be cured of all your ills."

One evening towards the end of the month the patient felt suddenly inspired to eat as if she were healthy. She ate with a better appetite than she had known for years, to the horror of her sister who could not imagine what the consequences would be. The only consequence was, however, that she spent a peaceful night asleep.

The next morning she went to see Fr. Leopoldo who was delighted. "The Lord has granted you a great boon. Praise Him always."

From that time on she had no more trouble.

In 1942 Signora Ada Zanotto was very worried about her only son who was fighting in Africa and of whom she had had no news for some time. She tried all official sources but still heard nothing. In her trouble she went to Fr. Leopoldo.

"You are a widow, aren't you?"

"Yes, Father."

"And he is your only son?"

"Yes, Father."

"Well, then", he said happily. "He will write very soon. You will have a happy Easter."

Much impressed by his knowing she was a widow and had only the one son, she experienced a feeling of confidence that quietly replaced her fears. It was only a few days more to Easter. Soon after she came back from Mass on Easter Sunday the post arrived with a letter from her son saying that he was a prisoner and in good health.

Alfonso Zannini suffered acutely from 1927 to 1941 with a pyloric ulcer complicated by cystitis and colitis. During his time as porter at the Capuchin Friary he asked Fr. Leopoldo daily for his prayers and received the same reply, "Have faith! You will get better."

Seeing one day that he was not really convinced, Fr. Leopoldo said quite definitely. "Have faith! You will be cured. I tell you this in God's name. I know what I am saying."

In 1941 Zannini was *in extremis* and received the Last Sacraments. After much hesitation an operation was undertaken, though without any certainty about the result. In fact all went well and in a short time he was perfectly fit as Fr. Leopoldo had foretold.

In 1934 Signora Anna Selvaggini, of Venice, was dangerously ill with intestinal poisoning. Due to mistaken treatment, frightful complications set in accompanied by numerous abscesses. The poor woman was in continuous delirium. She had recourse to Fr. Leopoldo, who wrote to her:

Do not be frightened. You should know—and mark my words well—that you have many more years to live. You will get better. Be of good heart, therefore: Jesus and Mary are with you.

The recovery was almost instantaneous, and twenty-five years later, Signora Selvaggini is still in excellent health.

Signora Maria Meneghello was admitted to a clinic in Padua in July 1933. After careful examination, Prof. Fasiani diagnosed an intestinal tumor and decided to operate, even going so far as to fix the day and time. Her husband arranged for Fr. Leopoldo to come and hear her confession and give her his blessing the day before the operation. He did so, but finding her depressed and frightened, he remained a while in private prayer and then clapped her happily on the shoulder.

"Have faith! God has changed the cards. Have faith and don't worry!"

Next day she was prepared for the operation, but the surgeon suddenly thought he would wait a bit. In the afternoon he examined her again and found no trace of the tumor. The patient showed no further symptoms and was discharged in perfect health.

Lino Menegazzo, of Padua, writes: *In 1935 I went to confession to Fr. Leopoldo. I had been recalled to the colours and was so depressed by this that I wept in his presence. He consoled me and gave me a medal of Our Lady. "The war will be terrible," he said, "but you will survive."*

War came and in 1941 I was again recalled. I suffered a lot from sickness and operations. While still convalescent, I was posted to Albania and on the way across the Adriatic we were attacked by a submarine, but the attack failed. I fought in Albania and later against the Slav partisans. A hundred times death was my neighbour, but I always remembered Fr. Leopoldo's words, which gave me courage. When it was all over, I was able, albeit broken in health, to return to the bosom of my family.

On 23rd March, 1932, very early in the morning, a gentleman who was a confidant of Fr. Leopoldo's, visited him in his confessional. He saw immediately that he was very sad.

"What's up, Father? Are you unwell?"

"No, no! I'm perfectly well."

"Well, has something happened?"

"No, nothing has happened to me", he said, but he sobbed aloud.

Finally he managed to get out of him that the previous evening, at his prayers, "God opened my eyes and I saw Italy in a sea of fire and blood."

Covering his face with his hands, he continued through his tears, "Please God, I may be wrong! Please God, I may be mistaken!"

After a bit he pulled himself together. "No! I was not mistaken, alas! Italy will be a sea of flame and blood."

From then on whenever the future of Italy was mentioned he covered his face with his hands and cried, "God have pity on Italy."

On several occasions Fr. Leopoldo let it be more or less clearly understood that the Capuchin Friary in Padua would be destroyed. In 1940 he was quite definite about it. In June of that year Alvise Franceschini asked him if Padua would suffer aerial bombardment.

"Yes. It will be hit many times."

"And the Friary?"

"Alas, the Friary too will be badly hit... but this little cell (his confessional) will not. Here God has shown so much mercy to souls that it will remain as a monument to His kindness."

It is a matter of history that Padua suffered considerable bombing which caused terrible damage and very many casualties. On 14th May, 1944 the friary and its church were hit by at least five large HE bombs. The church was almost completely wrecked, as was a large part of the friary. Miraculously untouched were the statue of the Madonna and Fr. Leopoldo's confessional-cell. There were no casualties.

The above are but some episodes, but there were innumerable occasions when Fr. Leopoldo saw into the future for the benefit of his penitents. On most occasions it was done so discreetly, without putting any emphasis on it, that the beneficiary was unaware of it at the time and only remembered the prediction when it came true. In the use of this gift, as of others, he sought only the good of souls and the greater glory of God.

CHAPTER XVI.

THE SANCTITY OF FAMILY TIES

Our Faith teaches us that the reason for the privilege of the Immaculate Conception of the Virgin lay in her divine maternity. After her Son, the Blessed Virgin was to be the moral cause of the salvation of mankind. To her was given all righteousness and holiness so that the human race should have its salvation, in due proportion, from her as well as from her Son, should have that is, the grace of God in this life and eternal glory in the next.

FR. LEOPOLDO

Family upbringing leaves an indelible mark on the soul. It is virtually impossible for anyone to escape the moral influence of his upbringing, which will be felt up to an advanced age. Fr. Leopoldo's family was of noble origin, morally sound, well educated and determined to bring up its children in the peace and love of God and Man: the effect on him was to arouse an indefinable tenderness and a feeling of the nobility and sanctity of the family ties that remained a living and operative force throughout his life.

On becoming a Capuchin he cut himself off completely from his family and saw his relations only very rarely, yet he remained united to them in love and prayer and was sensible of the separation to the end of his days. Only a greater love, that of God, could have made him accept such a sacrifice.

Separated from his natural family, he wanted to make the family life of his penitents as sound and holy as possible so that they should experience the holy joys of home life that he himself had renounced.

For him the family was something grand. In 1909 he wrote: "The first, most sacred, most noble and most necessary form of society is the family. God sanctifies it, completes it and perfects it so that our nature is thereby not diminished but supported."

He wanted young men to prepare themselves with purity for family life and advised them in this matter. Untold numbers of young men owe it to his fatherly wisdom, or severity if the occasion demanded, that they were saved from dangers that might have spoiled their whole lives, and were able to taste the joys of a sound Christian family life. *Betrothal and marriage,* he wrote to one, *are the sources of good habits. So says St. Paul under divine inspiration. You must always love and do everything you can for the good of the future companion of your days. For us believers, you see, matrimony is a sacrament, in other words something essentially sacred. Therefore God stands between husband and wife. That is the measure of sacredness, strength and faithfulness of the love you owe your fiancée and future bride. When I talk to engaged couples, or married people, I remind them as clearly as I can of these great truths. Our Faith teaches us how much love one should have for one's wife: as much love—it is St. Paul who speaks—as Our Lord Jesus Christ had and has for us.*

To Armando Bredolo: *You are greatly preoccupied by a serious matter: the marriage you are about to embark upon. I am very glad to hear it, for it means that you are giving the proper weight to the serious step you are about to take. With marriage one begins a new life, that is, a new way of life altogether. But do not worry: embrace this new life as the wherefore of your temporal existence. At the basis of your affection let there be truth and justice and then Divine Providence will guide your steps.*

You will have the privilege of forming a good family. One who lays firm foundations can build solidly upon them. Your practising of your religion is your firm foundation. Continue in this and Jesus and Mary will always be with you.

So great was his esteem for the beauty and grandeur of this aspect of human life that he showed the greatest severity towards those who would drag it in the mud. Anyone who tried to abandon some poor woman after misleading her with vain promises had to repair the injustice at once or never set foot in his confessional again. No argument on that point! Any silly young dandy who aped the gallant was given such a lecture that he did not want a second. "I flay them," said Fr. Leopoldo.

Except in rare cases he apportioned the greater part of the blame to the man since, he said, God has given man a more stable function in life and therefore more responsibility.

Woe to anyone advancing theories that diminished the sense of responsibility in such matters, pleading the force of passion and so forth. "God gave man means sufficent to control himself: to say otherwise is to try to fool him: but you can't fool God."

He used every means available to encourage the growth of truly Christian family life, for the example of Christian families in society would serve to defend the Gospel and revivify the Faith. A man from

Padua, who had long been one of Fr. Leopoldo's penitents told him one day of his decision to leave the world and enter religion. He imagined that Fr. Leopoldo would be glad and would encourage him to carry it out. Instead, he said thoughtfully, "What you tell me is a very serious matter. Let us consult God in a novena of prayer and then I'll give you the answer."

At the end of the novena he said firmly, "No. You can leave the habit to me. You are called to a normal family life. You must live in society and represent the believing, practising Catholic Christian in it. You will preach, not in words but by your example. You will be a living, objective proof that one can be a practising Christian even though living in the midst of the world and its affairs. If you do not heed my words, I cannot guarantee your eternal salvation."

At times he seemed to receive supernatural enlightenment in order to show his penitents the way of life they should choose and that they should marry and have a family.

"In His good time," he said to one, "God will send you a wife."

"But, Father," replied the man, who had been seriously ill for seven years, who lived in the greatest squalor and was on the point of being evicted with the rest of his family from their home on account of their debts, "why say such things to me? You know my circumstances. Do you imagine I can think about starting a family?"

"Don't worry! Let God do as He wishes. He and His blessed Mother will arrange it. You'll get better—and if that needs a miracle, a miracle there'll be. God will cause you to leave your family and will give you an honoured position in society. Have faith in what your confessor tells you. Confessors don't tell lies; they don't talk at random, for it is God Who prompts them to speak. What I have told you, will happen. No syllable of God's words can be altered."

In due course everything happened as Fr. Leopoldo had predicted.

* * *

When newly married couples came to him on their wedding day to seek his blessing, it was moving to see the joy with which he received and blessed them. He would give them a medal of the Madonna accompanied by fatherly advise, urging them especially to be frequent at the Sacraments so that their love could continue in the grace of God.

* * *

For already existing families his efforts were directed towards the maintenance of peace and harmony, dealing where necessary with moral difficulties which threatened. To a Paduan lady he wrote: "Let me remind you of the comforts of Faith, that is of Him Who knows all human desires whatever they may be and Who is, in so far as they are right and good, their first author, since He is the author of the natural as well as the supernatural order."

He was always ready with good wishes and a blessing for those who had a proper affection for their family. To Nino Bertotti he wrote: *Your letter was welcome for another reason, to wit that, separated from your wife and children as you are, you have them constantly in your heart and are always aware of the sacred duties of a husband and father. May the love of a husband and a father be always, after the love of God, the* raison d'être *of your life. You can easily imagine what a comfort it is to us priests to see such deep family love.*

To a lady in Rome: *When I read your husband's words expressing all the affection which should bind for ever those who in the words of the Gospel are two souls in one body, they were a great comfort to me.*

He was particularly pleased when he found conjugal affection reinforced by religious sentiments. *Your note brought me very welcome news*—he wrote to Signora Benetti—*I was most pleased about the religious action you and your family undertook with such great piety. Keep this religious sentiment always and your family will always enjoy true love, the fruit of God's blessing.*

On other occasions when the love and harmony in a family were threatened, he was able to restore peace. Many were the families on the point of breaking up who found salvation in Fr. Leopoldo's confessional. It did not matter how deep or wide the rift might be, it was only necessary for husband and wife to come to him: they could not resist his words, instinct with nobility and love. They left him, happy and determined to resume their life together as it should be.

A typical case of his bringing peace to a home is narrated by a man from a village near Padua.

In 1907 I left my family house to live in that of my wife, the only child of elderly parents. After some months in this new home I was regretting terribly having left the home of my own beloved parents. I was, in fact, so homesick that I knew no peace. Everyone could see from my face that I was unhappy, but no one knew why, not even my wife who did her best to make me happy.

After some years I felt I could not bear it any longer and went to Fr. Leopoldo. Immediately he said, "Listen to me and have Faith. All this is the work of the devil who is trying to make you miserable by getting at your weak points. Forget the whole thing. Pray and all your troubles will disappear."

His words brought me immediate peace. All my unhappiness disappeared and from that moment I have been so happy among my wife's family that I would not go back to my old home for all the gold in the world.

The family is not always, alas! a haven of peace. When there is no religion to inspire mutual give and take, where there is no real love to make each partner make sacrifices for the other when necessary, then egoism, fierce and brutal, takes charge and family life becomes a hell. So often in these cases the man becomes cruel and oppresses the woman. Fr. Leopoldo was made very unhappy by such cases and rose in wrath against the husband. In this connexion Signora Mezzadri, a widow from Padua, writes: *Occasionally in exceptional circumstances I used to bring to Fr. Leopoldo's notice cases of unfortunate women bullied by their husbands. He reacted violently in defence of the wife and her family rights, using very harsh words about bullying and brutality and so-called men's privileges. "God does not let evil go unpunished," he would say. "The guilty can never escape, especially not the oppressor of the weak."*

One day a man in his late fifties came to confession to Fr. Leopoldo. He was a dreadful fellow who hideously maltreated his wife. Suddenly

Fr. Leopoldo, unable to contain himself any longer, got up and said, "You are a criminal!" The man took offence and demanded that he withdraw the words.

"I withdraw nothing. More, I repeat it in God's name," said Fr. Leopoldo firmly, drawing himself up.

The man broke down. "You are right, Father. I am a criminal." Whereupon Fr. Leopoldo heard his confession and sent him away transformed and happy.

Back at home, he told his wife the whole story and she came later to thank Fr. Leopoldo.

Another incident, tragic in its outcome, indicates how severe God can be in defence of a woman betrayed...

My husband had been deceiving me for some time with another woman. Seeing that I could do nothing to change things, I went one day to Fr. Leopoldo. He listened to my story and consoled me, urging me to have Faith.

After some time, as my husband had not changed his ways, I returned to Fr. Leopoldo who again told me to pray and have faith. But things went on as before and there was no sign of an end to this sinful liaison, so I went a third time to Fr. Leopoldo and told him I could not bear it any longer.

Fr. Leopoldo became serious, apparently lost in sad thoughts. After a long silence he suddenly said in a firm voice: "There! God's justice has been done. Go home. Everything will be once more as it should be.

Much impressed and somewhat preoccupied, I went home where I was joined by my husband in a state of great agitation. He embraced me in tears. His mistress had suddenly died and the shock had brought him to himself and we had peace in the home thereafter.

Fr. Leopoldo was certainly not so one-sided that he always blamed the man for any family discord, but he did say that God, having made man the head of the family, had also given him more grace to enable him to govern his small realm in wisdom and peace.

He had a particular compassion for widows, left desolate and often without means. In this connexion Signora Mezzadri writes: *I had been told that Fr. Leopoldo was a man's confessor but that he did also occasionally hear the confession of women. Women who had been to him declared themselves very satisfied, so I decided to go myself.*

I should never have believed that any man, least of all a religious who had spent his life in the cloister cut off from the daily life of the world, could have so much understanding of a woman's mind and be so able to adapt himself to her sensibilities.

Woman, by nature weak and in the need of support, easily discouraged, often persecuted especially if alone, tends at certain times to despair, even to losing her faith and her contact with God. But he knew how to dispel the clouds, to revive hope and courage, and how to bring one back to the light and to faith in God's help.

And what a fine appreciation he had of family ties.

"How dreadful it is," I said once, "to be alone at times like Christmas and Easter when everyone else has a family!"

"I understand, my daughter. I understand. It's very sad. You know, even though I have been a friar since my youth, I long for my family on these occasions. But God comforts us and blesses us."

Fr. Leopoldo was a saint, but a saint who understood human language; who knew, with the perceptiveness of innocence, all human needs and desires and longings, though he raised them all to God and sanctified them.

* * *

The family is complete when there are children. The hearth without children, or with an only child, is a cold hearth and does not know peace and love. Anything opposed to this principle was anathema to Fr. Leopoldo and he tried to make it so for his penitents as well.

When a new life was in danger, he could obtain a miracle from God.

In 1933 Signora Carenza contracted acute nephritis during pregnancy. The case was serious and Professors Bertino and Scimone of the obstetrical clinic declared that the pregnancy should be terminated in an effort to save the mother at least. The husband put the case to Fr. Leopoldo who immediately said, "No, no! God doesn't want that sort of thing. Have faith! All will go well. Just have faith."

The husband, a thoroughly Christian man, ignored the verdict of the doctors and put his faith in Fr. Leopoldo. His faith was rewarded, for, contrary to all human expectations, the pregnancy came to a succesful and normal end with the birth of a boy who, in thanksgiving, was called Leopoldo.

Cencio Marconi, of Padua, writes: *In 1927 I went to Fr. Leopoldo to seek a special favour. My daughter Luigina was about to have her second baby and, since the first delivery had been very difficult and dangerous for both mother and child, everyone at home was frightened of what might happen.*

Straightaway Fr. Leopoldo said with absolute certainty, "Have faith! All will be well. I tell you this officially in the name of God. You know what 'officially' means? Well, have faith!"

When the birth was due, my daughter felt no pain but certain symptoms made it apparent that a natural delivery was impossible. She was taken then to the maternity clinic where Professor Bertino examined her carefully and declared that natural delivery was impossible and that he would try to operate the next day, though this would possibly be fatal for the child.

Hearing this, I remembered what Fr. Leopoldo had told me and, turning to the crucifix hanging on the wall, I implored God for the promised miracle. At that very moment my daughter's labour started and the birth took place naturally and with the greatest ease.

After her fifth most difficult pregnancy Signora Carenza of Rome, was in very poor health, suffering from organic weakness, anaemia and nephritis. Prof. D'Aprilia, her gynaecologist, said he would not accept responsibility in the event of another pregnancy, since this would undoubtedly prove fatal. The Carenzas however, having four sons and missing the two girls who had died in infancy, wanted a daughter and put their faith in Divine Providence.

In due course, however, the mother's health gave cause for so much worry that her husband decided to put the case before Fr. Leopoldo. Arrived in Padua on 28th January, 1937, he went straight to him and explained the situation, asking him to obtain the favour that nothing should happen to his wife.

Fr. Leopoldo gladly promised to pray for her: then after raising his eyes to Heaven as though in ecstasy, said with certainty, "Go in peace, and assure your wife that all will go well right to the end without any intervention. What is more, afterwards she will be completely cured of all her ailments."

"Father I am most grateful for your assurance, but... well, we would like a girl to take the place of the two who died."

As kind and calm as ever, Fr. Leopoldo answered without hesitation, "Your wishes will be granted in this as well."

"Father, I believe absolutely all that you have told me, but my wife will almost certainly think I have made it up to calm her. Could you possibly put in writing what you have told me?"

"Of course!" He took pen and paper and wrote a note for Signora Carenza repeating what he had told her husband.

On 1st March the much-desired daughter was born and was given the names of her two sisters and the additional name of Leopoldina in memory of the favour received. To complete the picture, from that day on Signora Carenza suffered no more from her former ailments.

The note from Fr. Leopoldo is framed and treasured as a most precious relic.

Signora Anna Gazzi, of Stellata Po, was about to give birth to a child. For many days she had been in bed in acute pain. In view of her now alarming condition, the doctor wanted her to go at once to hospital. But Signora Gazzi, who knew Fr. Leopoldo, did not want to take such a decision without writing and asking his opinion. In the meantime the doctor and her relations were urging her in view of her worsening condition to allow herself to be taken to hospital. But she would hear nothing of it: an inner voice told her to wait.

Finally a telegram came from Fr. Leopoldo in Padua.

"Go to hospital. All will be well."

She allowed herself to be taken. The senior physician, Prof. Doni, examined her and straightaway told the husband and parents that there was no hope of saving her. In the meantime the pain was increasing and was accompanied by high fever. After trying every possible treatment, the Professor said that only a miracle could save her.

All her relations stood about her bed weeping and in despair for her life. She alone remained calm, secure in the knowledge that what Fr. Leopoldo said would come true.

Contrary to all human expectation, the miracle happened and she gave birth naturally to a daughter. Everybody admitted that there must have been divine intervention.

Before they had time to tell Fr. Leopoldo about the joyful outcome, he topped it all by sending another telegram:

"Congratulations on birth of daughter."

No half measure about this miracle, either. In spite of the doctors' prognostication that a long convalescence would be necessary for Signora Gazzi to recover from her illness and exhaustion, she was discharged fit after four days.

The child was christened Leopolda and as soon as possible brought to the delighted Fr. Leopoldo for his blessing.

Dear to God and to all good men, children were also especially dear to Fr. Leopoldo, and they reciprocated his affection. Prof. Rubaltelli wrote in 1943: *I got to know Fr. Leopoldo through my children who often went to see him and ask his blessing. He was always calm and patient and pleased to see them. He would give them a holy picture and encourage them to be good and obedient.*

They were really attracted to this humble son of St. Francis and the friary was often the goal of their daily walk from which they returned happily enthusiastic. In spite of their tender age at the time, they have never forgotten him but each day say a short prayer asking for his protection and keep his picture adorned with fresh flowers.

On 14th April, 1938, Signora Amalia Levoratti, of Padua, went into the church of S. Croce with her small son. Fr. Leopoldo was kneeling before the altar of St. Antony deep in prayer.

"How I should like him to bless my child," she thought, "but I dare not disturb him."

As though in answer to her thought, Fr. Leopoldo got up and came to them, caressed the child and blessed it, and then went back to his prayers. Signora Levoratti was too astonished even to say thank you, but when they were outside again, said, "My son, remember that today you have been blessed by a saint."

Fr. Leopoldo loved children and young people, but he always recommended to parents that kindness in their upbringing should be leavened with severity when appropriate, as indeed God says very clearly in the Bible. He deplored those parents who from misguided compassion allowed their children to grow up without correction or punishment.

A fellow Capuchin relates the following incident.

One day in the sacristy a woman asked Fr. Leopoldo for a blessing for her son who was so undisciplined.

"How old is he?"

"Fifteen."

"Punish him," he said, and dismissed her.

She left in tears and, meeting me outside, told me what had happened.

"If it will make you happy," I said, "I will bless your son, but see that you don't forget his words, for he really knows what he is talking about."

Afterwards I went and found Fr. Leopoldo.

"Father, that woman was really upset."

"When boys of that age are naughty, there's no other way," was all he said about it.

Chapter XVII.

OUR LADY

In the natural order Mary is a daughter of Adam. In her, therefore, as in all mankind, there should be the sad effect of original sin. The Blessed Virgin, however, by a unique exception in her favour, was made free of the taint. What should have been the birthright of mankind has become hers alone: all others are excluded and she is the sole heiress, enjoying alone all that mankind should have inherited. She alone can give glory to God and say, "I am the Immaculate Conception."

Fr. Leopoldo

Fr. Leopoldo had a great love of Our Lady, a love that sustained him though his life of suffering, was light to his mind and warmth and comfort to his heart. Not even those who lived with him could describe accurately the extent and depth of this love. The tone of voice when he spoke of her, his expression when he looked at a picture or statue of her, cannot be described: one had to experience them to realize the ardour of his love.

He was fortunate in having a mother also devoted to the Madonna, who dedicated him to her at birth and sowed in his heart the seeds of a love that was to grow to such proportions. "I was consecrated to Our Lady as a child, and she has been of particular help to me in my vocation," he said.

By nature logical, he did not want to base his love on a sort of vague sentimentalism which would evaporate and change with circumstances and moods, but on a sound knowledge of her grandeur. Mariology became, therefore, his favourite subject for study throughout his life. From the time he was a young student at Padua his favourite reading was Grou's *Interior Life of Jesus and Mary*. He meditated on it and asked his companions for explanations of anything he was not clear about. Later on, he studied treatises dealing with Our Lady alone and acquired a wide and well-based knowledge of Marian culture. He studied particularly the passages in Scripture dealing with the Blessed Virgin and waxed indignant at any interpretations which did not correspond to her real greatness. He meditated upon them and constantly sought new interpretations which would be homogeneous and fit in with his concept of the Mother of God. He asked explanations of those of his penitents who were knowledgeable in this field. There is still in existence his correspondence with Mgr. Giuseppe Perin, a Professor at the Padua Seminary, on the subject of scriptural texts of difficult interpretation dealing with the Madonna. He considered it his duty to know all the truth in order to increase his love. From his colleagues who were experts in the matter he would ask what the great Doctors of the Church had to say about the greatness and privileges of Our Lady, and is saddened him that the greatest Doctors such as Thomas and Bonaventure had not explicity defended the Dogma of the Immaculate Conception. When the Capuchins of the Province of Venice published the *Mariale,* the first volume of the works of St. Laurence of Brindisi, in which the Saint exalts the Madonna, he was overjoyed, read the book immediately and spoke of it with great enthusiasm.

Throughout his life he cherished the idea of writing a book about the Madonna to show her as co-redemptress of the human race and the channel of all grace. He thought a lot about it and often spoke about it in a manner that made it clear that his ideas were worthy of the great work that existed in his brain. He also asked for prayers for this intention.

Mgr. Canon Zanocco writes: *When I think of the discussions Fr. Leopoldo used to start after confession about the privileges and greatness of Our Lady in the scheme of redemption, I bitterly regret that my poor memory will not allow me to recall them in all their beauty, high-mindedness and clarity. He seemed to live on love of Mary.*

In 1927 in order to fix his ideas on the subject, he wrote on a picture of the Blessed Virgin: *I, Fr. Leopoldo Mandić Zarević, firmly believe that the Blessed Virgin as co-redemptress of the human race is the moral source of all grace, since everything we receive comes from her fullness.*

He hoped that his work would help to add a new diadem to Our Lady's brow by the proclamation of the dogma of Our Lady Mediatrix of all Grace. Unhappily his work in the confessional did not permit him to complete the book and his notes have been lost. A real pity, for his acute intelligence and great love would certainly have produced a valuable work. Articles written by him for the *Bollettino Francescano* are ample indication of this.

Fr. Leopoldo loved and honoured Our Lady in every way. He had a picture of her in his confessional adorned with flowers which he tried to renew every day as a symbol of his daily-renewed love.

He celebrated Mass at the Lady Altar every day, and on Saturdays whenever permissible he said the votive Mass of the Immaculate Conception. Every day he recited the Little Office and several rosaries. For reasons of health he was not allowed to get up at one in the morning for Matins, but he managed to get permission to do so on the vigils of the feasts of Our Lady.

Whenever he passed before a statue or picture of the Madonna he made some gesture of reverence. In his days, as was customary in all the friaries, there was a small chapel in the garden dedicated to Our Lady: he used to visit it every day, bringing a flower picked in the garden and remaining some time in prayer. When his doctor, supported by the authority of his superiors, required him to take a half hour's walk outside the friary every day, he always started by going to the nearby parish church of S. Croce to spend some moments in prayer before the *Madonna della Salute.* Each Sunday and Holy Day of Obligation he went without fail to the Basilica of St. Justina to venerate Our Lady of Constantinople. He knelt on the marble steps of the altar and remained up to half an hour absorbed in prayer. Sometimes during confessions or just talking to somebody, he would excuse himself for a few moments to go and pray at the Lady Altar, coming back beaming with joy.

In his love for Our Lady, Fr. Leopoldo had very firm convictions about her power and her kindness. He knew that in Heaven a mother's heart was watching over him. To a lay brother, Fra Giorgio of Bassano, he wrote once: *The Blessed Virgin was present at the Crucifixion as the mother of the Divine Victim. There can be no doubt that from her place in Heaven she is also present at the unbloody sacrifice offered daily on the altars for mankind. We have therefore a mother's heart in Heaven.*

He wanted his penitents to see her in this light too. He wrote, for example, to Signora Rosa Salvagnini: *May the Blessed Virgin, co-redemptress of the human race, that is the universal source of all good, be always with you with her mercy.* And to Achille Tognon: *Have recourse to the Blessed Virgin whose supremacy, as our Faith tells us, all must acknowledge.*

He saw in her mankind's only sheet-anchor, the only means by which the human race could be saved from the destruction it merited by its faults. *If the Immaculate Virgin does not save us, we are already lost: unless she intercedes with the Son, God's justice cannot give way to His mercy.* Or again: *The life of grace comes to us from her through Christ the divine fruit of her womb: this life was generated at the foot of the Cross in the most appalling martyrdom that a mother's heart could ever experience. We are in truth the children of her tears.* Children, he knew, whom she could never abandon.

He exhorted those who were suffering to have recourse to Our Lady in the certain hope that she would not repulse them. To Luigi Bordignon he wrote: *You have always repeated to the Mother of God,* Monstra te esse matrem, *Show yourself to be a mother. Once more you have moved her maternal heart: the favours you have received up to now are but a sample of greater ones to come.*

To Signora Assunta Botti: *Today is the Vigil of the Annunciation. Even Our Lady, the Blessed Virgin, in spite of being a virgin and immaculately conceived, knew on this earth the sorrows of a mother: she will be able to console you. She, the consolation of all the children of Eve, will show you her mother's heart.*

By word of mouth, too, he was constantly urging love and devotion to the Blessed Virgin. He spoke often of her to his penitents. He often asked priests how they explained Our Lady's greatness and privileges in their sermons and if he detected any inaccuracy, particularly in relation to her virginity or the Immaculate Conception, he corrected them gently but with great firmness.

When he was at the friary at Thiene from 1899 to 1903, he used in his humility to work with the lay brothers, washing dishes and cleaning the church and the friary. While they were working he wanted them to pray, especially by reciting the Litany of Our Lady. When they came to *Causa nostrae laetitiae* he used to pause, raising his eyes to Heaven, and for a time would be absorbed in something like a state of ecstasy.

When one of the lay brothers asked him why he always stopped at this point, he repeated "Our Lady, cause of all our joy" and remained a long time, his face radiant and his eyes raised to Heaven.

There was something delightfully childlike about his love for Our Lady, whom he treated as a very small child might treat its own natural mother, referring to her all his sorrows and difficulties and those of other people as well.

A lay brother from the Basilica at Loreto used to visit him on his annual visit to the Venetian Province and was always given messages for Our Lady. "When you get back, go straight to the Holy House and tell the beloved Mistress that Fr. Leopoldo sends his respects and love."

Sometimes he would write her letters asking her help. They were simple affairs but overflowing with childlike love and confidence in her ability to arrange anything, and he would "post" them at the foot of her statue.

That his love was not one-sided nor his confidence misplaced, there is abundant evidence. Not only did Our Lady give him consolation in his spiritual difficulties and sustain him in his physical sufferings, she also gave him direct answers to prayer.

In 1927 Signora Adelina Milazzo, of Padua, was very worried because her sons needed jobs and there seemed to be no hope of getting any. Another woman had charitably done her best to help, but that had also been in vain.

When she recounted her troubles to Fr. Leopoldo, he said, "Go at once to St. Justina, go to the altar of Our Lady of Constantinople and say to her, 'Your servant Leopoldo has sent me. Do what the lady could not.' Don't say anything else. But go immediately. Understand? Go straightaway."

Full of faith, she did exactly as she was told, repeating his words verbatim, and went home confident that Our Lady would listen to Fr. Leopoldo's request. The next day all the difficulties disappeared as if by magic and her sons got the employment they wanted.

In 1928 a five-year-old girl from a village near Padua was seriously ill with double parotitis. For days she lay in bed, her hands crossed behind her head, not uttering a word, her glassy eyes fixed on a picture of the Madonna on the wall. With the greatest difficulty she managed to swallow a little milk.

The doctor tried everything but declared there was great danger of the infection spreading and causing meningitis.

On 22nd October an uncle of the child's went to Fr. Leopoldo and told him of her pitiable condition. Fr. Leopoldo grew very sad, bowed his head almost to his knees and remained a long time in that position. Then he got to his feet, radiating joy and said, "Excuse me a moment. I'll be back soon."

He was away five minutes and came back saying gaily, "Don't worry, your niece will be cured."

At the moment a servant arrived with a big apple which Father Leopoldo blessed and gave to the uncle. "Take this to the child and make her eat it, and then come back and tell me how she is."

The uncle hurried back to the house and to the sickroom where his niece lay as before motionless. "Look what a lovely apple Father Leopoldo gave me for you!"

The child took her hands from behind her head, took the apple, sat up in bed and ate it with hearty appetite. She was cured.

When the uncle went straight back to Padua to tell Fr. Leopoldo, the latter was delighted. "It was Our Lady!" he said. "It was Our Lady! Praise and thank her always."

A Paduan who had not been to the Sacraments for years was finally touched by grace and came to Fr. Leopoldo to confession. For his penance Fr. Leopoldo told him to say a *Salve Regina* before the Lady Altar.

"I'm sorry, Father, but it's such a long time since I said any prayers that I've forgotten the words."

"I told you to say a *Salve Regina*."

"Forgive my insistence, Father, but I just don't know the *Salve Regina*."

"Say a *Salve Regina*," repeated Fr. Leopoldo with finality.

The man left the confessional rather disgusted, but finding himself by the Lady Altar, knelt at the rail without thinking. Suddenly in his ear an unearthly voice began prompting him syllable by syllable until full of joy and peace he had completed the penance given him.

Giulio Businaro, of Padua, got to know in hospital in Castelfranco Veneto one Alberto Bedin who was completely paralysed. He was very sorry for him and spoke about him to Fr. Leopoldo who knew him very well, offering to drive him over to see him. Fr. Leopoldo accepted with pleasure, but when the time came to start did not want to go. Businaro was by no means pleased, but Fr. Leopoldo said, "I'm not going because he wants to be cured and the time isn't ripe. You go and tell him to have faith in Our Lady. She will cure him, but not yet."

Two years after Fr. Leopoldo's death Bedin suddently left his bed, cured.

A railway worker lay at death's door in Padua hospital. For more than forty years he had not approached the Sacraments and he would not hear of it now.

The Sisters sent for Fr. Leopoldo but he was rudely repulsed. He did not lose heart, however, but with the faith that procures miracles, prayed and made others pray to Our Lady, Refuge of Sinners.

Next day the patient complained that "that little friar" was always before his eyes, and asked that he be sent for again. Full of joy, Father Leopoldo came and reconciled him to God.

He lived on another five days, demanding that Fr. Leopoldo should constantly be with him, and saying, "He is an angel, that friar."

Giacomo Lampronti, of Udine, writes: *I had told Fr. Leopoldo of my worry that my wife was still far from the Faith, being bound to her Jewish traditions. He gave me a small medal of Our Lady saying, "Take it to your wife and tell her to keep it. It is a relation of hers."*

Contrary to my expectation, my wife not only kept the medal but also came with me to Fr. Leopoldo's Jubilee Mass.

Fr. Leopoldo had also told me, "Don't be insistent with your wife. By Our Lady's intercession God will give her the grace." And so in due course it turned out, for today my wife is a Catholic.

In March, 1933 the small son of Salvatore Damiata, an Army NCO stationed at Padua, was afflicted with acute otitis. In spite ef every care and cure, the child got steadily worse and the doctor considered the case very serious.

On 14th March the child seemed at death's door and his father rushed round to Fr. Leopoldo and begged him with tears to save his son. Fr. Leopoldo consoled him and urged him to have faith; then, raising his eyes to Heaven, remained some time in prayer. Then suddenly he smiled and turned to the anxious father. "Go home in peace now, Sergeant, and give thanks to Our Lord and Our Blessed Lady."

Damiata went home happily to be met by his wife running out of the house, crying, "Salvatore, come quickly! He's cured! About half an hour ago he suddenly sat up in bed and said, "Mummy, I don't feel ill any more, I feel hungry."

All this happened just when Fr. Leopoldo was telling him to go home and thank Our Lady and Our Lord.

In July, 1934 one of Fr. Leopoldo's dreams came true. Some of his penitents were going to Lourdes and wanted him to come with them at their expense.

He went off radiantly happy and seeming years younger. During the journey he spent his time going round the train which was carrying the sick, for they all wanted him to hear their confession. An extraordinary thing happened at Turin where they made a stop en route. Mgr. Guido Mazzocco, Bishop of Adria and Rovigo, describes the incident.

In July, 1934 I had the good fortune to make the pilgrimage to Lourdes in the company of Fr. Leopoldo. On the way there we made a stop at Turin and visited the Cottolengo [1] *together. I shall never forget the veneration shown to him by the Sisters and the patients in this town of sorrow and love. As he passed through the narrow streets and visited the various "families" where so many unfortunates were gathered together, everyone ran to meet him, and knelt and tried to kiss his hand and ask for his blessing. Yet up till that moment none of them had seen or even heard of him.*

In Lourdes he spent his time praying and hearing confessions and taking part in the public worship. He was able to say Mass at the Grotto and it is evident that he received some special grace from the Madonna, though all we know is what he wrote on a picture of her, that she had given him to understand that he must start his spiritual life anew since everything he had done so far had been nothing.

The days passed like a flash and on 13th July he was back in Padua. He arrived at the railway station in company with Don Luigi Callegaro, the Parish Priest of Cornegliana, near Padua. Augusto Formentin, with his seven-year-old grandson Angelo Bernardi, came to collect them in his cab. Coming through the Via Dante, they came upon a tram and trailer approaching from the other direction. There was not room between the tramlines and the columns of the arcade for the cab to pass. The street was crowded and a lot of people shouted at them to stop, but neither the tram nor the somewhat spirited horse would do so... and they passed each other untouched.

Everyone crowded round so that the cab had to stop. As soon as they saw who was there, people said, "Nothing happened because Fr. Leopoldo was in the cab."

---

(1) St. Joseph Cottolengo (1786-1842) founded in Turin in 1832 what was then called the "Little House of Divine Providence" with a few beds in poor surroundings, very little money but a great deal of faith. Faith was rewarded by private benefactions and contributions from other charitable institutions and the place was able to expand, taking more and more sick to look after whom the Saint founded small but devoted religious congregations. It has now become a whole city of 10,000 sick, known popularly as "the Cottolengo" and has given rise to others, including one at Padua. In general the patients are those who cannot obtain admittance elsewhere, those with incurable diseases, deformities and so on.

Embarrassed, he said, "No! No! We are a couple of priests just back from Lourdes and it was Our Lady who saved us." Nevertheless a large number of people escorted them as far as the Friary.

Before letting the cab go on with Don Luigi, Fr. Leopoldo asked the driver how it had happened.

"It seemed to me that the road just became wider," he replied.

Two days later Don Luigi and the driver went back to the place and measured the distance between the tramlines and the columns and were more than ever convinced that only a miracle had let them through.

Several times Fr. Leopoldo reminded Formentin and his grandson of the incident, always ending by saying, "It was Our Lady who saved us."

In this way, and in many others, Our Lady testified to the truth of the saying that was constantly on Fr. Leopoldo's lips, "I rely on the powerful intercession of Our Lady, on her mother's heart, for everything."

CHAPTER XVIII.

VICTIM FOR HIS PEOPLE

The august Mother of God is in truth co-redemptress of the human race and source of all grace. In fact on the one hand we have in her the most perfect obedience to God's laws and, after her Son, the most perfect innocence: He impeccable by His nature, she impeccable by grace. On the other hand we see her as Our Lady of Sorrows, as He was the Man of Sorrows. If, therefore, by eternal decree of God, the Immaculate Virgin was the moral victim of sorrow as her Son was the physical victim, and if God's avenging justice found no shadow of fault in them, it follows inevitably that they were paying the price of the sins of others, that is of mankind.

FR. LEOPOLDO

We shall now try to throw some light on a great mystery of grace operating in Fr. Leopoldo. He had a double life: one as a confessor, known and appreciated by thousands of persons; the other private, known only to God and a few chosen confidants, the offering of his entire being in order to obtain from God the grace of the return of the schismatic Eastern Churches to the Catholic fold. In silence and completely hidden, he achieved an enormous amount, enough to put him in the ranks of the great Apostles of Unity. What he achieved can only be seen in part, since the mysterious workings of grace are known to God alone.

God called him to this great work, but made the method of achieving it clear to him only a little at a time. In fact, for a long time Fr. Leopoldo did not fully understand God's call to him. He had left his father's house and become a Capuchin in order to follow a sublime ideal which seemed to him to be the supreme end of his life: to become, that is, apostle of the eastern peoples and lead them back to the Catholic Church. He studied lovingly and tried to become a vessel of election of the grace of God so that he might pour out on the prodigal children of the East the superabundance of heavenly gifts.

This was in fact the mission to which God called him, but in His Divine Providence He wanted his cooperation not in the mission field but in prayer and sacrifice in Italy, spending his life for the salvation and perfection of many souls in the Sacrament of Penance.

Such mysterious workings of Providence are often found in the lives of the Saints. St. Theresa of Avila, St. Theresa of Lisieux and St. Philip Neri, to cite only a few, were anxious to work in the missions among heathens, but the two Theresas spent their lives shut up in their convents, and St. Philip spent his in Rome educating young people. Nevertheless they were also great missionaries, and had all the merit thereof, saving innumerable souls. It was revealed that St. Theresa of Avila brought as many souls to salvation as St. Francis

Xavier; and St. Theresa of Lisieux was made universal Patroness of Catholic Missions.

Such was also God's design for Fr. Leopoldo, who was a great missionary in his chosen field although spending his life shut up in his confessional.

It was because of his missionary ideals that he became a Capuchin. There were other Franciscan friaries at Castelnovo, but the Capuchins seemed the most suitable and he was able to know from his own experience that the Orthodox were not shy of them.

Other Orders worked in this field, of course, but it is a fact that the Capuchins did more over a wider area, from Russia to Abyssinia, than any other Order. They are still to be found wherever they have not been expelled by Moslems or Communists.

Once a Capuchin, he learned more and more what his Order had done and was doing and became daily more enthusiastic about the task he proposed for himself, always thinking about it and often discussing it with his companions. Mgr. Cuccarollo writes: *As a student Fr. Leopoldo was already yearning for his future work among the schismatics. He often spoke about it and confided in us that he wanted to convert them through devotion to Our Lady which he would encourage by word of mouth and by the printed word. To this end he studied hard at Balkan and other languages.*

On 18th June, 1887, while he was still a student at Padua, occurred an event that was a milestone in the development of his missionary vocation. God called him and, as with the young Samuel, manifested His will. Was it a real vision? Did he physically hear the voice of God? Was it internal enlightenment? The answers to these questions will never be known, for he spoke to nobody about it, neither then nor at any other time. Only fifty years later to the day, after saying Mass at the Altar of St. Gregory Barbarigo in the Cathedral at Padua, he wrote on a picture of Our Lady:

In solemn memory of the event: 18th June, 1887-1937. Today is the fiftieth anniversary of my hearing for the first time the voice of God calling me to pray and work for the return of the schismatic Eastern Churches to Catholic unity.

It seems therefore that it cannot just have been a new access of his desire to bring the East to salvation, but some really exceptional divine manifestation to be remembered, even as to the date, all his life.

From that day on his heart knew no peace. It seemed to him that the vast teeming East with its nations differing in customs, in dress and in political life but pratically all in schism, stretched out its arms to him for help. They were his people. In innumerable instances he refers to them in writing as "mio popolo" or "mia gente". God had chosen him for the salvation of these people and had told him so clearly. The task was enormous, enough to discourage anyone from even starting, but he had heard God's voice and wanted to fulfil his mission. (1)

As soon as he was ordained he asked his Superiors full of enthusiasm for permission to make his dream come true. As we know, however, they thought differently. It could not have been otherwise, for his constitution and health would not have allowed such an apostolate, though he had never admitted it to himself because God had spoken to him and he could not forget that God had used the weak young David to dispose of Goliath. Nevertheless, he bowed to authority and waited for God to clear the way and show him how he was to accomplish

---

(1) Some idea of the size and difficulties of the task may be obtained from the following summary. For a thousand years everything had been tried and, though at times reunion seemed imminent, it always fell through and the gap became wider. Differences of custom and tradition, racial dislikes made things so difficult on both sides that the problem appeared insoluble. From 863 when Fozio started the schism made definite in 1054 by the Patriarch of Constantinople, Michael Caerularius, the Eastern Church had gradually come more and more under political influence, becoming a national Church. With the fall of Constantinople in 1453 the Churches which had been under the Patriarch broke away and became independent: there were then the Bulgarian, Greek, Serbian and Russian Churches, and a lot more, each with its independent Patriarch but each more or less dependent on the civil authority. Then came Communism which on principle swept them all away but later found it politically expedient to recognize the Churches and the Patriarchs but made them absolutely dependent upon the State whose principles, and the methods of applying them, they were bound to uphold. This brought the situation to an impasse that only the hand of God could break. The masses of people, often good and religious, would have no difficulty in returning to the Catholic Faith, but their priests and patriarchs are bound with chains that are too heavy to be easily broken.

the mission entrusted to him. In the meantime he passed through various friaries in the Veneto Province and it twice seemed that God had at last put his foot on the path, that is when he was sent to Zara and Capodistria, but each time nothing came of it and he was recalled to the Veneto. During this period he tried to prepare himself in every way for what God wanted of him and to prepare others for the apostolate.

In fact when he was for four years Director of the Capuchin Students in Padua he wrote: *The object of my life should be the return of the dissident Eastern Churches... therefore, so long as obedience to my Superiors leaves me in the position of Director of our young people, I shall do everything possible in the circumstances to prepare the apostles who, when the time comes, will be engaged in this work.*

Many of his students did in fact embrace his ideal. One of them, Fr. Tarcisio of Bovolone, wrote to him in 1939 from Brazil where he was a missionary: *I had prepared a letter for you on Church Unity to tell you that although our prayers do not seem to produce much result in the East, here in Brazil many Greek Orthodox, of Arabian origin, embrace Catholicism easily, have their children baptized by us and want them brought up in the Roman rite.*

In 1923 came the last step in the direction of the longed for East. Fr. Leopoldo was sent to Fiume to deal with the confessions of Slavs, Serbs and Croats who were flocking to that port. Had the moment arrived at last? No! All that had come was the time for the definite clarification of God's will through the orders of his Superiors. In fact he had not been there a month when out of the blue came the order from the Father Provincial to return to Padua for good. The Provincial, Fr. Odorico of Pordenone, was also Fr. Leopoldo's spiritual director and knew him very well, but through a variety of circumstances already recorded in this book he had come to understand God's will with regard to Fr. Leopoldo and now as his Superior communicated it to him. Among other things, he wrote: *God is demanding yet another sacrifice of you, but I am sure that you will repeat our Divine Master's* Ecce, adsum! *and* Fiat voluntas tua. *You must come back to Padua. This is not the first time this has happened: St. Anthony wanted to go and preach to the heathens and find martyrdom among them, but the winds of Heaven brought the ship in which he was sailing for Africa to our shores. No doubt he needs you now at his side. Accept therefore the will of God and come back to your niche here.*

Fr. Leopoldo obeyed and came back at once. The end of his missionary dream? No, rather the final clarification of his true mission for the salvation of his Eastern brethren.

For some time already God's plan had been taking shape in his mind. He had clearly understood that God wanted to use him as part of a great plan for the salvation of the dissident East, and that he would be used in a particular way. God did not want him to go among those peoples and bring them back by his preaching to the one fold; He did not want him to write books or pamphlets to this end; He wished him to offer himself as a sacrifice to obtain the grace necessary for this great object. Others might go there, and preach, and talk and discuss and perhaps, before mankind, get the credit: all he had to do was to sacrifice himself. It did not matter whether anyone knew what he was doing for his separated brethren; it did not matter if all his work and suffering and tears remained unknown for ever: all he had to do was to sacrifice himself. God, Who had chosen him for this work and sown the seed in his heart, He would know—and that was enough. Only God could—can to-day—achieve what no human effort could ever manage: Fr. Leopoldo's path was to earn as far as possible by his sacrifice the grace necessary for such an act of mercy.

He accepted with generosity and in silence made his sacrifice.

Without faith one cannot understand the greatness and merit of this action, but for the faithful it is the greatest thing a man can do, not before mankind but before God. All good done to souls comes from God's grace and therefore the greater merit comes to him who by his sacrifice earns it.

Fr. Leopoldo, understanding the divine plan so far as it affected himself, accepted it in full, not for human glory which might never materialize, but solely for the glory of God. He realized that God wanted *his* sacrifice and from then on spoke to no one of his mission: only his own confessor and a couple of close friends were in the picture. He wanted to be like Jesus Who sacrificed Himself alone for the salvation of mankind.

This change was noticed by other members of the Community. Brother Osvaldo of Fontaniva writes: *In 1900 I was with Fr. Leopoldo in the friary at Thiene. He talked to me about the East and told me to pray to Our Lady to obtain for him the favour of being allowed to go and convert the schismatics. Years later I was with him again in Padua and asked him one day how it was that he had formerly spoken with such enthusiasm of going to the Missions and now never mentioned it.*

"Some time ago," he answered, "I happened to meet and give Holy Communion to a very holy person. Afterwards this person said to me, 'Father, Jesus has told me to tell you that your East is in every soul that you help here in Confession.' So you see, my dear chap," he went on contentedly, "that God wants me here and not in the mission-field, just as He wanted St. Philip Neri in Rome."

"I was born," he once said to a friend, "among a people that does not think as we think, but I live for that people. Pray to Our Lady to obtain for me the favour that when I have completed my work here in Padua I may be able to carry my old bones to my people and do them some good. For the moment there is no question of my leaving Padua: they want me here, but I am like a caged bird and my heart is across the sea."

Exactly. He realized that God wanted him to stay sacrificing his whole life to the hearing of confessions in that little cell and that this sacrifice was the ransom he was asked to pay for the salvation of 'his' people. He himself put it several times in writing. In 1935 he wrote from Vicenza "*...every soul that comes to me will be for the present my East.*" And again in 1941, "*Every soul that needs my ministry will be as it were my East.*"

He continued to take a great interest in everything to do with the return of the Eastern Churches, but of his vow and of his supreme sacrifice not a word was spoken. For many years he devoted himself to supporting Sister Maddalena Bredo of Padua, the foundress of the *Poverelle di S. Francesco d'Assisi per l'Unità della Chiesa,* sustaining her in the years of preparation through the most painful contradictions and misunderstandings, but never uttering a word about his own work. It was only after his death that Sister Maddalena got to know that he had the same ideal of Church Unity and had given his whole life in sacrifice for it.

Fr. Leopoldo heard God's call to the great work and it was in fact a new vocation for him within the Franciscan vocation. He often repeated it to himself, as though to revivify the theme of his existence; he wrote it on little slips of paper, or on holy pictures, which he kept in his breviary so that every time his eyes fell on them he was reminded of his special vocation.

There was no doubt about the divine call. On 2nd February, 1918 he wrote, *I believe and therefore I speak: Christ Our Lord is the Redemption: I, His unworthy minister, am truly His minister in the redemption of the Eastern Schismatics. Lord, Thou knowest all: Thou art Thyself the author of my will.*

Clearer still on 22nd July, 1923: *Before God I am certain, from the truth of events and the voice of my confessor, that my mission, as ordered by Providence which orders everything firmly and smoothly, is the salvation of my people.* And then, as though adding an exhortation to himself. *Remember you are sent for the salvation of your people.*

On 11th August, 1925, at two o'clock in the afternoon: *By the grace of God it is perfectly clear to me what work I am called to: that is, I understand that I am called to the salvation of my people.*

In 1937, happening to be at the friary in Venice, he wrote: *The will, the very desire, be it more or less urgent, to obtain the return of the Dissident Easterners to Catholic unity is the same divine vocation which Divine Providence has granted me... Before God I must have no further doubt about whether or not I am called for this work. In fact this has already been made abundantly clear to me.*

On 31st January, 1941, the feast of St. John Bosco: *Before God: I have no doubt left: in the same way as my vocation to the priesthood, I am chosen for the salvation of the Eastern people, that is the Schismatics. I must therefore respond to the divine goodness of Our Lord Jesus Christ who deigned to choose me so that, through my work as well, the divine promise may be finally redeemed that there shall be one fold and one shepherd.*

On more than one occasion God showed him by special signs that this call really represented His Divine Will and, at the same time, His pleasure at the way His servant was answering it. On 7th October, 1912 Fr. Leopoldo wrote: *Today at Holy Communion I clearly understood, from a mass of facts and evidence, that I am called to the work of the redemption of my people. That is, Our Lord and Our Lady want to save the errant sheep: among those called to this work, they want me also to be numbered.*

And on 11th June, 1928: *Today in making the spiritual Communion I experienced, unless I am mistaken, a sense of the divine pleasure from which I clearly understood that, on account of my vocation, I am called to the apostolate so that the Eastern Dissidents may return to Catholic unity.*

The same feeling must have manifested itself on two other occasions in that month since two other dates are added: *19th June p.m.* and *27th June 4 p.m.*

There is no doubt but that God had really called him to cooperate by his silent sacrifice in the redemption of the Eastern peoples. Father Leopoldo considered this vocation a supreme gift of God and wanted it to be the whole object of his life, using all his energies to that end. He put it in writing on innumerable occasions, but unfortunately only a few examples can be cited.

On 31st August, 1908, at the Seminary at Vicenza where he was helping to hear the confessions of priests in Retreat: *Truly before God and the Blessed Virgin, confirmed by oath, I have undertaken in honour of the Co-redemptress of mankind, to use all my strength in this life, under obedience to my Superiors, towards the redemption of the Dissident Eastern people from schism and error.*

21st August, 1914: confirmed 3rd August, 1928 at 6 p.m. *The object of my life must be the return of the Eastern Dissidents to Catholic unity. That is, before God, in the faith and charity of Our Lord Jesus Christ Who expiated the sins of the world, I must direct all my energies, so far as my poor condition allows, towards the goal of making some contribution to that great work through the merits of the sacrifice of my life.*

24th April, 1915: *Today while celebrating Mass I offered myself to Our Lord Jesus Christ for the return of the Eastern Dissidents to Catholic Unity.*

That same Lord Jesus Who expiated the sins of the whole world, expiated their sins as well: it is therefore my desire and purpose that the object of my life, the reason for my whole existence, should be to serve this divine charity of Christ Our Lord.

In 1935, once more at the Seminary at Vicenza: "...*In the grace of my vocation in favour of the Eastern Dissidents, I bind myself by a vow that from now on the whole purpose of my life shall be to obtain that as soon as possible the words of Our Lord Jesus Christ that there shall be one fold and one shepherd shall be true of the Eastern Dissidents.*

And just before his death he wrote again: *The whole purpose of my life must be the Divine Plan; that is, that I too in my small way bear something to the end that one day, in accordance with the dictates of the Divine Wisdom which orders all things with gentle strength, the Eastern Dissidents may return to Catholic Unity.*

Fr. Leopoldo did not limit himself to believing that his vocation and the whole purpose of his existence should be the return of the schismatic Eastern Churches, he confirmed this with a vow frequently renewed. We do not know when he made the original vow, for the holy pictures and odd slips of paper on which he renewed it in writing have in great measure been lost. The first surviving document is dated December, 1905, and already speaks of renewal. Some sixty-six such papers have survived, many of them bearing numerous dates and one can only suppose that when time pressed, instead of writing it all again in full, he merely added the date to a renewal already written. One might be tempted to think of this constant written repetition of the vow as no more than the manifestation of an *idée fixe,* were not such a notion inconsistent with the unmistakeable evidence we possess of a temperament that was sound and well balanced in every other respect.

It is easy enough to make a vow, but then one has to fulfil it, and Fr. Leopoldo naturally wanted to do so as nearly perfectly as possible. To start with he must be as worthy as possible of the vocation, putting all his intensity and fervour in making the best use of the graces given him.

Every single action of his was directed towards the furtherance of his task and we know from his writings on holy pictures and so on that it was not just a once-made general intention but an intention renewed daily and even more often, frequently in different places. Finding himself in a new church, before a statue or picture of Our Lady for example, he would be moved to renew his intention in words of the greatest ardour.

But more than frequently renewed vows and fervently expressed intentions, something concrete had to be done towards the achievement of the object. After a great deal of thought and prayer and consultation with confessor and spiritual director, he found the way to direct all his work to the desired end.

It was this. Every penitent who came to him for confession was met by him as though he were one of the Eastern schismatics returning through him to unity with Rome; that is, everything he did for that particular penitent was offered to God to obtain the return of one schismatic. This meant a sort of double intention: to do his best for the soul actually in the confessional and to offer the good thus done for the benefit of one unknown and unspecified schismatic.

This work in the confessional was not only a work of charity inspired by love of God, it was also a matter of obedience to his Superiors. For every penitent who came to him he renewed his intention of performing an act of obedience in hearing and comforting them: the merits of such acts of obedience he again applied to the return of the Eastern Dissidents to the fold of Peter.

Fr. Leopoldo was well aware of the value of obedience. He had studied St. Francis on the subject and St. Ignatius whose letter on obedience he had copied by hand and kept in the confessional. He knew that no human action prompted solely by one's own will, however virtuous it may seem, is as acceptable to God as an act of obedience to one's Superiors done for the love of God. He knew that in obedience he had a far more effective means of reclaiming 'his' people than any sermons he might have preached among them or any books he might have written for them.

The other great practical means to realize his object was prayer, continuous fervent prayer to obtain the desired result from God's mercy. He also exhorted his penitents to pray for this intention. "Our fathers prayed for this," he said once, "and we pray for it and others after us will pray, and I hope that the day is not far off when there will be one fold and one Shepherd."

To the constantly renewed intention, to his work in the confessional and his obedience he added the offering of himself as a sacrifice for his people. Anyone who has read about his more than fifty years in the confessional, in itself a sacrifice, and about the physical sufferings of heat and cold and ill-health born with such resignation and even with joy, and who realizes that he never had more than five hours rest in the twenty-four, spending the rest of the time in the confessional or at prayer, will realize also that this offering of himself as a victim was no mere form of words but was something quite genuinely carried into effect.

Nevertheless the one means by which Fr. Leopoldo was *certain* of obtaining the return of the Dissidents to unity with Rome was the celebration of Holy Mass. We have already seen what a sublime view he took of the Mass and how he made it the core of his existence. In his unshakeable faith he knew that he was offering God a gift so great that anything he asked for must be granted: anything he could ask for was nothing in comparison to the Victim he offered. Thus, the most perfect possible celebration of the Mass became his surest way of fulfilling his mission to the Eastern Churches.

His ideas on the subject were perfectly clear, albeit not expressed in conventional terms since he wrote them for himself with no thought that they would one day become public. *Remember that your mission is the salvation of your people, not from any merit of your own, for it was Christ who died for souls not you: your mandate comes from your office, but merit does come into it to the extent that the more perfectly you carry out your office, the greater will its efficacy be.*

He meant that the merit of the Sacrifice of the Mass derives solely from the bloodless sacrifice of Christ and that the priest is simply the agent through whom Christ offers himself: he knew nevertheless that application of this merit to souls is also a function of the holiness and degree of perfection of that agent. Therefore he wanted to celebrate as nearly perfectly as possible so that the merit could be applied in the greatest measure possible to the great cause: his own merit was thus united to that of the Divine Victim.

As late as a year before his death he put it in writing again: *I must respond to the Divine Goodness of Our Lord Jesus Christ who deigned to choose me so that also through me as His minister the divine promise may come true that there shall be one fold and one Shepherd.*

I say "through me as His minister" in the sense that when I celebrate Mass for this intention, the Divine Love offers Himself for the Dissidents and thus accomplishes their redemption.

Fr. Leopolodo was not able to make this intention every day as he would have liked to, for justice, charity and obedience mostly imposed other intentions. Twice a month he could always manage, since the Capuchin Rule allows its priests two free intentions each month, and generally Fr. Leopoldo used them for this purpose.

Even this was not enough, however, and he also tried to make the utmost use of his daily Mass. Since the Mass has an infinite value before God, there may be as it were, some merit left over after the needs of justice and charity have been met. This surplus was always intended for the cause.

On 19th October, 1935 he himself put in writing: *I bind myself by vow as follows: Every time I celebrate Mass, unless prevented by charity or justice, all the merit of the Holy Sacrifice will be applied to the return of the Eastern Dissidents to Catholic unity. When justice or charity demand otherwise, once their needs have been met, any remaining merit shall be applied for the same intention.*

Although he knew it was a purely personal vocation and thus to be carried out privately, Fr. Leopoldo's ardour in the matter occasionally burst out beyond the memoranda written for himself and led him on occasion to confide in others. He once said to such a confidant, "I feel myself called to work for the Eastern peoples. God in His wonderful Providence has given me the means to do so in the Holy Mass. You help me as well when you hear Mass and go to Holy Communion. You earn the same merit thereby as I do. Never forget that every man has a duty to save his fellows."

On another occasion he said to the same person, "This morning I celebrated Mass for my people, and I am certain that they have already felt the effect of that great sacrifice."

* * *

Fr. Leopoldo found another means to further his cause in his devotion to Our Lady. We have already seen how great that devotion was, what high ideas he had of her greatness and what filial confidence he had in her. Here again he was not content with vague sentimentalism but based himself on sound principles of Marian theology.

"I believed therefore I have spoken," said the prophet. The apostle can with perfect truth apply these divinely inspired words to himself. On the basis of divine Faith I apply them to myself.

I believe in this dogma of Catholic Faith: that the Blessed Virgin Mary is a second Eve, as we believe that Christ Our Lord is a second Adam. I believe therefore that the maternal providence of the same Blessed Virgin Mary constantly watches over the Church in accordance with the charge given her by her Son dying on the Cross: "Woman, behold thy son... Son, behold thy mother." In heaven together with her Son Who unceasingly intercedes with the Father, she too is ever interceding, completing in Heaven what she began on earth at the foot of the Cross.

The most holy Virgin has so much love and care for the human race that she is as it were a victim of her own heart in her love for us. But since her love for us is caused by the love of God, she, in the fullness of her beatitude, intercedes for the salvation of mankind so that as we have the Son pleading for us with the Father, so also we have her as advocate with her Son with Whom also she intercedes with the Father for the salvation of the human race.

Fr. Leopoldo saw this loving care for mankind as particularly directed towards his Eastern Dissidents. On 21st May, 1914 he wrote: *I believe by divine Faith that you, O Blessed Virgin, are most solicitous for the Eastern Dissidents and I wish to cooperate as much as possible with your maternal love. All my actions shall have this intention.*

He saw quite clearly that Our Lady's mission and his own were different, she being Co-redemptress with Christ while he was but a minister. For that reason he wanted to place all his work in her hands, an intention that was renewed again and again on slips of paper or on backs of holy pictures. If at any time he felt that circumstances prevented him from dedicating himself as fully as he would have liked to his mission he appealed to her. *You know the circumstances of my life and its difficulties: please take my cause into your hands.*

* * *

Faith, only profound and unshakeable faith, sustained Fr. Leopoldo in this hidden work, the same faith that assured him that his effort did have the effect of hastening the desired unity between the East and Rome. He had no doubts about this.

A year before his death he wrote to Fr. Odorico of Pordenone, his spiritual director: *...I have the East always before my eyes and I feel that God wishes me to celebrate the Sacred Mysteries, saving where justice and charity demand otherwise, so that the great promise of one fold and one Shepherd may in due course be fulfilled. And it certainly will be. This is what I think about it: God moves His ministers to apply His merits to the Eastern Dissidents, so that He is praying for them to the extent that we celebrate the Sacred Mysteries for that intention. That means, then, that He Himself is praying through us, and we know from His own words that God the Father always answers His prayers. The great event will therefore infallibly happen. My task therefore is to work towards the realization of this great prophecy. There you have my ideas on the subject.*

The goodness of the Blessed Virgin and her maternal care for the Eastern peoples who have such great devotion to her were for Fr. Leopoldo a guarantee of their return to the fold. He wrote: *O most Blessed Virgin, you said in your Canticle, "The Lord hath received Israel His servant, being mindful of His mercy;" I too firmly believe that the reunion with the Eastern Dissidents will take place.*

In 1910, to a friend: *The older I get the more I am convinced of the importance of the apostolate of prayer for the Eastern Dissidents, that is the Schismatics.*

The most Blessed Virgin, to whom those peoples are greatly devoted, certainly has and will have great care of them and will obtain for them from her divine Son the gift of the true Faith.

Now since in the order of things established by God, and in the ordinary course of Divine Providence, every good must derive from prayer, all who pray for this intention become ministers and agents of Divine Providence and at the same time truly ministers and agents of the maternal heart of the Mother of God in favour of those strayed peoples.

Anyone who has the generosity to exercise this apostolate will find every favour with God.

Once after celebrating Mass for "his people" he told a friend, "*Thinking of the greatness of the Divine Victim offered to the Father, I exclaimed, "Now refuse me—if you can!"*"

Certainly God, who had kindled so ardent a flame in his heart, cannot have failed to hear his prayer, and one day we shall see that in his hidden work, whose scope is known in its entirety to God alone, Fr. Leopoldo was among the greatest Apostles of the East.

CHAPTER XIX.

GOLDEN JUBILEE

Satan's words to Eve were nothing but lies and deception and she by her acceptance of them was the occasion of the sin of mankind. By contrast, the angel's words to Mary were pure truth and justice: the Virgin knew her mission, and with her great Fiat became the real cause of the salvation of mankind.

So a mother was given to Israel and we should repeat what in other circumstances came from the lips of the ancient People of God: "Valiant men no longer were seen in Israel, and her glory returned when Debbora appeared and a mother was given to Israel."

FR. LEOPOLDO

On 3rd May, 1938 Fr. Leopoldo celebrated the fiftieth anniversary of his profession as a Capuchin. It was a domestic celebration, entirely spiritual, in which he tasted the joy of renewing after so many years of sacrifice to God his original immolation with the same holy enthusiasm with which he had made it fifty years before.

Before the High Altar of the small friary chapel, surrounded by his brethren, in a voice charged with emotion, he asked their pardon if in those fifty years he had ever borne himself other than in the way demanded by his vocation. He then renewed his Profession, promising God to start anew, with renewed fervour, his road to perfection.

The Father Guardian, Fr. Marcellino of Cartigliano, made a brief but moving reply, saying among other things:

"Today you are celebrating the fiftieth anniversary of your first consecration to God. Fifty years! Half a century! Normally the entire working life of a man. And these fifty years not spent in the world in ease among pleasures and amusements but in the religious life which is a life of sacrifice and continuous immolation. Fifty years of faithful service of God in a life of poverty, obedience and chastity. Fifty years of such a life embraced with joy and lived with serenity and heavenly joy. These fifty years really deserve to be considered in the first place by yourself to give glory to God on their account, and then by us that we may rejoice with you and with you bless the Lord.

"You will understand that my aim at this time is not to flatter your vanity, for such a thing does not exist; nor is it my intention to offend your modesty by speaking of your interior life, of your spirit of prayer and mortification, of your love of God and your neighbour; I make no pretence of revealing or discussing what only the four walls of your cell know, what only God knows; all I want to do is to recall your fifty years of life in religion and to join in giving thanks to God who gave you the strength to live these years not just in word but in deed and in truth."

Fr. Giacinto of Trieste, at that time Father Provincial and now Archbishop of Gorizia, wrote to him from Venice: *Your Father Provincial wishes to be the first, as is only right, to send his heartiest congratulations and best wishes on the fiftieth anniversary of your Profession.*

In themselves fifty years of life are nothing particular, and they are less than nothing if they are ill-spent, but fifty years of religious life lived intensely for good are equivalent to sanctity and eternity.

You, dear Father Leopoldo—allow me to say it though you may think otherwise—have spent these fifty years of the religious life as follows: incessant striving to rise daily higher in the ascent to seraphic perfection; scrupulous observance of your vows and even the most insignificant tasks; all your time spent in prayer, study and the work of your apostolate. And what an apostolate! One which has known neither halt nor hesitation but has been a very real and continuous sacrifice to God.

Your particular apostolate, to which you received a very special vocation, is the direction of souls. It is not necessary to repeat what is obvious to all. Always in your confessional, at every hour of every day. Terrible daily routine in which you kept for yourself not even one hour, but gave all for others. Bishops, priests, monks and nuns, pious laymen and poor sinners, all turn to Fr. Leopoldo as their favourite confessor because they discern in him a brighter ray of the Divine Mercy welcoming them with discretion and kindness, pardoning all, opening their hearts, comforting them and inspiring with renewed hope in Heaven.

How much merit you must have acquired, dear Fr. Leopoldo, with the just Judge who records every detail in the Book of Life. How many souls are and will be eternally grateful to you and will pray for you.

Fifty years spent like this call for no regrets: they are years full of real life, and merit the sincerest congratulations which I offer you in my name and on behalf of the whole Capuchin Province of the Veneto which rejoices with a son who does her so much honour.

To the congratulations I should like to add—since you do not yet want to sing the Nunc dimittis *nor do we want you to—all our best wishes for many more years of fruitful apostolate for the glory of God, to the comfort of so many souls, and the honour of the province and our Order.*

May our seraphic Father St. Francis, greatly honoured by the virtues and labours of his son, bestow upon you his most generous blessings.

Fr. Leopoldo enjoyed this happy celebration, but he did not stop to think about the good achieved in so many years of religious life: he thought only of turning to his dearest Mother, the Blessed Virgin, to ask her for renewed strength to live with ever increased intensity the life of sacrifice freely chosen by him in his youth. On a picture of the Madonna he wrote:

Today, the fiftieth anniversary of my religious profession, I renew my vows in honour of the Sacred Heart of the Divine Shepherd and of the Most Blessed Virgin Mary since she has, by divine decree, been given to us as Mother. Therefore, to serve her maternal love, I renew my vows.

On 22nd September, 1940 Fr. Leopoldo celebrated the fiftieth anniversary of his ordination.

This event deserves special mention because of the spontaneous and universal tributes of esteem and affection which it evoked, and which all gave very convincing proof of the immense achievement in good works that had been Fr. Leopoldo's during fifty years in the priesthood.

When on that morning he celebrated Mass the Capuchin church was crowded to the doors. All classes were represented, clergy and laity, rich and poor, learned and ignorant—all had thronged to the church to give expression to their love and gratitude.

After the Gospel of the Mass Mgr. Guido Bellincini preached a sermon of congratulation, an impressive discourse, during which this accomplished orator, without causing embarrassment to the naturally modest Fr. Leopoldo, fixed the attention of his listeners on the many virtues of the Jubilarian and on the apostolic work accomplished by him to the benefit of innumerable souls; he stressed, too, the heavenly gifts which Fr. Leopoldo had received in such abundance and which he had used with very wonderful effect in the confessional, yet always with great humility.

As for Fr. Leopoldo, he was completely absorbed in his thoughts and apparently unaware of what was going on around him; probably he was concerned only with the consideration of the supreme grace of having been able to celebrate Mass for fifty years.

After Mass he went into a room adjoinig the church because those present wanted to offer their congratulations. It was a moving scene with every one crowding round trying to kiss his hand or at least his habit. Moved and embarrassed by so much demonstration of affection, he shrank into himself and raised his eyes to heaven, repeating, "All for my sins! All for my sins!"

From all over Italy came letters and telegrams by the armful, from the highest ecclesiastical and lay authorities as well as from the humblest individuals. They all expressed the same thoughts: joy for the grace received by him and gratitude for the spiritual help received from him.

A particular joy was the receipt of the Papal Blessing.

The Father Provincial, Fr. Girolamo of Fellette, now Bishop of Padua, wrote to him: *The happy occasion which is being celebrated with brotherly enthusiasm and affection by colleagues, acquaintances and admirers cannot find the Father Provincial absent.*

Fifty years of priestly life, especially such as yours have been, contain and express so much that is sublime and holy that they deserve to be recalled as an example and edification for all.

You have not been the lazy servant who buried his talent, but the good and faithful servant who made it increase tenfold for his Lord. In the exhausting daily ministry of the Sacrament of Penance, undertaken with such constancy by you, you showed your spirit of sacrifice and self-denial, your zeal for God's glory and your total dedication to the good of your neighbour.

And this is written in gold letters in the Book of Life and will be your crown in Heaven.

It is proper also for us, your brethren, to rejoice with you for all this good which pleases the Church and does so much honour to our Order.

Led by the Cardinal Patriarch of Venice, all the Bishops of the Veneto sent him their congratulations and best wishes.

The then Bishop of Padua, Mgr. Carlo Agostini, wrote: *I send you my sincere and cordial congratulations, and I join you in thanking God for all the good—and it has been very great—which your example and your ministry have achieved in these fifty years, and I wish you many more years to come in which you may work for God's greater glory, for the perfection of your crown of merits and for the good of souls.*

May every blessing comfort your life and multiply the fruits of your apostolate. Pray for me.

The Mayor of Padua, G. Solitro: *Allow the Mayor, in the name of the people of Padua, to present his most sincere congratulations and best wishes on the occasion of your sacerdotal Golden Jubilee.*

All the local papers carried long articles exalting the humble Capuchin as one of the great benefactors of the city.

On 30th September the clergy wanted to pay their own special tribute. Numerous priests assembled in the friary church so that he could say a special Mass for them. After Mass they adjourned to the neighbouring room and offered their personal greetings. The following address was read by Mgr. Giuseppe Schievano, Archpriest of Padua Cathedral, in the name of them all:

Reverend Father Leopoldo, you are at this moment surrounded by a notable part of your spiritual family. The bonds that bind us are holy, strong and deeply felt. Only at the last day will it be known what sacrifices you have made, how much good you have done to our souls, how many turmoils you have calmed, how many sorrows softened and comforted. When we were beset by doubts, discouragements and weaknesses, you always welcomed us within those poor walls that represent the sacrifice of your life and the resurrection of so many souls, and like the good Samaritan you have bound up and healed our wounds.

If we could make one criticism it would be that you have been too good to us. Yet your inexhaustible kindness is a double lesson for us: it reminds us of our duty to respond generously to the Father who, through His minister, deals so generously with us; and it reminds us of our duty to use the same measure of generosity towards those souls who come to us.

Your kindness reminds us that it is charity alone that wins souls, charity which makes us like to Christ, Who albeit able to triumph by force, prefered the way of love, to the extent of renouncing triumph if love could not be served. Such love has been the inspiration of your whole life.

Fr. Leopoldo spent these days in holy joy, thanking God for the good done to souls by such demonstrations of faith, but untouched in his humility. If anyone commented on the scale and spontaneity of the rejoicings in his honour, he answered, "They give me nothing and take nothing from me. All this is not for me, it is for the Habit."

Truly humble, he did not scorn praise, but accepted it gratefully in the firm conviction that it was not directed at him personally but at the Habit he wore and at the Supreme High Priest Whose humble minister he had been for fifty years.

To Domenico Morassuti he wrote: *Like so many of my dear friends, you overwhelm me with praise. I am bound to accept such sincere proofs of friendship: may it all be to the honour of the Eternal High Priest, Our Lord Jesus Christ, of whom we priests who are but men of flesh and blood are merely a shadow that fades with time.*

Therefore in the tokens of affection and esteem which I have received in the last few days I have seen Our Lord honoured in my humble person albeit aware that this same humble representative of Him, who alone is worthy of praise, was full of secret faults.

I felt, as I feel now, the full contrast between the voice of conscience which is the voice of truth, and the praises which have been offered me.

I accept these tokens and am very grateful for them. They will always be cherished memory of so much great affection. But they are only for Him who does not disdain praise and who will accept it even at the hands of this humble writer.

And to Prof. Giovanni Soranzo: *For how many things does my conscience upbraid me after fifty years of the ministry! I am obliged to accept the compliments of my friends, but all for Him who is the first Priest in His Divine Person. Praise be to Him always.*

So even the unanimous and enthusiastic praise he received from everyone only served to increase his humility and give greater glory to God.

CHAPTER XX.

IN THE LIGHT OF GOD

The Church of God, whose task it is to bring mankind to salvation, has the right and duty to come to the aid of human society. She must have, therefore, in this field as well, people to represent her and fight in God's cause. She has therefore need of militant Catholics in the ranks of Catholic Action.

FR. LEOPOLDO

Fr. Leopoldo's life was rapidly drawing to its close. To those who congratulated him on the magnificent celebrations for his Golden Jubilee, he replied, "Yes, but they were farewell celebrations."

For so many years he had been a tireless worker in the Lord's vineyard, had sown the Word of God with heroic sacrifice in so many souls and had joyfully reaped an abundant harvest. Now God wanted to call him to his rest and reward in Heaven.

But before he should taste the joys of Paradise, God wished him to endure with His Son the agony of Calvary, for only from this bloody height can souls safely embark on the sure way to Heaven. It is a commonplace that the greater a soul is before God, the harder is the last stage of the journey. In the furnace of suffering the last vestiges of human dross must be purified, so that the soul may pass directly from earthly exile to heavenly home.

So it was with Fr. Leopoldo.

His frail constitution had always meant that he was afflicted with sufferings, often very severe, but in his last two years these sufferings were immeasurably intensified.

In the winter of 1941 the stomach pains, which had troubled him virtually all his life, became very much worse. It was thought to be a gastric ulcer. In the meantime, the unfortunate priest, unable to take any nourishment, was getting weaker and weaker until he could no longer stand.

"I feel now," he said to a penitent, "that Leopoldo has not much time left, but my spirit is still that of a child."

So often during his life when anyone urged him to cut down the exhausting work and take some rest he had answeerd, "We'll get our rest in Heaven, when our heads rest on the Divine Heart of Jesus."

This moment was approaching for him.

Kept going by sheer will-power, he managed to continue his work for a time, but eventually he had to give way and take to his bed.

He was subjected to a rather drastic therapy.

He suffered agonies not to be understood by anyone unacquainted with his spiritual ardour. The physical suffering was nothing compared with the moral agony. So many souls were awaiting his ministrations, so many hearts needed his comfort and consolation, and he had to remain lying uselessly in bed.

One day, unable to control his ardour, he got up and went down to hear the confession of someone who had come a great distance to see him. But his strength was leaving him and on the way back to his cell, he had to stop halfway up the stairs, exhausted and trembling. Another member of the community happened to come by.

"What on earth do you want to go down to the church for in your weak state?"

"What could I do? Someone came from a great distance and was waiting for me..."

He had to be more or less carried back to the infirmary.

He heard more strongly than ever the voice of God calling him to the salvation of the Eastern peoples and he knew that the means to this end was his ministry to souls, so that not to be able to go down to his confessional was agony indeed. God increased this desire in him in order to increase his merit. From his bed he wrote again, his handwriting shaky, "*On account of my vocation I feel myself called to the salvation of the Eastern people and then to the ministry of the confessional.*"

He prayed unceasingly for enough physical strength to be able to attend once more to his ministry. His rosary never left his hands and his lips were constantly moving in silent supplication to Our Lady, Health of the Sick. His penitents too, were enlisted to pray to this end. He wrote to Signorina Caterina d'Ambrosio: *Pray to our Blessed Lady for me that she will deign to give me back my former health so that I can once again attend to souls. Please pray with all your heart. Importune the Sacred Heart of Jesus and His infinite charity to give me the necessary health to serve Him as confessor.*

To Angelo Marzotto: *Thank you for your kindness. Our Lord will reward you, as he promised. Tomorrow is the feast of our great Patro-*

ness. I shall try to pray for you and your wife with all the faith permitted me. I know well what your feelings are for the present humble writer. In your esteem for me, please pray with your wife that our Blessed Lady will remember me. Ask her to have pity on me. You know of what I stand in need. Let us be united in devotion to Our Lady: let her be Mother to us all.

As if his physical sufferings and frustrations were not enough to crucify his pour soul, spiritual trials were added. As has already been noted, spiritual aridity was not infrequent with him, but in the last two years of his life it was almost continuous and brought him almost to a state of acute emotional tension.

He had recourse to his spiritual director, Fr. Odorico of Pordenone, who answered from Fiume on 22nd January: *I am sorry to hear you are ill and trust that it is only a temporary affair. I recommend, however —in fact I order you to take proper care and allow yourself to be treated. I know how much you suffer when you cannot exercise your sacred office, but this, too, comes at Our Lord's hands. You can see that Jesus really loves you because He has, as the saying is, touched you on the raw. Thank Him for this gift: He wants to prepare your soul and render it ever more acceptable to His Sacred Heart.*

Father Leopoldo also wrote to his intimate friend Don Giovanni Calabria, (now, too, a Servant of God) a letter so touching that he was induced to come to Padua and comfort his sick friend although he himself was far from well. They remained a long time closeted together in the infirmary cell. What these two great souls said to each other nobody knows, but certainly Fr. Leopoldo derived great comfort from it, for a new serenity was thereafter apparent in his bearing.

With God's help and the protection of his Mother, the trial passed. Slowly Fr. Leopoldo began to recover; the pain eased and he was able to take nourishment and to start building up his wasted strength.

As soon as he was well enough to stand, Fr. Leopoldo returned to the confessional, but his feeble movements and more than usually bent frame foretold a relapse before long.

He wanted to carry on working as he had done before his illness, but it was physically impossible in his weak state. This was agony for him, the more so since his superiors set a limit to the time he might spend in the confessional so that he should get some rest.

His heart bled, but he submitted humbly to obedience: only he demanded the prayers of all his friends that the Lord should take the matter in hand.

Don Giovanni Bussoni wrote to him from Canoscio (Perugia) on 21st August, 1941: *I put the matter to the Capuchin Sisters, particularly to the one I think is closest to God. After many prayers, they gave me today this exact answer: Tell the priest that God will take care of his souls either by providing another confessor or, as a reward for his obedience, by giving him back his health and inspiring his superiors to give him greater freedom in the exercise of his ministry.*

The summer passed thus, but with the first cold of winter Father Leopoldo began again to suffer terribly. His painful ascent had not yet brought him to the summit of Calvary. Once more came the agonizing internal pains accompanied by the inability to take food.

Once more he went on as long as he could, trying to conceal his suffering for fear he should be forbidden the confessional. But finally the illness was too much even for his heroic will and he was obliged to take to his bed. As in the previous winter, spiritual trials were also not wanting whereby Our Lord wished to bring him to the highest peak of perfection.

The thought of the many souls awaiting his ministrations before the door of his confessional, and waiting in vain, caused him agonies of suffering such as can only be measured by a soul desirous of bringing everyone to God. Often people would arrive from great distances to hear the words of comfort and absolution from his lips as only he knew how to pronounce them. Many came up to his infirmary cell where, in spite of exhausting pain and other weakness, he welcomed them as lovingly as ever. But this privilege could not be granted to all, and to the others he wrote, with trembling fingers, a short note. A few words breathing the most lively charity and begging forgiveness that he could not come down to them, as if it were his own fault.

Sometimes, unable to master his own zeal, he made the supreme effort of going down to the church, but often he had to be carried back to bed.

Soon the news of his alarming state of health spread, and everyone was saddened by it. There was a continuous stream of people coming to the friary to enquire, and in their faces could be read the sorrow and fear of losing their beloved Fr. Leopoldo. Among this visitors were distinguished members of the clergy and laity. The Bishop of Padua insisted on being kept informed of his condition, sending his Vicar General on several occasions, and came himself to impart his blessing.

But alas, despite all the care and treatment, Fr. Leopoldo's life was rapidy drawing to a close. He was ready to go when called, but his zeal for souls, to whose welfare he had without ceasing devoted his life, still devoured him. He often repeated the words of St. Martin, "Lord if you think I can still be useful to your flock, I accept the task: nevertheless, Thy will be done."

But God's will was that he should suffer more yet.

After a consultation with various professors, it was decided to try a blood transfusion in an attempt to bring back some strength to the weakened body. On 1st April he was taken to hospital. The first transfusion was dangerous because of his extreme weakness and was attended by three professors, each of them well aware that Padua expected from them the miracle of saving their beloved priest.

The transfusion went well and was followed in due course by seven others. Everyone wanted to give blood, but the choice fell on the lay brother Fra Ruggero and the infirmarian Marco Ercolini.

Father Leopoldo did begin to improve, gaining strength by slow degrees, and it seemed that mortal danger was past.

In the meantime, as soon as the newspapers mentioned that he was in hospital, people came flocking to his bedside to express the universal prayer and hope for his rapid recovery. His bed became a throne whence shone the radiant example of his patience and resignation to the will of God.

One day his spiritual director, Fr. Odorico of Pordenone, came to see him and found him in tears.

"Why are you weeping?"

"I am weeping because I find myself the object of so much attention from the professors and attendants and sisters and from the people who come to see me. But why all this for such a wretch as me?"

"It is not for you," said Fr. Odorico, "is is all for the Habit of St. Francis."

At this Fr. Leopoldo immediately calmed down. Apparently he had only just become aware of the devotion borne him by people of all classes and he feared it as a temptation against humility.

Fearing that the stream of visitors would be bad for him since he badly needed rest, the doctors forbade all visits and fixed a signed notice to that purpose on the door of his room, but it had no effect. People could not do without their Fr. Leopoldo and would not hear of prohibitions. In the city he was the sole topic of conversation.

He himself welcomed them all, heard confessions, gave advice and comforted those in need, albeit so weak that he could barely make his voice heard.

Mgr. Carlo Margotti, Archbishop of Gorizia, wrote: *One day I came to Padua to visit Fr. Leopoldo who was in the municipal hospital there. Not knowing the way, I took a taxi. Hearing the address, the driver said, "I suppose you are going to see Fr. Leopoldo?" Later he added, "That man is a saint."*

After a month in hospital Fr. Leopoldo came back to the friary.

He seemed much better, being able to stand and walk. Already his hopes were high. In fact, however, his fate was already sealed. Careful X-ray examination had revealed that a tumour, previously unlocated, was growing in the oesophagus. No effective cure was possible.

He knew nothing of this and as soon as he was strong enough he started hearing confessions again, sometimes going down to the church but otherwise receiving penitents in his cell in the infirmary. He felt himself reborn, and cherised with all his former enthusiasm his dreams of a fervent apostolate and the conversion of his Eastern schismatics.

But his illness, at first hidden, became more manifest, and each day its effects were more apparent. Often a sudden crisis would cause him such excruciating pain that he fainted: every day it became more and more difficult to take any nourishment, even liquid, since it caused the most painful spasms.

This was the supreme trial which was to make him worthy of the loving welcome of his Lord which could not now be long delayed. As before, physical pain was accompanied by trials of the spirit.

During his life he had often said to the sick, "Courage! Trust in the Lord, for Jesus is both doctor and medicine." So now, seeing that all human efforts were in vain, he turned to Jesus and His Blessed Mother, asking if it should be agreeable to them that they should come to his aid.

He had recently written to Don Giovanni Calabria and got the following reply: *The grace and peace of Jesus be always with you whom in my poverty I always remember. Your letter troubled me and moved me by the kindness and charity it evinced towards this humble priest. May God recompense you as He knows how, turning it all to your spiritual account. In my poor way I have prayed, and still pray, that the Divine Physician, if it be His will, give you the health so necessary for you to continue to minister to souls seeking Him. I have said Mass for this intention. I, too, have great need of prayers for my poor soul.*

In spite of all the pain and suffering, Fr. Leopoldo continued undeterred to hear confessions and did so with so much attention and welcome for his penitents that everyone was moved.

Giuseppe Rampazzo writes: *On 30th June, 1942 I went to confession to Fr. Leopoldo in his cell in the infirmary. He was in some pain and had difficulty in walking, yet he insisted on accompanying me to the door of the friary and overwhelming me with signs of affection.*

Arrived at the door, I thanked him for his kindness. With a sad look such as I had never before seen on his face, he asked me:

"Do you know why I came to the door with you? Because we shall not see each other again."

"But I shall be back at the latest in a month."

"May be. But we shan't meet again."

When I did come back a month later Fr. Leopoldo was already in Heaven.

And Giovanni Mattiello: *On one of the last days of his life I went up to his cell to confession. I told him that my wife was also anxious to go to confession. I was greatly moved at the time and can never forget the incident. Immediately, with a great effort, he went down to the church and heard her confession.*

But the pains, the sadness and the anguish of spirit grew ever worse and in this crucible of supreme trial Fr. Leopoldo found solace in turning to Our Lady. He had loved her so much she could not possibly forsake him.

He prayed constantly to her and asked others to do so as well.

In July he wrote twice to a friend urging him to pray to Our Lady for him. The combination of his own suffering and the love and faith with which he regarded the Blessed Virgin make it impossible to read the letters without emotion.

Today you prayed to Our Blessed Lady for me. (This was in fact true, but Fr. Leopoldo had no human way of knowing it). *Stand secure in the Faith. This Faith tells us that in the Blessed Virgin we have a Mother. Although I cannot claim any rights in the matter, since when man stands before God he is nothing, in fact he is sin since he is the real author of sin, nevertheless God's mercy is infinite and I therefore count absolutely on mercy through the intercession of Our Blessed Lady. I certainly need it, for I am aware of all my weaknesses. But the Blessed Virgin is Our Mother and that is enough.*

A few days later: *I have the most crying need that Our Blessed Lady will have pity on me. May her mother's heart look at me and have pity on this poor creature. You know my state of health. I will hope in her, before God, even if she has to leave my prayers unanswered. She is a mother. She is the moral fount of mercy, the Mother of Mercy rather. Therefore I will hope in her. She is a mother, and that is enough. Please intercede with her for me.*

The Blessed Virgin, as a good mother, did not leave his prayers unanswered but was always at his side to sustain him in his great trial.

At the beginning of July Fr. Leopoldo had the great consolation of being able to see once more his spiritual director, Fr. Odorico of Pordenone. From his words he derived great comfort and support in overcoming the tribulations which all but overwhelmed him.

Although subjecting His servant to the severest trials, God did not abandon him, but comforted him with extraordinary graces and favours, making it clear to him that his great suffering was destined to accomplish even greater perfection in his soul.

Fr. Leopoldo was aware of this. Two days before his death he wrote: *Put my case to the divine charity of the Sacred Heart of Jesus. May He, Who deigns to give me signs of that infinite charity, have mercy on me; may I become His perfect servant.*

Fr. Leopoldo had always had a great fear of death and now that it was approaching with rapid strides he felt all the agony of that fear, a fear largely inspired by his own humility. A few days before he died he said to a fellow Capuchin, "I have always been afraid of death. And why not, when even Jesus trembled before it and asked that the bitter chalice might be removed? However, what worries me is not the physical disintegration so much as the thought of the Judgment after death, for I am a sinner. May God have mercy on me."

The evening before his death he suffered a tremendous crisis which, however, passed and left him calm, saying, "The Lord wants it like this: His will be done. Only may He have mercy on me!"

He had another, most noble reason for wishing to live longer. He was so devoured by zeal for the salvation of souls: he sacrificed himself to an heroic degree for them and would have liked to live till the end of the world in order to continue his apostolate in the confessional and give glory to God by reclaiming sinners for Him. He had always asked God to be allowed to work up to the last moment and to die in harness. This wish was granted him.

In the three months of life remaining to him after his return from hospital, he continued his ministry to all intents and purposes as it had been before his illness, his confessional being replaced by his infirmary cell where he received a constant stream of penitents. People could not understand how he managed in his present physical condition, which excited the pity of all who saw him, to have the moral strength to welcome everyone with the same kindness and attention without once showing the least sign of tiredness or irritation.

The day before his death he heard, among others, the confessions of some fifty priests.

Another favour he had always asked was to be allowed to be conscious up to the end in order to be able to dispose his soul for the final great step. Fr. Luca of Carrè, OFM Cap, writes: *It was the evening of 29th July, 1942. After a very hot day, the air was still heavy and muggy. Two young friars had accompanied Fr. Leopoldo into the garden so that he might get a bit of the fresh evening air. We sat down on a low wall by a well. Conversation was slow and halting, for Fr. Leopoldo could hardly hold himself upright. His voice was charged with subtle overtones. We spoke about one of our number who was sick and who from his age and the nature of his illness, was reduced to a state bordering upon unconsciousness. After a moment's silence, Fr. Leopoldo said sadly, "A miserable business, to appear before God unconscious." He said it so emphatically that I have never forgotten it. The next morning, watching him accompanying silently with his lips the Prayers for the Dying, I realized that his plea to be allowed to appear before God perfectly conscious of his own actions had been heard.*

His last night on earth was spent by Fr. Leopoldo almost entirely in prayer. The Brother Infirmarian stayed with him a long time until he was sent away. "Go and get some rest, you are tired. I'll give you the Blessing." About midnight another Brother, Fra Giorgio of Bassano, came in and found him at prayer. He stayed with him a bit and asked him to hear his confession. In a mere thread of a voice Fr. Leopoldo answered his usual, "Here I am! At your service!" After they had prayed a bit together, Fr. Leopoldo said, "You go to bed too, but look in first at the infirmary chapel and pay my respects to Our Lord."

He was alone. Did he know that his last hour was come? Nobody can say he did, for he gave no clear sign, but he certainly had some awareness of it. The sensitiveness which his soul had developed, and his close union with God as the result of a whole life of preparation, must certainly have given him some indication of what was going to happen. That night must have been devoted almost entirely to preparation for meeting his God.

30th July, 1942. As was his habit, Fr. Leopoldo was up very early to make his preparation for Mass and spent nearly an hour in prayer in the infirmary chapel. At half past six he went into the sacristy to vest, but a sudden attack caused him to faint. He was carried to bed. He came to and seemed to regain strength, even wanting to get up and say Mass, but almost immediately another attack brought him to death's door. Perfectly conscious he received Extreme Unction from the Father Vicar, Father Marcellino of Cartigliano, with perfect resignation to the Divine Will. In the meantime the Father Guardian had arrived who then recited the *Commendatio animæ*—the prayers for a departing soul—to which he added three times the *Hail Mary* and then the *Hail, Holy Queen.*

Slowly, his voice growing ever weaker, Fr. Leopoldo repeated the prayers word by word. With his last breath he repeated, "O clement, O loving, O sweet Virgin Mary," and died.

One cannot doubt that Our Lady, whom he loved so much and had recourse to so often, was at his side at this moment to accompany him before the throne of God to receive the reward of his heroic virtues. Such anyway the impression of those present. Fr. Beniamino testifies: *I was present during his last moments and I have no hesitation in believing that his passage into eternity was helped by a vision of the great Mother of God.*

Fr. Leopoldo was dead. But there was no sign of it on his face. He might have gone quietly to sleep. In the solemn majesty of death, he as almost transfigured, rather, so great a peace and so much nobility were to be seen on his countenance.

It was seven o'clock in the morning.

The sad news spread like lightning through the city and the villages, raising a wave of sorrow and the cry, "A saint is dead!"

Almost at once began an influx of people wanting to take a last look at his mortal remains. Labourers from the fields and factories competed with high civil and ecclesiastical dignitaries to express their great sorrow.

No longer would Fr. Leopoldo's hand be raised in absolution to wipe away so many sorrows, no longer would his lips pronounce the words of resurrection and comfort, no longer would his glance penetrate and illuminate souls.

All felt they had lost a guide, a consoler and the father of their souls, but the sorrow they felt was a calm sorrow, almost turning to joy with the realization that from his place in Heaven he would follow and protect them more closely than ever.

The whole of this day too the crowds were enormous. Not only the room itself and the church, but the whole Piazza di S. Croce was teeming with people. Round the body itself the scene was most moving: everyone wanted to touch it, or place rosaries, holy pictures and other objects of piety on it to be kept thereafter as relics. Everywhere one heard the same phrases. "He was a saint! He did so much good for my soul! Father Leopoldo, pray for us!"

Even children approached the body, kissing it without fear. One small girl stood gazing for a long time and then turned to her small companion, "Look! Isn't he like Jesus?"

Those who had given the matter any thought had expected some sort of demonstration when Fr. Leopoldo died, but nothing on the scale of what actually took place. It was calculated that on that one day alone 25,000 people passed before the bier. Police were necessary to control the crowds. It was only with the greatest difficulty that the doors could be closed that evening, for people were still coming in their hundreds.

The next day, 1st August, the funeral took place.

The church was opened at five o'clock and the influx of visitors began at once, repeating the scenes of the previous day. Masses were said without pause until 10 o'clock and Holy Comunion was given to thousands.

At 9 o'clock the body was brought into the church, which was immediately packed. The square, too, was black with people. All the City Authorities, civil and ecclesiastical, were present. The Bishop, unavoidably absent, was represented by his Vicar General, Mgr. Giuseppe Pretto. The Mayor was also present: "Where the people are, there must their Mayor also be." And the religious Orders and Convents were also well represented.

The Father Provincial, Fr. Girolamo of Fellette, arrived and saw at once that it would not be practicable to have the service in the friary church since not more than a small part of those present could get inside. At the request of many people, he decided that the service should be transferred to the Servite church where there would be room for all.

A procession was immediately formed, the bier being carried by priests of the friary. The mass of people moved a human river towards the new venue while numerous police kept order. For more than two hours traffic had to be suspended in the main thoroughfare of the city since it was packed solid with people following the cortège.

As the cortège passed, people appeared at windows, many throwing flowers, while many of those in the streets knelt. Those who could do so, touched the bier and crossed themselves.

Arived at the Servite church, the funeral service was celebrated by the Provincial assisted by members of the Community, but it was found that even this great church could not hold all those who wanted to attend.

Mgr. Giacomo Gianesini pronounced the funeral oration during which many were moved to tears. He described Fr. Leopoldo's daily work in the following terms.

"He has not left behind writings and publications to draw the attention of the learned, but on the souls of innumerable people thirsting after justice and peace he has written in indelible characters words and memories that will never fade; he did not move crowds with the flow and force of his eloquence, but with evangelical simplicity he gave to thousands upon thousands of penitents words of kindness, of forgiveness and of new life; he did not sail the seven seas nor force his way through desert or jungle in search of souls to win for Christ, instead people of every age, of every class and condition, from near and far, came to him to find the Jesus whom they had lost; he founded no charitable institutions, but like the Good Samaritan poured the oil and wine of Christian Charity in generous measure into wounds both material and moral of so many suffering hearts. He bound their wounds; in hearts darkened by sin or doubt he caused the sun of truth to shine anew; to souls burdened by the weight of human suffering he brought that peace which the world cannot give, the peace of Jesus; he was not endowed with exterior charm, but he had another charm, one which does not fade with the years but in chosen souls grows ever stronger, the charm of kindness, of virtue, of sanctity, a charm which informed his every word and gesture and which conquered all who had the good fortune to meet him."

After the ceremony the cortège was reformed and moved to Piazza Castello where the final farewell took place. By public demand, the body was not buried but placed in a sarcophagus above ground.

For several days all the city newspapers devoted long articles to the deceased, mourning the loss of so great a figure. Two articles are quoted in part.

Avvenire d'Italia 1st August. *The Sorrow and Gratitude of the City.*

Now that Padua has lost her humble, almost invisible guide, a deep void is felt amongst us. To feel this and to mourn his loss not only constitutes homage and gratitude to Fr. Leopoldo for his daily work amongst us, it is also an act of faith in the sublime sacrament of grace which he dispensed so generously in the name of Jesus Christ.

The sighs which rise from so many hearts and the tears which fall from so many eyes are witnesses to the pure joy which he gave and continues to give to souls.

The demonstrations of affection and grief at his funeral today constitute a solemn proclamation, are the highest apotheosis of the divine ministry of confession. To any unbeliever who considers confession too great a burden, or as something hateful, we can say, "Look! Today a people weeps and prays because it has lost one who was a minister of this sacrament of forgiveness, reconciliation and peace."

Il Gazzettino 2nd August. *Fr. Leopoldo's imposing funeral.*

Crowds in and around S. Croce, crowds in the Corso Vittorio Emmanuele, in the Prato della Valle, in the Via Umberto and the Via

Roma, crowds in the Servite Church, all because the people wanted to be present at the funeral of the Capuchin Fr. Leopoldo, all bearing witness to the fascination that is exercised by spiritual forces working on souls through the simple, straightforward ways of the Lord.

Strangers, people from Trieste, Milan, Turin, Rome and as far afield as Naples, because in so many years of his apostolate the humble Capuchin, who occupied so little space in this world, whose body was as it were the mere physical elements of a body held to this earth solely by the great faith which informed it, this humble friar was able to dispense full-handed consolation to all who came to him in Padua to be reconciled to God on the occasion of pilgrimages from every part of the country. People who wished to honour him and join in the public expression of gratitude to one who would certainly not have wished it in his lifetime though, from Heaven, he could more easily appreciate the motive of so many grateful hearts.

Letters of condolence arrived from all over Italy, from all classes of people, mourning with one voice the loss of their spiritual father and proclaiming the sanctity of his heroic virtues.

Space forbids the quotation of more than a few.

The Most Reverend Fr. Donatus, Minister General of the Capuchins, wrote from Rome: *I am not surprised at the popular "canonization" of our lamented Fr. Leopoldo, as I should not be surprised were the Church, the one competent authority in the matter, one day to recognize this verdict officially. During the few days I was in Padua I had the distinct impression of being in the presence of a saint, albeit hidden away in his profound humility, in a fervent interior life,* abscondita cum Christo in Deo. *For our beloved Veneto Province it is yet another glory, but I am well aware that it is also a great loss. In Heaven Fr. Leopoldo will be the protector and mediator for his beloved Province and for the whole Order, while he can rejoice in the reward he has earned to crown his holy life.*

His spiritual director, Fr. Odorico of Pordenone, from Fiume: *We have lost a saint! I knew Fr. Leopoldo intimately for more than sixty years and can say that from his seminary days his soul belonged to God. He was always the same, always united to the Lord.*

One can say without fear of contradiction that his life was lived in God, with God and for God, with the lively desire to apply the merits of Our Lord to the good of souls. Since early youth all his actions were offered through Mary to God for the return of the Eastern Schismatics to union with the Catholic Church.

The words of his intimate friend Don Giovanni Calabria were few but moving: *The venerable and saintly Fr. Leopoldo is in Paradise watching over us, praying for us and waiting for us. His death was a great personal sorrow for me.*

Signora Giulia Tessaro, of Padua: *The death of Fr. Leopoldo has moved and saddened us profoundly. In the morning, I went to see the body and I wept and prayed, overcome with grief. In the afternoon I came again with my husband and son, exactly as if it were a pilgrimage to the tomb of a saint. And he really looked like a saint, so peaceful was he. We have lost a great benefactor, a valued adviser, and the source of our consolation. How often have I been to him with despair in my heart and come away completely at peace.*

We shall never forget him, but we shall continue to turn to him, for we have such need of his intercession. We feel that a saint has died. This is the general opinion of the people of Padua and of the enormous crowd, including people from all the neighbouring villages, which has been gathering in the last few days to pay homage to his blessed remains.

The *Trigesimo* (1) was the occasion for another great demonstration of affection.

Since the friary church and that of the Servites had both proved too small for the actual funeral service, it was decided to have the *Trigesimo* in the Basilica of St. Anthony so that all could attend.

It was a moving affair, the basilica being packed out as it is only on very great occasions. Most of those present were Fr. Leopoldo's spiritual children, gathered together to give expression to their grief at the loss of their guide, counsellor, consoler and spiritual father.

In the centre of the black-and-silver draped sanctuary stood the

---

(1) Commemorative service celebrated 30 days after death.

catafalque surrounded by massed flowers and flowering shrubs and flanked by ten elaborate funeral candles.

Among those present were the Bishop of Padua and representatives of the Cathedral Chapter, clergy of the Basilica, representatives of all Religious Orders in the city and high civil dignitaries.

The solemn Requiem was celebrated by Fr. Clemente of S. Maria in Punta, Provincial Secretary at the time.

At the end of Mass the V. Rev. Don Giuseppe Andreotti, a professor at the University of Padua, gave the funeral address in which he magnificently portrayed in a voice charged with emotion the singular virtues of Fr. Leopoldo, laying especial stress on his humility and his fervent zeal for souls.

Among other things he said, "How different are God's ways from ours! The whole history of religion demonstrates how much He abhors material greatness, pomp and worldy power, loving instead humility, showering upon the humble the abundance of His gifts, and choosing humility as the foundation upon which He builds, as the field for His divine operations and the instrument for the realization of His designs.

"Today we are commemorating a man who is one of the best proofs of this divine economy. If Humility had to take human shape it could not do better than take that of Fr. Leopoldo.

"For a long time he appeared even to the members of his own community to be a star of the very smallest magnitude, following its appointed path in silence and unobserved. Seen through the proper lens, however, he appeared as a star of the first magnitude, and the lens which allowed one to observe, study and recognize all the splendours of this star, by which I mean all the treasures of heart and mind of Fr. Leopoldo, was Confession."

After reviewing all the wonders achieved by Fr. Leopoldo in the lowliness of his cell during his many years of ministry, and considering the many lessons he had left, particularly for those who like himself devoted themselves to the salvation of souls through the Sacrament of Penance, he concluded his address as follows.

"'A Saint has died!' was the cry raised by a whole people when his death was announced. No wonder, for Fr. Leopoldo was one of those sovereign spirits whom one should approach, as the poet says, on mentally bended knees; he was one of those privileged spirits who reach a high peak of Christian virtue, a peak all the higher in comparison with the depth of mediocrity from which we view it.

"Let us also say, 'Fr. Leopoldo was a Saint' and if it is permitted to express a wish, which I believe to be that of all of us, laity and clergy alike, it is that the dear remains of Fr. Leopoldo should soon return to his place of work, to that small cell whose unadorned walls, poor arm-chair and cheap *prie-dieu* will for ever remind us of the mystery of love, the mystery of charity."

The anniversary of Fr. Leopoldo's death was celebrated in the friary church in the presence of a great crowd. Before the service, the celebrant, Mgr. Giuseppe Pretto, Vicar General of the Diocese, gave an address which included the following.

"A year has passed already since the death of our beloved Father, but his memory has not dimmed. Gratitude and veneration for him remain alive in the hearts of all who knew him. Today's commemoration which has brought so many of you together is clear proof of this. This same commemoration, while offering a welcome opportunity to express the lively sense of gratitude to Fr. Leopoldo for all the good he did to our souls, invites us also to persevere in the spirit of faithfulness and love of Our Lord which he knew so well how to instil in the hearts of all who came to him.

"The fame of Fr. Leopoldo's virtue is daily spreading wider, and this too is a benefit which he continues to work among us and for which we should be grateful."

All the local papers had references to the anniversary. On 31st July, under the title *Fr. Leopoldo*, the *Gazzettino* carried the following.

To day, no less impressively and with the same large crowd taking part, Padua renewed its tribute in honour of Fr. Leopoldo.

Fra Masseo once asked St. Francis, "Why does everyone follow you, and everyone want to see you and hear you and obey you? You are not good to look at, nor learned, nor noble. Why then does everyone follow you?" The same question, appropriately rephrased, might be put when one thinks of the fascination exercised by Fr. Leopoldo in the silence of the friary of S. Croce. Small, negligible, halting in gait and in speech, not a preacher, nor a writer, never holding office within his Order, a man of no attractions and of no apparent importance by worldly standards, he was yet sought after and venerated as a saint.

And he was a saint, above all on account of his humility. In his presence one knew at once that there was nothing unreal about his exceptionally humble bearing, that he had to a superlative degree a genuinely low opinion of himself.

He possessed a very tender heart, most sensitive to spiritual trouble, to poverty and all forms of suffering. He was full of Christian humanitas *which made him feel a man among men, a neighbour to all: and he loved them all without distinction and wanted to bring them all to his own heights, not with elaborate methods and formulas but with the utmost simplicity.*

It was for this reason that so great and varied a mass of people came to him, and for each soul he had the appropriate word.

Very early, before the sun was up, he celebrated Mass and then went immediately to his confessional, that tiny cell which he left only when it was once more dark. That was where his apostolate lay, that was where he dispensed brotherly exhortation, wise counsel and comfort. No one left there unconsoled.

It is known that on several occasions he accurately foretold the future, but he did not want people to know about it. People esteemed him a saint, and he had his work cut out to counter this belief which he abhorred.

Generously indulgent with others, Fr. Leopoldo was very strict with himself in the matter, for example, of fasting and abstinence and vigils. He ate, not the necessary minimum but something less, and this perhaps hastened his death.

Yesterday's ceremonies in honour of Fr. Leopoldo are evidence that the truly humble and unassuming benefactors of mankind live on in death.

CHAPTER XXI.

«MEMORIA IUSTI ERIT IN ÆTERNUM»

Asked one day whether Our Lord's words about taking up our cross and following Him meant we should undertake special penances, Father Leopoldo replied, "Special penances are not necessary. It is enough that we bear with patience the tribulations which life brings, the misunderstandings, the ingratitude, the humiliations, the sufferings, caused by changes of season or circumstances. They are the cross which sin has placed on the shoulders of man and which God willed as a means to our redemption.

"But in order that these tribulations be efficacious for our soul's good, we must not seek to flee them entirely, always wanting to be in the right, having immediate recourse to medicines, to relief from burdens, avoiding the summer's heat by retreating to the mountains or the sea (unless it is really necessary) and protecting ourselves by any means from the winter's cold. This is not the proper Christian spirit; this is not accepting our cross and following Jesus but fleeing from it. People who suffer only what they cannot somehow avoid are not thereby acquiring merit."

After his long day of work, Fr. Leopoldo left us for his final rest in God, but his memory has not faded. For the great majority of mankind including those who in their grandeur and power in life seem almost immortal, the tomb means the end of everything on earth. Tombstones may be inscribed, more or less truthfully, monuments may be raised in stone or bronze to defy the centuries, but they cease to command people's interest or to raise a spark of feeling or affection.

But it is not so with those who in this world abandoned all for God, consecrated themselves entirely to Him and, with heroic sacrifice, sought only His glory. God has undertaken to keep their memory fresh, for—in the words of the Psalmist—"The memory of the just man shall not perish; men shall remember him for ever."

This promise had been, and is being, kept in a wonderful manner in the case of Fr. Leopoldo.

The solemn manifestations at his funeral were not only the last tribute of affection and gratitude from a whole people, they were also the beginning of a new life of love and affection which grows daily.

On his earthly pilgrimage he had always wanted to remain completely hidden and never wanted people to talk about him, and God granted this wish; but after his blessed death humility had nothing more to fear, so God wished to glorify him to an exceptional degree.

His tomb became at once a place of pilgrimage and is always heaped with flowers. So, too, the confessional cell. Fr. Leopoldo had said that the church and the friary would be bombed, but not the confessional cell. "God has shown to much mercy to souls here that it must remain as a memorial to His kindness."

Was this the expression of a pious hope, an affection for the poor walls which had been the scene of his long sacrifice and had become almost a part of him, or was it the expression of a clear prophetic vision granted by God?

The fact remains that the cell was untouched among the bombed ruins and is still there to testify to God's goodness and the virtues of His faithful servant. Fr. Leopoldo is no longer there with his poor body martyred by illness and sacrifice, but he is there in spirit, in his great spirit. One really feels his presence, everyone is agreed about that. Many people say they have visited famous shrines and admired the buildings and trappings but have not experienced what they feel here. "Here I feel the presence of God, I feel overcome by a desire to be better, to love my neighbour, to be at peace with everyone but above all with Him." For many this is the beginning of a reformation of life. How often have people passed through that cell to go on into the church and ask for someone to hear their confession.

One incident shall be recorded. A group of foreigners was standing about listening to one of the priests talking about the great sacrifices Fr. Leopoldo had made for the conversion of souls. A little to one side an elderly distinguished-looking man was listening attentively. Suddenly his eyes filled with tears and he said aloud for all to hear, "And I haven't been to confession for forty years..." He went back alone into the little cell where we can imagine that the spirit of Father Leopoldo welcomed him with his customary enthusiasm. Be that as it may, very soon the man was asking for a priest to hear his confession.

Many non-Catholics visit the cell and hear about Fr. Leopoldo's great work. Often they become thoughtful, ask for a picture of him. For more than a few, the visit to the cell has been the starting point of conversion to Catholicism.

Fr. Leopoldo is really still present in his confessional cell and welcomes all who come to him. Around him, even more than previously, a whole world of souls is in motion. In a corner there is a large book in which many people write down their needs or desires for him. One could almost say they talk to him, for what they write is informal and frank. They feel that he is there and have complete confidence that he will hear and comfort them.

These volumes, and there are many, are filled with human sorrows, material wishes, spiritual anguish, physical suffering, family disasters. But another aspect strikes the reader, the number of requests for purely spiritual graces: the grace of a good confession, the reform of a sinner, the grace to keep away from sin... Fr. Leopoldo is still at his old job of bringing souls to God and getting them an increase of grace.

Another thing which strikes one about these books is the affectionate tone of the writings. They are no stereotyped phrases, but warm, loving words addressed to a father, a brother or a friend, the expression of a feeling experienced by everyone who remembers Fr. Leopoldo.

They all say, "I feel near him. I don't feel impelled to honour him but to love him." And this is true of everyone without distinction of age or class, though young people and children are especially fond of him. How many mothers come to bring their children who will not leave them in peace till they are brought! And when they come and see a picture of Fr. Leopoldo they greet it with cries of familiar love and respect and perhaps run off to get him a flower.

This is true not only of the people of Padua but also of people from all over the world. One page of one of the books, for instance, bears the signature of a Cardinal, the thanks of a Jewish journalist from Paris and the petition of a woman from the Philippines.

* * *

In his life time Fr. Leopoldo remained shut in his confessional-cell to attend to the souls that came to him to make their peace with God. Now, this is not enough. He wants to cover the world in his search for souls to bring back to God—and he is not doing badly, for there is hardly a corner of the globe where he is not known.

Humanly speaking it is inexplicable how, after a life that was completely hidden from world, a life in which he did nothing spectacular and undertook no work that could draw public attention, within a very short time after his death, knowledge of him and devotion to him should have spread so widely and so rapidly. The short biography has been translated into fifteen languages, always at the pressing demand of the faithful, and edition has followed edition. Various editions of this work have appeared: the sixth German edition, for instance was already exhausted in July 1960. The Novena prayers appear in no less than thirty different languages.

Various institutions in his name have been opened in different parts of the world: free schools, associations for the teaching of Christian Doctrine, orphanages, hospitals for the needy. The last in Italy and in Brazil at Belo Horizonte.

Fr. Leopoldo has penetrated behind the iron curtain and the peoples there have adopted him as patron and have frequent recourse to him in this hour of trial. They defy any danger to have a picture of him or a relic. The Jugoslav Capuchins have translated the biography into Croatian and Slovenian and with admirable patience cyclostyled three editions. In the Near East, too, Fr. Leopoldo is venerated. Even Mahommedans invoke him and ask our missionaries for his picture.

Fr. Leopoldo is thus fulfilling in Heaven the mission to the Eastern peoples which he could not explicitly do on earth.

He hears and answers innumerable pleas from all over the world as well. Innumerable letters of thanks from every continent testify to this.

Urged by the vast popular movement centred round Fr. Leopoldo, the Church started in 1946 the Process of Beatification.

The Diocesan Informative Process was completed in 1952 and reported to Rome and the documentary account of its transactions is now in the possession of the Sacred Congregation of Rites awaiting the Apostolic Process.

Many are the cardinals, bishops, prelates, priests and religious houses, and laity of all classes and conditions who have written to the Holy Father asking for the glorification of the humble Servant of God as a shining example of the love of God and his neighbour, a love for which he sacrificed his whole life in the humble but so effective ministry of the confessional.

Whether he will be canonized or not awaits the decision of the Church. One thing is certain, that innumerable people in every corner of the world devoutly wish it.

Faxit Deus!

CHAPTER XXII.

ECHO FROM THE EAST

"...when better days dawn (as they certainly will), the magnificent figure of Fr. Leopoldo will be the sure guide to peace of hearts and souls in God, since he knew, as few other men in our time, how to infuse the peace of God in the confessional into hearts saddened and broken with suffering."

† CARD. LUIGI STEPINAC
(1898-1960)

Krasic,
26th Sept., 1959

Fr. Leopoldo had considered the purpose of his whole life to be to achieve the salvation of the dissident Eastern peoples by their return to Catholic Unity. To his end he had sacrificed himself daily in a severe martyrdom. He desired, as far as his strength allowed, to gain this grace for his separated brethren. But his sacrifice, his prayers, his fervent vows, all remained hidden, known to God alone.

Now after his death we have the first marvel. God wanted everyone to know what he had done; in a truly inexplicable way the account of his hidden sacrifice penetrated near and far into the East, causing considerable stir. A mysterious voice sounded in the heart of these people telling them that for more than sixty years one of their number had been offering himself to God as a victim for them. All this merit is before God and the resultant blessings will come down on us.

The name of Fr. Leopoldo, previously unknown, has become a pledge of grace and salvation. In Hungary, Bulgaria, Greece, Turkey and other Near East countries, in Egypt, Eritrea and many other African countries, to say nothing of India and the Far East, the servant of God is known and venerated.

Jugoslavia needs special mention, particularly Slovenia and Croatia, where one can say there is scarcely a house without a picture of him.

In the face of enormous difficulties the Slovene and Croat Capuchins have translated the biography; the Croatian version has run through three cyclostyled editions. Many articles have appeared in Catholic papers and diocesan magazines recounting incidents from his life, particularly those relating to his apostleship of reunion. He is often publicly commemorated and prayers for his beatification offered at meetings of clergy and the faithful.

High ecclesiastical authorities also regard Fr. Leopoldo as a new light born of their native land to bring peace and comfort.

Cardinal Stepinac, Archbishop of Zagreb, martyr for freedom and the faith, himself wrote an introduction to the Croatian biography.

"God has chosen the weak things of this world to confound the strong," says St. Paul to the Corinthians. These words can be applied to Fr. Leopoldo.

This man, of no great physical stature and of weak constitution, was a giant of the spirit, which spirit he used in the service of God to lighten the burden for innumerable souls, to awaken their attention to the things of eternity and to encourage them in virtue.

Those who read the biography of Fr. Leopoldo are compelled to wonder and to praise God, Who is inscrutable in His designs, strong in putting them into effect, holy in operation, and infinitely good to His creatures. This book will be of immense spiritual value to all who know God, and will strenghten their Faith, Hope and Charity in these days when there is a conspiracy at work to erase the consciousness of God from the minds of men.

Above all it will be a great joy for the Croatian people since it was a son of our land whom God in His goodness has been pleased to guide into a way of life which was a supreme example to us all, particularly in its lesson of perseverance in good.

† LUIGI STEPINAC
Abp. of Zagreb

Zagreb,
12th July, 1946

On 10th October, 1946 Mgr. Butorac, Bishop of Cattaro, wrote to the Bishop of Padua.

I consider it an honour to be able, by this letter, to introduce myself to Your Excellency as Ordinary of the Diocese of Cattaro, the diocese which gave birth to that great Capuchin Fr. Leopoldo Mandić. He is the glory of our two dioceses; let us hope that he will intercede for us before the throne of God.

It is already some months since I instructed my clergy to offer public prayers for the beatification of Fr. Leopoldo.

The Croatian Capuchins have translated the interesting Italian biography written by the Venetian Capuchins, who best knew this modest soul that never wanted to be talked about, but alas! there are very few copies since they have not yet been able to print it.

For my part I say Mass for his beatification and I have complete faith in his powerful intercession.

May I express my deep gratitude and esteem for Your Excellency's exceptional zeal in the Cause of Fr. Leopoldo. We in the meantime are praying unceasingly that God will deign to glorify His servant.

On 25th September, 1952, the Bishops of Jugoslavia, meeting at Zagreb, sent a letter to the Pope asking that the Beatification Process be opened, assuring him that the glorification of this son of their land would bring great comfort to the faithful in the tribulations of the present day and would be a sure pledge of the return of the many Christians who have strayed far from the fold of Peter.

The letter is signed by all twenty-one bishops present.

The following wrote personally to the Pope:

Mgr. Garković, Bishop of Zara
Mgr. Butorac, now Bishop of Ragusa
Mgr. Vovk, Bishop of Ljubljana
Very Rev. Fr. Magjerec, Rector of the Illyrian College of St. Jerome
Mgr. Heilbach, Professor of Theology at Zagreb.

All emphasize the work of Fr. Leopoldo for the redemption of the Eastern peoples and see in his beatification a powerful means towards Catholic Unity.

* * *

Such great ardour in making sacrifices for the salvation of the Eastern peoples became, as it were, the keynote of Fr. Leopoldo's apostolate as is clearly brought out by the Papal Decree authorizing the Apostolic Process.

This document is of such importance and brings Fr. Leopoldo's work so well into focus that we reproduce it in its entirety.

PAPAL DECREE

AUTHORIZING THE APOSTOLIC PROCESS FOR THE BEATIFICATION AND CANONIZATION OF FATHER LEOPOLDO

(Private translation)

St. Paul, Apostle of the Gentiles, fired by zeal for the salvation of his Jewish brethren, went so far as to say: "It has ever been my wish that I myself might be doomed to separation from Christ, if that would benefit my brethren, my own kinsmen by race." (Rom. IX, 3.)

These words can be applied to the Servant of God, Fr. Leopoldo, professed priest of the Order of Friars Minor Capuchin, because of the very special love he had for his brethren separated from Catholic unity.

He was born on 12th May, 1866, at Castelnovo near Kotor in Dalmatia, and at his baptism was given the significant name of Bogdan (Adeodatus). His parents, Peter A. Mandić and Caroline Zarević, were noted for their integrity of life, purity of faith and cultivation of piety, and they took pains to provide the twelve children sent them by God with a sound Christian education.

It was within this family that the Servant of God began, from a very early age, to cultivate the Christian virtues, especially devotion to the Blessed Sacrament of the Eucharist and to the Virgin Mother of God, as well as obedience and purity. At eighteen he left his family and the world and entered the Venetian Province of the Capuchins among whom he was given the name of Leopoldo. He made his profession of simple vows on 5th May, 1885, and having duly completed his studies was ordained priest on 20th September, 1890.

Understanding clearly that he was called by Divine Providence to work for the return of his separated brethren, especially those of the

Eastern Churches and those among his own people, he allowed nothing to distract him from becoming a fit instrument for this purpose. On being transferred, while still a young priest, to another friary of the Province, he thought that he was to go to his native land to undertake at last his mission of bringing dissidents back to unity. But as soon as he knew that this was not to be, he submitted to the will of his Superiors, offering to God this disappointment, and himself as victim, for his separated brethren. Moreover, he bound himself by a vow, which he renewed at frequent intervals, to consecrate his whole life and all the labours of his ministry to this apostolate.

Even though he was unable to go to these eastern countries, Leopoldo was, in fact, none the less an effective apostle to their peoples. The prayer and supplication he offered for this apostolate, the sacrifices he made and the self-denial he practised for it, the difficulties he encountered, the anxieties and the physical and spiritual suffering he joyfully bore—all these are known only to God who reads our hearts and minds.

His way of life was simple. Having celebrated Mass at an early hour each morning, he went to his confessional cell and remained there for the rest of the day at the disposal of his penitents. He kept to this routine for forty years with never a word of complaint about the excessive cold in winter or the overpowering heat in summer, nor about the many aches and pains he continually suffered. He was afflicted with a stomach ailment which was later diagnosed as cancer and which spread to the oesophagus. He slept very little and when urged to rest longer, to spare himself or to take care of himself, he replied that it was not permissible for him to do so since he had to pray for his penitents and expiate the sins of others. Besides all his physical ills, he was sorely tried by spiritual conflicts and sufferings.

At length, having borne all these things with the greatest patience, and fortified by the Sacraments and prayers of the Church, he died on 30th July, 1942, in Padua where most of his life had been spent.

It is extraordinary how swiftly and how widely the reputation for sanctity of the Servant of God Leopoldo of Castelnovo spread and is still spreading in almost every corner of the globe. Clear evidence of this is provided by the very numerous letters requesting the introduction of his Cause which have been sent to the Roman Pontiff by cardinals, archbishops, bishops and major superiors of religious Orders and Congregations. Scarcely four years after the death of the Servant of God the Diocesan Process was opened, and the large number of witnesses examined in the course of the enquiry included six archbishops and bishops as well as a great number of priests, university professors and doctors of medicine.

The Sacred Congregation of Rites, having duly examined and discussed his writings, declared on 2nd April, 1954, that there was no obstacle to the continuation of the Process.

In due course, on 15th May, 1962, at the instance of the Very Reverend Father Bernardine of Siena, Postulator General of the Order of Friars Minor Capuchin, the Most Eminent and Reverend Cardinal Arcadio M. Larraona, Prefect of the Sacred Congregation of Rites and Relator of the said Cause, at an ordinary session of the same Congregation held at the Vatican, moved the resolution that the Commission for the Introduction of the Cause be approved, and gave an account of its progress. The Most Eminent and Reverend Fathers, when they had received the report and had heard the views of the prelates officially intervening in the Cause, particularly that of the Reverend Father Ferdinando Antonelli, O.F.M., Promoter General of the Faith, decreed *that the Commission be approved, if it so please the Holy Father.*

Accordingly, an account of these proceedings was on this day laid before the Holy Father, Pope John XXIII, by the said Promoter General of the Faith, and His Holiness, approving the motion of the Sacred Congregation of Rites, was pleased to sign with his own hand the Commission for the Introduction of the Cause of the Servant of God, Leopoldo of Castelnovo.

Given at Rome, the twenty-fifth day of May, in the year of Our Lord One Thousand Nine Hundred and Sixty-two.

ARCADIO M. LARRAONA, *Prefect*
ENRICO DANTE, *Secretary*

APPENDIX

FAVOURS RECEIVED

Owing to the vast numbers of favours attributed to Fr. Leopoldo only a tithe of the more interesting cases are quoted. In order to increase the effective content of the limited space at our disposal, many of the accounts have been condensed from the more detailed signed reports in the archives.

In conformity with Church ruling, we repeat that for these accounts no more is asked than the human faith one accords to the reports of serious and honest persons.

Typhus

Mario Barugolo was admitted to hospital with typhus in June, 1942. His condition grew worse and there were cardiac complications. By the end of July he was unconscious, with a pulse of 160 and high fever. The doctors considered his case hopeless. On 29th July he was not expected to live through the night.

On 30th he was still alive and his sister, having heard Fr. Leopoldo spoken of as a saint, went to Padua to ask his blessing for her brother, only to hear on arrival that he himself had died that morning.

Seeing her distress, one of the priests said, "Don't lose heart! Fr. Leopoldo's first favour from Heaven will be for your brother. Pray to him with faith."

Taking a handkerchief from her, the priest blessed it, placed it a moment on the body of Fr. Leopoldo and gave it back to her.

Returning at once to the hospital in Venice, she placed the handkerchief on the breast of her brother who was showing no signs of life. She and other members of the family began to pray Fr. Leopoldo. Improvement began at once. The fever dropped, the cardiac disturbances ceased, the patient regained consciousness and was soon completely well again.

Diphtheria

At the beginning of January, 1943 Sergio Soldà, aged seven, was struck by severe diphtheria. His distracted parents had one hope: at his birth Sergio had been miraculously protected by Fr. Leopoldo who was then still living. They prayed to him with the utmost confidence to save their child.

In the meantime the disease followed its course, which every one thought would end in death: already a tracheotomy had been necessary to permit breathing. The crisis was due during the night of 15th, but the doctors held out no hope of his surviving it.

The child's mother, in Padua, spent the night in prayer. At home in Monselice the father and other children went to Holy Communion in honour of Fr. Leopoldo. Back in the house shortly afterwards, the father heard an internal voice say quite clearly, "Your son is safe."

In Padua the child's uncle, Prof. Rubaltelli, telephoned the hospital expecting to hear the worst, but in fact was told that to everyone's astonishment the child had lived through the crisis. The improvement had started, and the child had started breathing freely, at the moment his father had heard the voice.

Duodenal ulcer

For six months Gino Franceschi had been suffering from a duodenal ulcer and the pain had reached the point that he could bear it no longer and agreed to an operation. He recommended himself with lively faith to Fr. Leopoldo and immediately felt better. On examining him again, the doctor found no trace of the ulcer.

Saved from bombs

At three in the morning of 8th February, 1944 Padua suffered an intense air raid. Great damage was done and there were many casualties.

The patients of the *Padiglioni* were assembled in the basement in a state bordering on panic. One of the doctors held up a picture of Fr. Leopoldo where all could see it and said, "Let us ask this holy priest to save us!"

They all prayed together and then, on a sudden inspiration, the doctor shouted, "Down, everybody!"

Hardly were they prone when the building was hit by a number of bombs. The blast, even in the basement, was so great that anyone standing would have been thrown against the wall and injured if not killed. As it was, no one was hurt.

Everyone attributed the doctor's sudden inspiration to Fr. Leopoldo, for normally in the basement there would have been no reason for lying down.

Hernia

"On 20th March, 1944, I was due to attend the funeral of my husband who had died on the 17th. For some years I had been suffering from a mild hernia, but as I knelt down to pray the evening before the funeral, it suddenly became acute and was accompanied by great pain.

In the morning, the doctor saw that it was strangulated and ordered me to hospital for an immediate operation since my life was in danger. In the meantime I sent the children off to their father's funeral and remained alone in the house.

I had always had a great devotion to Fr. Leopoldo and my husband had always been to him to confession, so I turned to him now and started to pray. After only ten minutes, while the bells of. St. Giustina were still tolling for my husband, I felt that the hernia had gone back into place of its own accord. Two hours later I got up and I have never had any trouble since ".

Padua, 7th April, 1944 — MARIANA MARCON ved. VISENTINI

Sinovitis

Signorina Facco's acquaintance with Fr. Leopoldo began somewhat miraculously in July, 1939 when she went to ask his advice. There were many women already waiting for his return to the church after the midday break and Signorina Facco was preparing to go away in despair for she had to be back at work and could not afford to wait her turn. Suddenly, however, Fr. Leopoldo arrived and, ignoring the others who were already crowding round him, called her to come first.

In 1942 she got sinovitis in one knee which resisted all treatment. She was away at the seaside doing a cure when she heard of Fr. Leopoldo's death. On her return to Padua she was no better and when the doctors wanted to put her leg in plaster she refused and started a novena to Fr. Leopoldo, dragging herself painfully each morning to his tomb. After three days of this she awoke one morning to find herself completely cured.

Stolen cow returned

"On 19th August, 1944, robbers came in the night and stole our milk-cow which was to all intents and purposes our sole support. As soon as we knew of this disaster in the morning, one of us rushed off to Padua and had a Mass said in honour of Fr. Leopoldo to ask him to have our animal returned.

That night at about eleven o'clock two strangers knocked at the door for us to come down and unlock the byre for the cow they had brought back."

Salboro, 23rd August, 1944 — ARTURO NERICCIO

Stolen ass returned

At two in the morning of 28th April, 1945, armed German soldiers came and took away the Pernumians' donkey. The wife turned at once to Fr. Leopoldo, praying before a picture of him she kept inside the front door.

As soon as the English arrived, the husband went out in search of the ass, covering forty to fifty kilometres a day on foot, but in vain.

During the night of the 3rd May the wife heard a voice calling her and saw Fr. Leopoldo standing before her with a child in his arms. He smiled and said, " Don't cry any more. Your ass is at Bastia di Rovolon, 20 kilometres away. But I want your two small daughters Maria and Agnese to say lots of prayers for poor sinners."

Next morning the husband rushed off to Rovolon and recovered the ass from a beggar who had found it abandoned in a ditch.

Instantaneous cure

In 1942, at the age of seven, Gabriella Tiso hurt her foot while playing. It apparently got better, but in 1944 began to hurt her again and she started to limp. Various doctors tried different treatments but the pain grew worse till the child cried day and night. She could scarcely put her foot to the ground and the whole leg was wasting away.

At Corpus Christi her mother managed with great trouble to get her to the nearby Capuchin church where she took her to the sacristy to ask for a blessing. One of the priests urged her to have recourse to Fr. Leopoldo, blessed the child in his name, and gave her a relic from his habit which the child kissed and hung round her neck.

Coming out of the sacristy, the mother noticed that Gabriella was no longer limping and asked her how she was. She replied that she felt no more pain. That evening she insisted on taking part in the celebrations and from that day to this has had no further trouble.

Cure of thrombophlebitis

On 6th August, 1945, Signora Teresa Bertelle, gave birth to a daughter. Everything went well, but after five days her right leg swelled up with acute thrombophlebitis.

The poor woman, who had five other children to think about as well, had to remain in bed in a state of desperate anxiety.

Wanting a blessing, she sent for Don Andrea, guardian of the Shrine of Our Lady of Grace of Piove. He duly blessed her and suggested having recourse to Fr. Leopoldo, starting a novena in his honour and placing a picture of him on the affected leg.

She did this, and the following morning at six o'clock she felt a sort of shock throughout her body. She tried to move the affected leg . . . and found it completely cured.

Instantaneous cure of glaucoma

For about a year Sister M. Teodora Frassetto had been suffering pain in her left eye. At first it was only occasional and not severe, but later it became continuous and very severe, causing sympathetic pain in the right eye and her whole head. She suffered this for some time without seeing a doctor for fear of hearing an unpleasant diagnosis. Finally in July, 1945, she was examined by an oculist who diagnosed it as a glaucoma requiring immediate operation if the other eye was not to be jeopardized.

But the Sister did not feel able to undergo such a delicate and difficult operation and waited, hoping for God's favour. A few days later, however, the pain was so great that she decided to fix a date for the operation.

She took with her a relic Fr. Leopoldo and on the way prayed fervently to him.

The doctor examined her and said in amazement, " My dear Sister, you no longer need an operation. You're cured, and you may thank God for it."

Osteomyelitis

In January, 1945 Signora Albina Trevisan, was attacked by osteomyelitis in the right jaw.

She was treated in the hospital at Castelfranco and had seven operations but to no effect. A terrible wound had formed and the pain allowed her no rest. Having read a life of Fr. Leopoldo, she turned to him, reciting the novena prayers continually.

On Christmas Eve she was discharged from hospital as incurable. That evening she placed a small relic of Fr. Leopoldo on the sore. She slept peacefully all night and awoke cured. The swelling was gone and the wound closed...

Asthma

Eighteen months old Gabriella Casarin had an attack of bronchial asthma. The specialists of Padua tried every treatment but without effect. The poor child was in a pitiful state. Her mother had recourse to Fr. Leopoldo and on 2nd May, 1945, came to the confessional-cell, prayed at length and touched his picture with a rosary. Then she went home quite certain that he would cure her child. As soon as she arrived, she hung the rosary round the child's neck and she was instantaneously cured and showed no further signs of the illness.

Chronic otitis

"For some years I had been suffering from a purulent discharge from the right ear which had been treated by various specialists in vain. Happening to be at Rovigo, I made an appointment to be examined by Prof. Rubaltelli who diagnosed it as 'chronic suppurating otitis media in the right ear with extensive caries.'

The professor considered a medical cure impossible—enough had already been tried—and proposed a radical surgical operation.

Worried by the thought of such a dangerous operation, I started a novena to Fr. Leopoldo and placed a relic on the affected part. Towards the end of the novena I woke up one morning to find I was in no pain and there was no discharge.

Another examination by Prof. Rubaltelli revealed that the affection had cleared up completely and so it remains after more than a year."

P. Sebastiano OFM Cap.

Padua, 5th May 1947

Arthritis

"In the winter of 1944 I began suffering arthritic pains in my right leg. Movement caused such agony that I could just about walk with the support of a stick. Various remedies were tried but brought no relief. They suggested I should appeal to Fr. Leopoldo and gave me a relic which I placed on the affected limb. A slow improvement began to take place. In spring when we changed our winter habit, the relic was taken off and immediately I became so much worse that I could scarcely walk at all. I begged Fr. Leopoldo's pardon and started to wear the relic again, whereupon the improvement started again and went on to a complete cure."

Bassano del Grappa, 15th January 1945 SISTER MARIA ASSUNTA

Saved from death and cured of deafness

On 2nd May, 1945, five year old Roberto Dottori fell through a skylight some twenty feet into the kitchen below and received a triple fracture at the base of the skull and displacement of the first cervical vertebra.

He was at once taken to hospital, but his condition was desperate. Some of the best known doctors did everything they could for him, but were unanimous in offering no hope of saving him.

The woman at whose house the accident had happened rushed to the hospital with a relic of Fr. Leopoldo which was at once pinned to the child's jacket.

The child's condition remained desperate. On the thirteenth day he opened his eyes, on the eighteenth he spoke his first words. The first miracle was accomplished, his life was saved.

But the injuries had left him completely deaf. A famous specialist after careful examination declared he would never hear again.

As soon as he could walk, his mother and grandmother took Roberto to the Capuchin Friary and to the confessional-cell of Fr. Leopoldo. Suddenly and for no apparent reason the child said aloud, "You will hear." From that moment he began to hear, gradually getting better until his hearing was completely normal.

Otitis

On 15th July, 1945, a child, Giuliano Torresin, had otitis so badly, that the local doctor sent him to hospital. His parents referred the case with great faith to Fr. Leopoldo. On arrival at the hospital, the boy was examined again and no trace of the disease was to be found.

"God is both Doctor and Medicine"

Edvige Bonanni suffered acutely from arthiritic pains in both arms and legs. On 30th July, 1945, she awoke with a start to hear a voice in her ear, "God is both doctor and medicine!" Recalling that this was characteristic phrase of Fr. Leopoldo's, she had the inspiration to place his relic on the affected limbs. As the relic touched them, the pain instantly disappeared. A year later there had been no recurrence.

Corn multiplied

In 1946 a poor family in Padua had managed to scrape together enough money to buy a sack of corn to supplement the inadequate bread ration. The father went at night into a nearby village to collect it and started to wheel it home on his bicycle without noticing that there was a hole in the sack. By the time he had noticed it, there were only a few pounds left. He came home in tears and the family spent the night in prayer to Fr. Leopoldo, for they had no material means of replacing the loss.

Next morning the mother went to see how much was left. She found a very empty looking sack in a corner and weighed the contents. Ten pounds. She put this in another sack and had another look in the empty one and saw there was still some. She weighed that. Another ten pounds.

So it went on, the apparently empty sack always producing more and the other sack getting fuller and fuller until the entire hundredweight was complete, plus an extra eight pounds!

Paralysis

Alberto Bedin as the result of a spinal lesion and rupture of the abdominal wall had been in bed, paralysed, for over nine years. Fr. Leopoldo had once saved his life by administering Extreme Unction and just before his own death, knowing Bedin to be still ill, sent him a note urging him to have faith for he would walk again.

Believing firmly what Fr. Leopoldo had written, Bedin bore his illness courageously, praying constantly to him and awaiting the promised cure. On 7th November, 1944, Bedin who was surrounded by other patients and nurses, felt Fr. Leopoldo presence, though he saw nothing. A voice told him to get up and walk. He bounced out of bed. The bystanders rushed to support him—he weighed nearly 250 lb.—but he cried " Out of my way! I'm cured," and began to run all round the ward and all over the hospital. Two years later he was still in perfect health, a living proof of Fr. Leopoldo's power.

Fatal illness cured

For four years Signorina Daniese had been ill with a blood disorder which left her in a pitiful condition. Eminent specialists had tried everything, including surgery, to no purpose. The patient grew worse and was bedridden and awaiting death. On the night of 4th August, 1946, she dreamed she saw her Parish Priest, who was also her confessor, who said to her, " Do you want to get better ? Then go to Confession and Holy Communion, and then go to Padua and have yourself blessed in Fr. Leopoldo's name in his confessional-cell."

On the night of the 6th a voice told her quite clearly, "Tomorrow will be the most fearful day of your illness, but bear it all with patience, for at sundown you will be cured."

Next morning she was driven to Padua, she made her Confession and received Holy Communion and was blessed in the confessional-cell. Her state at this time was such that it needed several people to support her. Then she was carried home and put back to bed.

During the day she got much worse and peritonitis developed. The local doctor could do nothing and insisted that she be sent to hospital the next morning.

Towards sundown the patient lay with horribly swollen abdomen, glassy eyes and a pulse that grew rapidly feebler.

Seeing that the sun was setting and that the promised cure had not yet happened, her faithful friend, Maria Chinchio, who had not left her side all day, turned in tears to Fr. Leopoldo and begged him to have pity on her friend. Suddenly the patient joined her hands, made some signs of the Cross in the air, and then, in her own words, felt a terrible blow at the back of her neck and heard a voice saying, "Don't be afraid, Rita! Get up. You are cured."

She got up. She was perfectly well.

News of the cure travelled like lightning, and people came from far and near to see her. There were many also who had long been estranged from God and who, when they heard of it, made their peace and returned to the Sacraments.

Sciatica

In the latter half of October, 1946, Signora Rossi suffered a severe attack of sciatica. No treatment was effective. The night of 30th October found the patient crying aloud in agony in spite of morphia. On the evening of the 31st, the nurse who came to give her morphia injections told her about Fr. Leopoldo and gave her a picture of him which the patient placed by her bed. About two in the morning the pain became once more unbearable. Signora Rossi took the picture of Fr. Leopoldo, kissed it and begged him to have pity on her. The pain ceased immediately and she was cured.

Puerperal septicaemia

A week after her child was born Elide Penolazzi suffered acute internal pain accompanied by high fever. The diagnosis was septicaemia in a particularly dangerous form. She grew steadily worse until she could no longer lift a hand and the doctor said that the end was near.

She and her familly all prayed to Fr. Leopoldo. That same evening, between sleeping and waking, she thought Fr. Leopoldo appeared, took her by the hand and raised her to a sitting position in bed, telling her she was cured. At first she thought it was a dream, but she was in fact sitting up in bed and in a few days was able to return to her household duties.

Pneumonia, meningitis and poliomyelitis

In 1946 four-year-old Antonio Baldan fell sick. The doctor diagnosed pneumonia and sent him to hospital, where meningitis and infantile paralysis were also diagnosed. "You have brought me a corpse," said the specialist. "Nothing but a miracle can save the child."

The nursing nuns gave the father a relic of Fr. Leopoldo and the novena prayers. The relic was placed on the child and the novena begun at once. Almost at once the child began to improve and to call for Fr. Leopoldo. In a few days everything had cleared up and the child went home completely cured.

Liver complaint

Signorina Teresa Pezzo had suffered for a long time from liver trouble. On 22nd October, 1946, in spite of persistent fever, she underwent an operation lasting three hours. After some days of hovering between life and death, she seemed to be improving and went to stay with her uncle, Mgr. Bartolomeo Pezzo at Bovolone. After a few days, however, a relapse left her as ill as before the operation, if not worse, and she was so weak she could hardy speak.

On 8th December, a Sunday, at the suggestion of a Capuchin priest, Teresa started a novena to Fr. Leopoldo, placing a relic on the afflicted part. On Tuesday evening she went to sleep at 11.30. As midnight struck, Fr. Leopoldo appeared to her. He was, she says, just like the pictures of him only much more beautiful and not wearing a stole. The light was out, yet the room was as bright as day. He approached her bed. Between joy and fear, Teresa cried out aloud.

"Don't be afraid," said Fr. Leopoldo. "You receive Holy Communion every day in bed, don't you?"

"Yes Father."

"To-morrow," he said, placing a hand on her shoulder, "go down to church for the 8 o'clock Mass and Holy Communion, for you are cured. And every day you must recite a rosary of the 'Glory be to the Father' as long as you live."

"Yes Father. I'll say two rosaries."

"Good! You have suffered a lot in your life, especially recently, but this will be repaid in the next. You must always do good in the world: should you have hard times, or sickness or pain, bear them with resignation and offer everything for the love of God."

"This is too good, Father."

"When does the novena end?"

"Monday."

"Then I shall come back at midnight on Monday, for I have a lot to say to you. Until then, my blessing."

He blessed her and disappeared with the words, "Praised be Jesus Christ."

Teresa shook herself. She thought she must have been dreaming, but she was cured: no pains, no swelling, no fever.

Her aunt, who shared her room, had heard everything she had said but not what Fr. Leopoldo had said, and had seen nothing.

In the morning Teresa, scarcely able to stand the day before, clattered down the stairs to the 8 o'clock Mass as instructed, and after a long thanksgiving came back to the presbytery to eat a hearty breakfast.

The cure caused a great sensation locally, for everyone knew about the illness of the priest's niece. Great excitement was caused, too, by the promised return of Fr. Leopoldo, and Teresa was charged with many questions to ask him.

At midnight 16th/17th December Fr. Leopoldo appeared again in a glow of brightness that made the room as light as day. He spoke to Teresa at a length about her spiritual life, recommending her particularly to pray. Then he answered the various questions put to him. As he spoke, Teresa wrote down the answers by the light he diffused, for the room was otherwise in darkness.

Her aunt, who shared the room, and a priest on watch outside the door, heard Teresa, but heard and saw nothing of Fr. Leopoldo.

As soon as he had vanished Teresa turned on the light. She had in her hand the piece of paper on which she had written at Fr. Leopoldo's dictation, but not the pen he had given her to write with. The aunt had heard the sound of the pen on the paper, but affirms that when the light went on Teresa had the paper in her hand but of a pen there was no sign.

From the answers he gave, one important fact emerges: Fr. Leopoldo complained that everyone prayed seldom and badly and insisted they should pray more if they hoped for God's blessing.

Naturally we have only Teresa's account of the visions and can only demand human faith in it, but the fact of her instantaneous cure remains, and that up till now she has had no recurrence of the illness that brought her to the edge of the grave.

Multiple cure

Signorina Zamildo Cantin at the age of 24 joined the novitiate of the Sisters of Mercy at Verona but later had to leave on account of ill-health. On 13th January, 1947, her complaints were diagnosed as colitis, cholecystitis, a misplaced kidney and spinal arthritis in the lumbar vertebrae. She was soon in a very poor way, hardly able to speak and with the spine so inflamed that the slightest touch was agony.

With lively faith the patient constantly prayed to Fr. Leopoldo, not to cure her but obtain the grace to bear her suffering with resignation.

However, on 27th March, as she was alone in her room, it occurred to her that the next Sunday was Palm Sunday and that she was going to miss all the Holy Week services which, up till then, she had always attended. This saddened her and she prayed to be able to attend instead of lying useless in bed.

Suddenly she remembered that in the drawer of a table near the bed there was a medal which had been placed on Fr. Leopoldo's body.

If, she thought, she were to place this medal on the affected parts, she would certainly be cured. But there was nobody at hand and she herself could not even stretch out an arm for it. "Oh well," she thought, "if Fr. Leopoldo wants to cure me, he can manage it without my having the medal." So she lay and awaited results.

A few moments later she felt a sort of shock throughout her body, followed by a sense of well-being and strength. She was cured. Not only had the swelling and painfulness disappeared, but she had also regained instantaneously her colour and strength as though she had never been ill.

She got up, went downstairs and out into the fields, and started working there to everyone's astonishmemt.

Examined again by her doctor, and X-rayed, she showed no symptoms of any of her previous ailments and has since been in excellent health, in fact better than before her illness.

Daughter cured

In August, 1947, Gianfranca Barbierato was ill with a chest complaint. Two local doctors insisted that an operation was necessary and sent her to a specialist in Padua.

Her family accompanied her on 5th September. Seeing that they were all worried, the child said "Don't be afraid. When we get to Padua Fr. Leopoldo will cure me."

Before taking her to hospital they went to the confessional-cell to ask for the grace of a cure. While they were waiting to get into the cell they saw against the wall to their left a small, old Capuchin with a white beard, bent and supporting himself with a stick, who appeared to be waiting for them. The sight was in some way a shock to them, although the old priest certainly was in no way frightening to look at. However, the child's mother told the child to kneel and kiss the Cross of his Rosary. The child did so and he placed his hand—his left hand, for the right hand held the stick—on her head and said, "Go in into the cell pray and get a blessing. Have faith, faith in God!"

Mother, father and uncle followed suit, kneeling and kissing the Cross on his Rosary.

The priest then disappeared and they assumed he had left by the door they had entered.

After praying fervently and receiving the blessing, the took the child to the specialist who examined her and wanted to know why they had brought her, for she showed no signs of any illness.

Overjoyed, they returned home, and it was not until some days later that anyone thought of looking carefully at a photograph of Fr. Leopoldo and realizing that it was he whom they had met.

To make sure, they want back to Padua and enquired if there were any other priest who might meet the description, but there was none.

Clearly Fr. Leopoldo had been pleased to appear to them and cure the child.

Typhus

Eight year old Santina Grotto had a great devotion to Fr. Leopoldo and always wore his relic. When she went to hospital with typhus in July, 1947, she continued to pray fervently to him, but her condition grew worse and she was given the Last Sacraments.

On the evening of 16th August she saw the figure of a Capuchin appear from above and approach her bed. "I am Fr. Leopoldo and I have come to cure you and all the patients in this room." (There were seven others). "I'll come again tomorrow evening."

Next evening he appeared once more. "Here I am again! You will get better, and then you will go to Padua and visit my confessional and write your name in the register you will find there. I urge you also to pray. Now make a good Sign of the Holy Cross."

The child did as she was bid and he disappeared.

Soon afterwards she was discharged perfectly fit, as were all the others in her ward.

It is worth noting that at that time neither the child nor her parents had been to the friary at Padua nor knew of the existence of the register in the confessional-cell.

Sinusitis

In 1947 Signora Augusta Toso was sent by her doctor to a specialist in Padua who, after an X-ray examination, decided she had severe sinusitis and should be operated upon the next morning.

Signora Toso in the meantime went to Fr. Leopoldo's confessional-cell and placed herself in his care. During the night the pain grew much worse, but she held a relic on the affected part and continued to pray.

At about four o'clock in the morning the pain suddenly ceased and she was able to eat, although for two days she had not been able to touch food.

Later that morning she kept her appointment with the specialist, who had her X-rayed again. The astonished radiologist, remembering what he had seen the previous evening, asked her if she had been to Lourdes overnight. She was completely cured.

Malignant tumour

Fr. Camillo, OFM Cap, was in the Mission at Angola in Portuguese Congo when in June, 1948, he was taken ill with acute pains in the lower abdomen. The local doctor diagnosed a tumour and sent him to hospital in Luanda.

Here he was examined on several occasions by three doctors including the celebrated Prof. Silveira Ramos who agreed in the diagnosis, the professor pronouncing the tumour malignant.

An operation was considered urgent but the climate unsuitable, so the Professor used his influence with the Governor to get Fr. Camillo a flight to Lisbon.

In the meantime Fr. Camillo, being told of the seriousuess of his case, placed a relic of Fr. Leopoldo on the affected place and started a novena. His fellow missionaries, and the nuns, and even the piccaninnies, all prayed as well.

The day after his arrival in the Colonial Hospital in Lisbon Fr. Camillo was examined by Prof. Sexas who found nothing wrong with him. X-ray and other tests confirmed this, and the patient had a good appetite and no fever. He was kept for a few days for osbservation and then dismissed.

He attributes the cure to the intercession of Fr. Leopoldo, having noticed an improvement throughout the novena until on the ninth day he felt no discomfort at all.

Displaced vertebra

In July, 1947, Ermenegildo Miatello fell from a cart and displaced a vertebra. He was in considerable pain, but after various treatments had proved ineffectual, the doctors said he would always have it. After five months of unbelievable suffering it was suggested to him that he have recourse to Fr. Leopoldo. This he did, with lively faith, and on the night of 10th January, 1948, he seemed to see Fr. Leopoldo who said, " You will soon be cured. Go to Padua to morrow morning and hear Mass in the Basilica of St. Anthony. In the morning the pain had gone and he was cured.

Child run over

On 8th October, 1949, the child Stefano Sguotti was riding home on a cart loaded with half a ton of sugar beet when he fell off and was run over by both front and back wheels.

There was non sign of injury but child was speechless and they feared internal lesions.

His mother was out when they got him home, but as soon as she arrived she ran to embrace the child and ask him what was the matter.

" I was run over by the cart with Fr. Leopoldo who was so small and neither of us was hurt. The wheel went over him first and then over me."

The parents had always had a great devotion to Fr. Leopoldo, praying to him daily.

Renal haemorrhage

On 6th June, 1949, the Lay Brother Fra Pacifico fainted in the streets of Cesena, falling awkwardly and injuring a kidney. Days later he was passing a great deal of blood in the urine and was admitted to hospital where renal haemorrhage and intestinal poisoning were diagnosed. On the 28th there was a crisis with great pain and considerable loss of blood which lasted throughout the night. Fra Pacifico prayed continually to Fr. Leopoldo.

The following morning, after the Chaplain had brought him Holy Communion, he was alone making his thanksgiving when he saw Fr. Leopoldo at his bedside. Fr. Leopoldo blessed him and said, "You are cured!" and then disappeared.

Fra Pacifico thought he had been dreaming, but shortly the pain and bleeding ceased. A few more days were spent in hospital under observation before he was discharged and resumed his arduous task of seeking alms in the city of Cesena.

" Give your children a Christian upbringing "

"Since 1938 I had suffered frequent epileptic attacks and on 21st June, 1950, while preparing dinner, I fell into the fire. I was alone in the house at the time and when my family returned they found me with my right calf horribly burned. The wound became gangrenous and it was decided to amputate.

You can imagine my despair.

I prayed to Fr. Leopoldo and kept a relic on the affected leg. One afternoon while I was half asleep I saw him at my bedside. He was bent and carrying a walking stick. Speaking very kindly, he said, "I have come to visit you. You must not die because you have small children whom your husband cannot bring up alone. Don't forget, however, to give them a Christian upbringing. That is why God is going to cure you." Thereafter he blessed me and went out of the room, stopping at the door to turn and remind me, "Don't forget what I said!" I awoke and felt a shudder through my whole body. At once the fever left me and there was no further talk of gangrene. Very soon I was completely cured."

CESIRA BERLATO

6 Juin 1951

Malignant tumour

In 1946 Attilia Macignato was operated on in Padua for an abdominal tumor, but it was found to be malignant and not removed. The abdomen was closed and she was sent home and told that there was nothing to be done.

She continued as before to invoke Fr. Leopoldo but the pains continued, although they were bearable.

In 1949, still suffering, she went to Argentina where, in 1951 she grew worse and was admitted to hospital. They found the tumor and wanted to operate. The patient continued to invoke Fr. Leopoldo who one night appeared to her, placed his hand on the affected part and said, "Don't be afraid! You will get better."

In spite of the fact that she was thereafter no longer in pain, the doctors carried on with the operation but found no tumor to excise.

Attilia remains in excellent health.

Empyema

On 7th April, 1952 Sister Romilda of the *Suore Maestre di S. Dorotea* was admitted to hospital with empyema over the left lung. For two months already she had been unable to lie down on account of the pain. Careful examination showed that there were serious complications and it was decided to operate and remove four ribs, part of the lung and one kidney.

During her illness Sister Romilda, who had always had a great devotion to Fr. Leopoldo, prayed incessantly to him. On the 8th May after a final—pre-operational examination, she addressed one last agonized petition to him as the theatre doors opened to admit her stretcher.

A shock passed through her body and the pain ceased. She sat up, crying, "I'm cured! I don't need the operation!" She was duly given another X-ray examination and it was found that all signs of the disease had vanished. She was perfectly cured.

Headhaches

For two years Signorina Agnese Manfron had been suffering from headaches that were sometimes so severe as to render her unconscious for hours on end.

All sorts of treatments were tried in vain and finally she was advised to go to a clinic for an extended period of observation. Not wanting to go at that time, she went home, but went via the Capuchin Friary where she spent a long time in prayer in Fr. Leopoldo's confessional-cell.

Next morning, 14th January, 1954, she was in the kitchen with other members of her family when Fr. Leopoldo appeared to her in front of the statue of Our Lady. He made her make the Sign of the Cross three times and then placed a hand on her head, saying, "No more medicines! Have faith!" Then he made her make another Sign of the Cross, signed her forehead with his thumb and told her to kneel and say three Hail Marys. Giving her his hand to kiss, he then disappeared.

Her family saw her do all this and heard her talking, but saw and heard nothing of the apparition.

She was in the meantime perfectly cured and the next day resumed the factory work she had to give up.

Gangrenous foot

Signora Carmela Bellettieri of Positano was admitted to Salerno hospital in September, 1955, with a diabetic sore on one foot. Treatment proved ineffectual and after five months the sore had become gangrenous and so deep that the bone was exposed. It was accompanied by great pain, allowing the sufferer no rest.

An acquaintance gave her a relic of Fr. Leopoldo to place on the affected part and urged her to pray. This she did and after three days the pain suddenly ceased and the sore began to heal.

In a short time it was completely healed and not even a scar remains to show the place where it was.

Chronic bronchial asthma

No treatment had any effect on Antonio Schiavo's chronic bronchial asthma.

On 2nd January, 1955, he sent his wife to the confessional-cell to pray for him and to have a shirt blessed. On her return he uttered a last prayer and, full of faith, put on the shirt.

The cure was immediate and there has been no relapse.

CHRONOLOGICAL TABLE

12. 5 .1866	Born at Castelnovo, Dalmatia.
13. 6 .1866	Baptized Bogdan (Deodatus).
16.11.1882	Entered the Seraphic Seminary at Udine.
2 . 5 .1884	Clothed as Fra Leopoldo at Bassano del Grappa.
3 . 5 .1885	Simple Profession.
20.10.1888	Solemn Profession at Padua.
20. 9 .1890	Ordained priest by Card. Domenico Agostini in the *Salute*, Venice.
1890-1898	Confessor in various Capuchin Friaries in the Province of Venice.
1899	Superior of the Capuchin Hospice at Zara. Later to Thiene.
1903	To Bassano del Grappa.
1905	Father Vicar at Capodistria.
1906-1942	Confessor at Padua.
1910-1914	Director of Philosophy Students at Padua.
1917-1918	Interned in Southern Italy.
3 . 5 .1935	50th Anniversary of Profession.
22. 9 .1940	Sacerdotal Golden Jubilee.
30. 7 .1942	Died in the odour of Sanctity.
16. 1 .1946	Opening of the Diocesan Informative Process.
18.12.1958	Peroration for the Apostolic Process in the presence of H. H. John XXIII.
25. 5 .1962	Papal Decree allowing the introduction of the Apostolic Process.

SOURCES

1. *Writings of Fr. Leopoldo.*

a) Letters, of which 220 are available. Owing to the little time at his disposal for letter writing, and the physical difficulty caused by arthritis, the majority are no more than notes on visiting cards, sometimes not even covering the whole card. There are, however, some on larger paper and they contain much food for thought.

Most unfortunately the letters he wrote to his spiritual director, in which he described his struggles in periods of spiritual aridity, were destroyed as a result of hostilities in Fiume during the second world war. However, twelve letters from his spiritual director in answer to letters of his have survived.

Inexplicably lost, too, are the letters Fr. Leopoldo wrote to the servant of God Don Giovanni Calabria, of Verona, in which he asked for spiritual advice. Here too, however, seven answers from Don Giovanni are available.

b) Articles published in the *Bollettino Francescano,* a monthly produced by the Capuchins at Padua for the spiritual education of Tertiaries. They comprise, (1) a series of eleven articles on the Mission of the Third Order published between December, 1907 and February, 1910; (2) a series of three articles on Our Lady, published between February and June, 1916, under the title "*Mary Immaculate, Queen of Peace*"; (3) two article, "*The Resurrection*" (April, 1912) and "*I am the Resurrection and the Life*" (April, 1941); (4) an article "*Saint Francis*" (October, 1911).

c) Writings relating to his vow for the reconversion of the eastern peoples. Sixty-six are available, written on odd sheets of paper or on holy pictures. Probably a large number have been lost.

2. *Accounts* written by persons who knew Fr. Leopoldo (181 pieces).

3. *Personal memories* of Mgr. SEBASTIANO CUCCAROLLO, OFM Cap., Archbishop of Proconneso (29 pieces).

4. *Twelve letters* from Fr. ODORICO OF PORDENONE, Fr. Leopoldo's spiritual director (see 1. above).

5. *Seven letters* from Don Giovanni Calabria (see 1. above).

6. Documents relating to Fr. Leopoldo's various postings.

7. The author's personal memories.

With the exception of Item 6 (in the Provincial Curia at Mestre) the above papers are all in the archives of the Vice-Postulation at Padua.

NOTES ON THE RELIABILITY OF SOURCES

All the accounts used are the personal memories of people who knew Fr. Leopoldo for greater or less time. They were all spontaneously offered, not "solicited." In addition, their reliability was investigated in terms of the moral and intellectual character of the writers.

The most important statements in this Life are based on the written accounts of persons well qualified to make them and whose reliability cannot be impugned. Among them are:

Mgr. Carlo Agostini, Bishop of Padua, later Patriarch of Venice. Account written at Padua on 9th July, 1944.

Mgr. Sebastiano Cuccarollo, OFM Cap., Archbishop of Proconneso. Lived with Fr. Leopoldo from student days and was for some years with him as a priest in Padua. Account written at Otranto, 10th May, 1943, when he was Archbishop there. Other accounts at various dates from Bassano del Grappa.

Mgr. Carlo Margotti, Archbishop of Gorizia. For many years a penitent of Fr. Leopoldo. Account written at Gorizia, 19th October, 1943.

Mgr. Vigilio Dalla Zuanna, OFM Cap. Lived a number of years with Fr. Leopoldo at Padua and was thereafter Minister Provincial, Minister General, Apostolic Preacher, Bishop of Carpi and, finally, Archbishop of Mocisso. Account written at Carpi, 28th March, 1944.

Mgr. Guido Mazzocco, Bishop of Adria and Rovigo. For many years a penitent of Fr. Leopoldo. Account written at Rovigo, 15th October, 1943.

Mgr. Giacinto Ambrosi, OFM Cap. Archbishop of Gorizia. Spent some years with Fr. Leopoldo at Padua and was later Minister Provincial. Account written at Chioggia, 27th March, 1944.

Mgr. Girolamo Bortignon, OFM Cap., Bishop of Padua. Was Fr. Leopoldo's Provincial. Account written at Belluno, 12th June, 1944.

Fr. Odorico of Pordenone, OFM Cap., a companion of Fr. Leopoldo from Seminary days, and later his Provincial and spiritual director. Account written at Fiume, 23rd June, 1943.

Mgr. Antonio Maria Bettanini, Professor at Padua University, for thirty-three years a penitent of Fr. Leopoldo. Account written at Padua, 24th May, 1943.

Mgr. Antonio Barzon, Canon of Padua Cathedral. Many years a penitent of Fr. Leopoldo. Account written at Padua, 12th Sept., 1944.

Mgr. Giacomo Dal Sasso, Professor at Padua Seminary. Many years a penitent of Fr. Leopoldo. Account written at Padua, 17th August, 1943.

Prof. Enrico Rubaltelli, Padua ENT Specialist. For many years a penitent of Fr. Leopoldo. Account written at Padua, 22nd March, 1943.

Fr. Venceslao of San Martino di Lupari, OFM Cap. Was Fr. Leopoldo's Provincial. Account written in Rome, 30th July, 1943.

Mgr. Rizzieri Zanocco, Canon of Padua Cathedral. Many years a penitent of Fr. Leopoldo. Account written at Padua, 12th Sept., 1943.

ACKNOWLEDGMENTS.

I have to thank who have so generously contributed to the successful completion of this work, in particular those who introduce it to the English-speaking world; the Very Rev. Fr. Bernardine of Siena, the Postulator General, for his wise counsel, and above all Fr. Umile of Valstagna for the intelligence and loving care with which he has gone over my text.

THE AUTHOR.

GRAFICHE
ERREDICÌ
PADOVA

Photographic documents

Fr. Leopoldo a few days before his death →